Reading Dante and Proust by Analogy

32
35

75, 104, 117, 120

LEGENDA

LEGENDA is the Modern Humanities Research Association's book imprint for new research in the Humanities. Founded in 1995 by Malcolm Bowie and others within the University of Oxford, Legenda has always been a collaborative publishing enterprise, directly governed by scholars. The Modern Humanities Research Association (MHRA) joined this collaboration in 1998, became half-owner in 2004, in partnership with Maney Publishing and then Routledge, and has since 2016 been sole owner. Titles range from medieval texts to contemporary cinema and form a widely comparative view of the modern humanities, including works on Arabic, Catalan, English, French, German, Greek, Italian, Portuguese, Russian, Spanish, and Yiddish literature. Editorial boards and committees of more than 60 leading academic specialists work in collaboration with bodies such as the Society for French Studies, the British Comparative Literature Association and the Association of Hispanists of Great Britain & Ireland.

The MHRA encourages and promotes advanced study and research in the field of the modern humanities, especially modern European languages and literature, including English, and also cinema. It aims to break down the barriers between scholars working in different disciplines and to maintain the unity of humanistic scholarship. The Association fulfils this purpose through the publication of journals, bibliographies, monographs, critical editions, and the MHRA Style Guide, and by making grants in support of research. Membership is open to all who work in the Humanities, whether independent or in a University post, and the participation of younger colleagues entering the field is especially welcomed.

ALSO PUBLISHED BY THE ASSOCIATION

Critical Texts
Tudor and Stuart Translations • *New Translations* • *European Translations*
MHRA Library of Medieval Welsh Literature

MHRA Bibliographies
Publications of the Modern Humanities Research Association

The Annual Bibliography of English Language & Literature
Austrian Studies
Modern Language Review
Portuguese Studies
The Slavonic and East European Review
Working Papers in the Humanities
The Yearbook of English Studies

www.mhra.org.uk
www.legendabooks.com

TRANSCRIPT

Transcript publishes books about all kinds of imagining across languages, media and cultures: translations and versions, inter-cultural and multi-lingual writing, illustrations and musical settings, adaptation for theatre, film, TV and new media, creative and critical responses. We are open to studies of any combination of languages and media, in any historical moments, and are keen to reach beyond Legenda's traditional focus on modern European languages to embrace anglophone and world cultures and the classics. We are interested in innovative critical approaches: we welcome not only the most rigorous scholarship and sharpest theory, but also modes of writing that stretch or cross the boundaries of those discourses.

www.legendabooks.com/series/transcript

TRANSCRIPT

1. *Adapting the Canon: Translation, Visualisation, Interpretation*, edited by Ann Lewis and Silke Arnold-de Simine
2. *Adapted Voices: Transpositions of Céline's Voyage au bout de la nuit and Queneau's Zazie dans le métro*, by Armelle Blin-Rolland
3. *Zola and the Art of Television: Adaptation, Recreation, Translation*, by Kate Griffiths
4. *Comparative Encounters between Artaud, Michaux and the Zhuangzi: Rationality, Cosmology and Ethics*, by Xiaofan Amy Li
5. *Minding Borders: Resilient Divisions in Literature, the Body and the Academy*, edited by Nicola Gardini, Adriana Jacobs, Ben Morgan, Mohamed-Salah Omri and Matthew Reynolds
6. *Memory Across Borders: Nabokov, Perec, Chamoiseau*, by Sara-Louise Cooper
7. *Erotic Literature in Adaptation and Translation*, edited by Johannes D. Kaminski
8. *Translating Petrarch's Poetry: L'Aura del Petrarca from the Quattrocento to the 21st Century*, edited by Carole Birkan-Berz, Guillaume Coatalen and Thomas Vuong
9. *Making Masud Khan: Psychoanalysis, Empire and Modernist Culture*, by Benjamin Poore
10. *Prismatic Translation*, edited by Matthew Reynolds
11. *The Patient, the Impostor and the Seducer: Medieval European Literature in Hebrew*, by Tovi Bibring
12. *Reading Dante and Proust by Analogy*, by Julia Caterina Hartley
13. *The First English Translations of Molière: Drama in Flux 1663-1732*, by Suzanne Jones
14. *After Clarice: Reading Lispector's Legacy in the Twenty-First Century*, edited by Adriana X. Jacobs and Claire Williams
15. *Uruguayan Theatre in Translation: Theory and Practice*, by Sophie Stevens
16. *Hamlet Translations: Prisms of Cultural Encounters across the Globe*, edited by Márta Minier and Lily Kahn
17. *The Foreign Connection: Writings on Poetry, Art and Translation*, by Jamie McKendrick
18. *Poetics, Performance and Politics in French and Italian Renaissance Comedy*, by Lucy Rayfield

Reading Dante and Proust by Analogy

❖

Julia Caterina Hartley

LEGENDA
Transcript 12
Modern Humanities Research Association
2019

Published by Legenda
an imprint of the Modern Humanities Research Association
Salisbury House, Station Road, Cambridge CB1 2LA

ISBN 978-1-78188-843-8

First published 2019

Copy-Editor: Charlotte Brown

CONTENTS

❖

ACKNOWLEDGEMENTS

The doctoral thesis on which this book is closely based would not have been possible without Manuele Gragnolati and Jennifer Yee, who had the faith (and courage) to supervise this ambitious project and whose attentive criticism ensured its quality. On a material level, the doctorate was made possible by generous funding from the Arts and Humanities Research Council.

Jennifer Rushworth paved the Dante-Proust Studies path and was always my first reader, from my PhD application to the thesis's final draft.

Edward Hughes, Ann Jefferson, Elena Lombardi, Roger Pearson, and Adam Watt all provided valuable feedback at different stages, as did Matthew Reynolds and my anonymous reviewer at Legenda. I am also grateful to Graham Nelson for his support in preparing this book and to Aydin Aghdashloo, who gave me permission to use his beautiful modern medieval diptych, *Vita/Mors* (2010) for the cover.

The solidarity and sense of humour of my fellow graduate students at Oxford brought joy to the years I devoted to researching Proust and Dante. Beyond Oxford, the international community of early career Proust scholars — or, as Cynthia Gamble has been known to call us, the 'Very Special Proustians' — has never ceased to motivate and inspire me. My monograph follows those of Jennifer Rushworth and Pauline Moret-Jankus, and I look forward to reading those by Synne Ytre Arne, Igor Reyner, and Richard Mason next.

Ali Rafiee pushed me forwards when the going got hard and was the one to suggest Aydin Aghdashloo for the cover (though I have yet to convince him that Proust is not 'boring').

This book is dedicated to my parents, two great booklovers and polyglots. It was growing up in an English-, Italian-, and French-speaking home that made me the inevitable comparatist that I am.

J.H., London, 25 March 2019

NOTE ON EDITIONS

❖

Works by Dante

The edition followed for Dante's *Commedia* is *La Commedia secondo l'antica vulgata*, ed. by Giorgio Petrocchi, 2nd edn, 4 vols (Florence: Le Lettere, 1994)

Conv. *Convivio*, ed. by Franca Brambilla Ageno, 3 vols (Florence: Le Lettere, 1995)
Inf. *Inferno*, in Dante, *Commedia*, ed. by Petrocchi
Purg. *Purgatorio*, in Dante, *Commedia*, ed. by Petrocchi
Par. *Paradiso*, in Dante, *Commedia*, ed. by Petrocchi
VN. *Vita nuova*, ed. by Domenico De Robertis (Milan: Ricciardi, 1980).

Citations from the *Commedia* are given as: Abbreviated canticle title. Canto number in Roman numerals, verse numbers in Arabic numbers.

Citations from the *Convivio* are given as: Abbreviated title. Book in capitalized Roman numerals, chapter in Roman numerals, paragraph in Arabic numbers.

Citations from the *Vita nuova* are given as: Abbreviated title. Chapter in Roman numerals, paragraph in Arabic numbers.

Works by Proust

The edition followed for Marcel Proust's *Recherche* is *À la recherche du temps perdu*, ed. by Jean-Yves Tadié, 4 vols (Paris: Gallimard, 1987–89)

Corr. *Correspondance*, ed. by Philip Kolb, 21 vols (Paris: Plon, 1970–93)
CSB *Contre Sainte-Beuve*, in, *Contre Sainte-Beuve précédé de Pastiches et mélanges et suivi de Essais et articles*, ed. by Pierre Clarac (Paris: Gallimard, 1971)

Citations from *À la recherche du temps perdu* are given as: Volume number in Roman numerals, page number in Arabic numbers.

Citations from *Correspondance* are given as: Abbreviated title. Volume number in Roman numerals, page number in Arabic numbers.

Citations from *Contre Sainte-Beuve* are given as: Abbreviated title. Page number.

Translations

Translations of *Convivio* are from Dante, *The Banquet*, ed. and trans. by Richard Lansing (New York: Garland, 1998), and translations of *Vita nuova* are from Dante, *Vita Nuova*, trans. by Mark Musa (Oxford: Oxford University Press, 1992)

Unless otherwise indicated, all other translations are my own.

INTRODUCTION

Dante Alighieri (1265–1321) and Marcel Proust (1871–1922) both have entire research fields to their name. As a senior colleague once put it, to write about them together is wonderfully unorthodox because these are authors 'accustomed to demanding a scholar's undivided attention'. It is precisely for this reason that approaching them with shared attention has much to offer. By reading Proust in light of Dante and Dante in light of Proust, we can see them with new eyes: a rare circumstance for these familiar faces of the Western canon. This book's comparative reading of the *Divine Comedy* (hereafter *Commedia*) and *À la recherche du temps perdu* (hereafter *Recherche*) was first inspired by a formal and thematic similarity: the use of the first-person protagonist and the question of his literary vocation. In both works, these combined features govern the characterization of the protagonist and his relationship with secondary characters, while also providing a *telos* and structuring principle to the narrative. In many respects, both plots centre on the interplay between protagonist, narrator, and author: the *Commedia* tells the story of Dante's transformation from being a sinner and a secular poet to being a saved soul and the author of the holy poem that we are reading, with the clear implication that writing this poem is in fact his act of atonement; the *Recherche* has been summarized as the story of how Marcel becomes a writer, or how the protagonist becomes the narrator.[1] But these are also works written in different languages and genres (one is a poem, the other a novel) and, most importantly, different historical and cultural contexts (early thirteenth-century Italy and belle époque France). Generally speaking, in literary criticism such differences tend to be awarded greater importance than any kind of similarity between two texts: one finds it easy to make the case for a comparison between Proust's *Recherche* and another 'modernist' novel, even if it differs in style and subject matter, because a continuity in genre and historical period is perceived; the same goes for studies of the *Commedia* in light of the classical or vernacular texts circulating at the time that Dante was writing, since these are considered part of the *Commedia*'s cultural context. But what this book aims to show is that a difference in contexts can be a valuable tool for critical inquiry, since it allows for the tension between similarity and difference that defines the heuristic process of analogy. Analogy, which I use as an umbrella term for metaphor and simile, draws its force from the conflict between the parallel that it identifies and the resistant differences between its two terms. In order to better formulate the method of this book, it is therefore useful to remind ourselves briefly of some key contributions to the theorization of metaphor.

Metaphor was seminally defined by Roman Jakobson as an internal relation of similarity between two terms, as opposed to the external relation of context, which is characteristic of metonymy (1987: 95–114). This broad definition allowed Jakobson to account for all forms of human discourse, while at the same time remaining in accordance with literary scholars and rhetoricians' accounts of metaphor as a trope, such as for example I. A. Richards's definition of metaphor as the putting together of 'two things belonging to very different orders of experience' (1936: 123). For the purposes of this book, the most pertinent re-evaluation of Jakobson's definition was offered by Paul Ricœur, who noted that the stress on similarity ('le travail de la ressemblance', 1975: 221) ignores that metaphor relies on a maintained tension between similarity and difference, and between what is metaphorically true and what is literally true. Metaphor, in Ricœur's account, is a contradiction that allows us to momentarily cast aside our prior categorizations (1975: 245–54, 310–21). Ricœur's argument can be illustrated with the opening pages of 'Un amour de Swann', in which Proust's narrator calls Madame Verdurin's salon a church in which the faithful must adhere to a Creed that dictates that all company beyond the Verdurin must be rejected for being too boring (I, 185). Women being more rebellious to this Creed than men, 'les Verdurin sentant [...] que cet esprit d'examen et ce démon de frivolité pouvait par contagion devenir fatal à l'orthodoxie de la petite église, ils avaient été amenés à rejeter successivement tous les "fidèles" de sexe féminin' [the Verdurins feeling [...] that their spirit of inquiry and the evil influence of frivolity could become fatal to the orthodoxy of the little church, had been impelled to ban the female 'faithful' one after the other] (I, 185). What makes the metaphor of the church so memorable is the conflict that the reader perceives between the accuracy of Proust's social satire and the preposterousness of comparing middle-class social habits to a religion. The existence of this parallel in spite of the gulf separating the tenor (the Verdurin salon) from the vehicle (a church) carries across the exaggeration of Madame Verdurin's demands on her social circle far more powerfully and clearly than if Proust had only used literal statements.

What I call reading by analogy is an approach to comparative literature which draws its force from this conflict between difference and similarity and which, rather than merely listing these differences and similarities, uses them to reach conclusions that could not have been reached had the two terms not been brought into relation.[2] Such an approach was announced by Gianfranco Contini in one of the earliest scholarly comparisons between the *Commedia* and the *Recherche*, the essay 'Dante come personaggio-poeta della *Commedia*' (1976), first published in 1958.[3] Contini introduces his argument as follows: 'Marcel Proust serve di metafora per un discorso non del tutto elementare su Dante' [Marcel Proust will serve as a metaphor for a discussion of Dante that is far from elementary] (1976: 33). In Contini's essay, Proust is a vehicle used to approach Dante, who is the tenor of the metaphor. In other words, the analogy is unilateral, with Proust being used to illuminate Dante. In this book, all analogies will be bilateral: I read not only Dante through Proust, but also Proust through Dante. This much more dynamic understanding of metaphor is best encapsulated by Richards's definition of metaphor as the 'interaction between co-present thoughts' (1936: 93) and subsequent scholars' developments of this definition. Richards established the key terms 'vehicle' and 'tenor', but he used them in a far more nuanced manner than common usage would lead us to believe, stating that a vehicle 'is not normally a mere embellishment of a tenor which is otherwise unchanged by it', but rather 'vehicle and tenor in co-operation give a meaning of more varied powers that can be ascribed to either' (1936: 100). These insights formed the basis for the interactive view of metaphor, which was outlined by Max Black as a three-step process: first, the presence of the tenor leads the reader or listener to select certain aspects of the vehicle; secondly, these selected qualities of the vehicle are projected on to the tenor; finally, a reciprocal projection also occurs from the tenor onto the vehicle (1993: 28). To go back to the example from 'Un amour de Swann', this means that when Proust calls Mme Verdurin's regulars 'les fidèles', he alters not only our understanding of the social rituals of the late nineteenth-century French bourgeoisie, but also our mental image of a church congregation.

After Black, the interactive view of metaphor was expressed in a less technical fashion by Denis Donoghue, who writes:

> We are engaging in a metaphor when we see, or think we see, or propose to see, one thing in light of another; it is an instance of perspective, not necessarily resemblance. [...] [T]he vehicle does not replace the tenor or indeed overwhelm it: what has existed still exists, in a mind generous enough to respect both. (2014: 84)

Donogue's words encapsulate the agenda behind my comparative study of Proust and Dante, that is, to offer a new perspective on both authors by reading them in light of each other. It follows from this aim that I shall not be undertaking a reception study. A study of influence would bring the focus resolutely on the *Recherche*, with Dante's relevance being confined to his role within Proust's pages.[4] I, however, am just as interested in Dante's text as I am in Proust's.

Analogies between Dante and Proust have been drawn by other scholars before me, some like Contini as a passing reference, and others devoting entire articles or chapters to their exploration.[5] The 'passing reference' approach does not do justice to both authors, since it draws on the second author only to bolster the argument on the main author under its focus. Thus, Contini (1976) refers to Proust in order to stress the metapoetic dimension of the *Commedia* and Leo Spitzer (1946) refers to Proust in order to stress the allegorical dimension of the *Commedia*, thereby reaching opposite conclusions.[6] In fact, as we shall see in Chapter 1, a deeper engagement with Proust's text reveals that the narrator-protagonist of the *Recherche* can neither be accounted for as the author of the book, nor as an allegorical Everyman, but should be understood as an ambiguous composite of both. Contini and Spitzer are thus defending their respective readings of Dante through a necessarily simplified version of the *Recherche*. The passing reference can on occasion be extremely insightful, such as in Steiner's essay on the 'gossip of eternity' in the *Commedia*, which observes that Dante's and Proust's masterpieces are both 'timeless, universal, because utterly dated and placed' (1978: 172). More frequently than not, however, the secondary author is not drawn on in his own right, but filtered by the critic's motivation to write about her or his main author.

Richard Bales compares Proust's novel to the *Commedia* in his chapter on the medieval aspects of the 'structure and scope' of the *Recherche*, which cites Samuel Borton's 'A Tentative Essay on Dante and Proust' (1958) as its forerunner (1975: 117–38). Bales's chapter, 'The Structure and Scope of *À la recherche du temps perdu*', is a great example for Proust scholars of the benefits of drawing on Dante for a better understanding of the *Recherche*. The *Commedia* allows Bales to describe the cathedral-inspired structure and totalizing ambitions of the *Recherche* and also to consider the ways in which the *Recherche* could be viewed as a twentieth-century version of Everyman's journey to salvation. Bales, however, does not engage closely with Dante's text, which is only cited through the mediation of Ernst Robert Curtius's *European Literature and the Latin Middle Ages* (1953).[7] As a result, while *Proust and the Middle Ages* offers new insights into Proust's novel, the same cannot be said for Dante's poem, of which Bales provides only a descriptive overview.

The present book is most closely aligned to comparative studies that devote equal attention to medieval and modern literary texts and their respective cultural contexts, such as Manuele Gragnolati's work on Dante and twentieth-century Italian authors Pier Paolo Pasolini and Elsa Morante (2013), and, closer yet, Jennifer Rushworth's monograph *Discourses of Mourning in Dante, Petrarch, and Proust* (2016). As expressed by Gragnolati in the introduction to *Amor che move*, his study does not seek to describe the influence of one author on another, nor to propose an intellectual history, but to shed new light on literary texts by placing them in dialogue (2013: 10). Jennifer Rushworth develops as a methodological tool the concept of interpolation, that is, the deliberate insertion of foreign or anachronistic material into a reading of a text (2016: 1–17). Thus, her first chapter interpolates Barthes into a reading of Dante's *Commedia*, while her second chapter, largely devoted to Petrarch, concludes with a Proustian interpolation. My methodology differs in so far as rather than looking at my authors in turn through separate chapters or sections, I read Dante and Proust together throughout the book, following Donoghue's definition of metaphor as the mind's simultaneous engagement with two terms. My argument is drawn from parallel close readings of passages from both texts concerned with or presenting similar issues. When Dante's and Proust's texts raise questions that can be related to wider debates in literary criticism, I draw on critical theory in order to nuance and clarify the discussion.

Although my approach to comparative literature differs in area of focus and methodology, it shares common goals with the projects of Gragnolati and Rushworth. To 'interpolate the medieval and the modern' (Rushworth), to conduct a 'diffractive reading' (Gragnolati via Donna Haraway), or to read by analogy, leads one to question prior assumptions based on literary genres or historical periods. Such a shift in perspective is all the more relevant in the field of Dante studies, which still bears the marks of its nineteenth-century origins.[8] Reading Dante with a modern author furthers the project of 'detheologization' inaugurated by Teodolinda Barolini, that is, 'a way of reading that attempts to break out of the hermeneutic guidelines that Dante has structured into his poem' (1992: 7). If we restrict comparative studies of Dante to his reception of classical authors or the

Bible, we are implicitly accepting the *Commedia*'s self-presentation as an inimitable sacred poem. If, ignoring what Dante claims his poem is, we read the *Commedia* instead as a work of literature among others, then it follows that we should be able to read it alongside works that came after it.

Crucially, approaching Dante via a twentieth-century author does not necessarily entail ignoring the socio-historical and literary context in which the *Commedia* was written. This is most notably evidenced by Albert Russell Ascoli's *Dante and the Making of a Modern Author* (2008), which offers an exhaustive and persuasive account of Dante's self-fashioning as an author by reading his entire *œuvre* through the prism of Arendt's, Barthes's, and Foucault's definitions of authority and authorship, while at the same time paying meticulous attention to the medieval models of authorship (*auctor*) and authority (*auctoritas*) available to Dante. As we saw above, it is the ability to hold simultaneously two different items and their respective contexts in one's mind that defines analogy as a heuristic device. It therefore follows that flattening out the differences between the *Commedia* and the *Recherche* (a significant part of which are a result of their different cultural and historical contexts), would severely diminish the analogy's potential for offering new insights. I have focused here on the benefits of reading by analogy for Dante studies, but the same applies to Proust studies. If we read Proust with a medieval counterpart rather than a twentieth-century author our perspective is broadened: we are alerted to different characteristics than those that arrest us when we approach him only in terms of his historical context.[9]

This book was first inspired by the analogy between Proust and Dante's use of the figure of the first-person narrator who becomes a writer (or rather, in Dante's case, a *poeta vates*). Once I began to consider the *Commedia* and the *Recherche* together, I identified further parallels that were worth exploring. I saw that both texts conceptualize literary creation as a journey and expressed this through imagery drawn in part from classical literature. At the same time, the journey metaphor is complicated in both texts by their non-linear treatment of temporality, which creates a resistance to the narratives' *telos*. Both works also use guide figures, whose relationship to the protagonist is very gendered. Finally, both works posit a relationship between artistic creation and personal redemption. The narrator-protagonists, their journey to writing, their guide figures, and their artistic redemption thus became the areas focused on in the four chapters that follow. In this respect I agree with Li's account of 'site-specificity' in comparative literature, that is to say: it is the combination of the texts that should determine the area of focus of a comparative reading (2015: 20–21).

In Chapter 1, I explore what kind of protagonist and what kind of relationship to the reader Dante and Proust create through their use of first-person narration. I will also consider what it means to write 'I' in thirteenth- and fourteenth-century Italy and what it means in nineteenth- and twentieth-century France. Dante's poem is widely read as the story of Everyman's journey to salvation, an interpretation justified by the Christian exegetical tradition. But I will show the limits of this reading, which in my view tends to ignore how innovative Dante was in transplanting the emerging individualized subject of lyric poetry into the Christian narrative of salvation. I will do this in particular through close readings of the opening two *canti* of the *Inferno*. I will explore, in contrast, the ways in which Proust seeks to create a faceless, anonymous protagonist, with little authority, who is closer to a universal Everyman figure than Dante's protagonist, focusing in particular on the opening pages of the *Recherche*. I will also analyze the different ways in which Dante and Proust blur the distinction between protagonist, narrator, and author, by considering in particular the passages of the *Commedia* and *Recherche* in which they name themselves. For Proust such episodes play a key role in heightening the ambiguity regarding the relationship between author and protagonist, whereas for Dante they serve to confirm the protagonist's identity as the explicit author (as opposed to implied author) of the text. I will reject the ubiquitous binary of Dante-pilgrim and Dante-poet, by showing that key passages in the poem (specifically *Purgatorio* XXIV and *Paradiso* XXV) draw their force from Dante's collapsing of the distinction between protagonist, narrator, and author.

Chapter 2 compares Dante's and Proust's use of journey metaphors. I will begin by considering their use of Ulysses, the quintessential traveller of Western literature, as a figure for the writer. I will then examine the metaphorical significance for both authors of the descent into Hell, for while it does take place on a literal level in the *Commedia*, it can also be understood in both works as representing an exploration of the self and of the past. I will then explore the strong similarities between both authors' use of flight imagery in the context of artistic creation. While Dante's language of flight draws on classical literature, Christian imagery, and vernacular poetry, Proust focuses on the recent invention of the aeroplane, creating an analogy between artistic and scientific innovation. However, we will see that while in Dante the point of destination is God, Proust's use of flight metaphors does not indicate any such higher alterity. As well as being driven forward by a journey towards writing, the *Commedia* and the *Recherche* also contain digressive and circular elements. I will therefore devote the last section of the chapter to the ways in which the two works resist their *telos* both thematically and in terms of narrative structure. I will consider in particular the *Recherche*'s chapter 'Les Intermittences du cœur' and *Purgatorio* II.

Chapter 3 complements the analyses in Chapters 1 and 2 by exploring the narrator-protagonists' relationship to guide figures. Characters such as Virgil and Beatrice play a paradoxical role, since on the one hand they are meant to highlight Dante's limitations, but on the other hand they also emphasize his poetic talent and uniqueness. I will compare this to Proust's similar use of predecessors and guides as foils (specifically Charles Swann and the grandmother), revealing the continuities between the medieval poem and the modern novel's treatment of gender. Indeed, as we shall see, both works present male mentors as rivals and female mentors as supportive figures putting the protagonist on the right path. The chapter also challenges the common perception that medieval representations of women are inherently more negative than their twentieth-century counterparts by underlining the authority with which Dante invests Beatrice.

In the final volume of the *Recherche*, Proust's narrator declares that art is 'le vrai Jugement dernier' [the real Last Judgment] (IV, 458), but how literally — or seriously — should we take him? By looking at Dante's and Proust's treatments of the notion of artistic redemption together, Chapter 4 will make a case against the idea that art replaces religion in Proust, exploring in particular the doubt, ambiguity, and humour present in the *Recherche*'s accounts of art, artists, and art-lovers. Having shown the ways in which the *Commedia* celebrates Dante's poetic genius and individuality in the preceding chapters, I will here consider the ways in which the poem reminds its readers that these must all be relinquished for the far greater privilege of encountering God. The chapter will thus come to show that while it may at first seem that both works celebrate the redemptive powers of art, they ultimately question them in different ways.

Important new facets and perspectives thus emerge when we read Proust and Dante together, rather than separately. Dante's innovative stress on individuality and poetic talent emerges the most clearly when we realize it is far more explicit than in Proust's introspective twentieth-century novel, which we come to realize is driven by a desire to transcend biography and the stress on individuality. It is the continuity and differences between Dante's and Proust's use of the journey metaphor that illuminate the psychological significance of Dante's journey to the afterworld and allow us to see how Proust's focus on intersubjectivity redirects the tropes he inherits from classical and medieval literature. By considering together the two works' elements of digression and circularity, we can conceptualize all the more clearly their respective narrative structures. The surprising parallels that emerge in Chapter 3 bring to light the pervasiveness of gender dynamics in European culture, be it medieval or modern, and Beatrice's authority is all the more striking because it surpasses that of Proust's female characters. Dante's unwavering Christian faith brings into sharper focus the fact that although Proust makes abundant use of religious language when speaking of art, this comes with a measure of doubt and irony. And the contrast between Proust's elevation of the human and Dante's elevation of the divine explains why the *Commedia* must fall silent when Dante encounters God. But this only becomes clear when we engage with the very fabric of these works through close reading. Jumping between them and interweaving them, this book will fuel an 'interaction between co-present thoughts' (Richards 1936: 93), so that you may see both texts with new eyes.

Notes to the Introduction

1. Of course, this linear summary is reductive and will be accordingly critiqued in Chapters 1 and 2.
2. The same argument has been made in this series by Xiaofan Amy Li, who writes that a comparative literary study should not merely aim to 'state how ideas, styles and pragmatics are similar to or different from each other', but rather 'what is more important is what these similarities and differences say about the texts or issues in question that cannot be revealed without comparing them' (2015: 21).
3. Another comparative article was published the same year: Samuel Borton's 'A Tentative Essay on Dante and Proust' (1958).

4. I have analyzed two of Proust's references to the *Commedia* in the *Recherche* (I, 166–67, and II, 6) elsewhere (Hartley 2017). For further analyses of Proust's references to Dante see: Pappot 2003, Teulade 2010, and Perrus 2014. See also Alberto Beretta Anguissola's entry for Dante in *Dictionnaire Marcel Proust* (Bouillaguet & Rogers 2014: 283–84. On the logical limitations of 'genealogical comparability', see Li 2015: 14–17.
5. The two other book-length studies devoted to Dante and Proust are Stierle 2008 and Rushworth 2016.
6. The comparison between Dante and Proust remains a site for the articulation of opposing interpretations today: *Poetics Today* 28.4 (2007) juxtaposes Gian Balsamo's suggestion that both in the *Commedia* and the *Recherche* the protagonist, thanks to the presence of a female beloved, becomes the narrator, with Joshua Landy's rebuttal of any such understanding of literary vocation in the *Recherche* (Balsamo 2007 and Landy 2007).
7. Bales 1975: 132–33 cites Curtius's interpretation of the symbol of the book in Dante, which includes quotations from the *Vita nuova* and the *Commedia* (1953: 326–32).
8. Exemplified, for instance, by the continued prevalence of the Poet/Pilgrim binary. (See the section 'Revisiting Contini' in Chapter 1.)
9. Comparative projects are usually undertaken between Proust and other twentieth-century authors. Notable examples include Large 2001, Azérad 2002, Tribout-Joseph 2008, and Hägglund 2012. Studies of Proust and earlier authors, or Proust and later authors, are for the most part reception studies. The essays collected by Karen Haddad-Wotling and Vincent Ferré (2010) exemplify the popularity and variety of this type of study among Proustians. Exceptions to the general tendency of comparing Proust with modern authors are Hughes 1994, Watt 2013, and Rushworth 2016.

CHAPTER 1

❖

The Narrator-Protagonist

Revisiting Contini

Dante's *Commedia* and Proust's *Recherche* are both first-person narratives of literary vocation. The *Commedia* tells the story of the poet Dante Alighieri's journey through Hell, Purgatory, and Paradise which takes place over Easter week in 1300. Through extradiegetic comments in which the narrative voice addresses either God, the Muses, or the reader, the *Commedia* also tells the story of its own writing, which in the *Paradiso* will be qualified as 'sacred' (*Par.* XXIII, 62, and XXV, 1). This has led Dante criticism to identify two Dantes: Dante at the time of action, referred to as the 'Pilgrim', and Dante at the time of narration, who is the implied author of the poem, and is referred to as the 'Poet'. *À la recherche du temps perdu* tells the life-story of an anonymous Parisian man roughly contemporary to Proust. This man desires to be a writer since childhood but experiences self-doubt throughout his adolescence and adult years. He keeps shying away from this ambition, until the very end of the novel, when as an older man he finds inspiration in the realization that his whole life experience has provided him with the material to write a book. The novel closes on this moment of inspiration. This has often led readers to conclude that the protagonist will write the book that we have just read, in other words, that he *becomes* the novel's implied author. As we shall see, however, the *Recherche*'s sustained ambiguity resists such a certain conclusion.

The fact that both works are concerned with the protagonist's literary vocation blurs the distinction between the character who narrates and the author. On top of this, the protagonists' similarities with their respective empirical authors lead to a further blurring of the boundaries between fiction and biography. In Dante's case, this is intentional: the implied author (that is, the authorial figure within the text) is explicitly presented as the empirical author of the text (that is, Dante Alighieri, the historical individual). One may therefore speak in his case of an 'explicit author'. In Proust's case, the confusion of fiction with biography is caused both by the narrator-protagonist's anonymity and by the biographizing tendencies of Proust's contemporary readers. Therefore, while Dante in the *Commedia* makes an autobiographical claim, in Proust's case the claim was made for him. In terms of the construction of the relationship between literature and biography, the key difference between these two works, therefore, is that the *Commedia* is built on a poetics of assertiveness while the *Recherche* relies on a poetics of effacement and ambiguity.

Dante's and Proust's use of first-person narration and a protagonist who is — or in Proust's case wants to be — a writer is precisely the concern of one of the foundational essays of modern Dante criticism: Gianfranco Contini's 'Dante come personaggio-poeta della *Commedia*'.[1] Contini opens this essay by suggesting that Proust's *Recherche* can serve as a 'metaphor' through which to approach Dante's *Commedia* (1976: 33). The ambiguity of Proust's novel relies on the double value of its first-person, who is both the subject of a unique and individual story and of a universal human experience. This double dimension, Contini argues, is also embodied by the very plot of the *Recherche*, which is that of a literary vocation: 'Il personaggio che dice "io" si riconosce come poeta, e la curva della vicenda consiste nell'evolvere dell'osservazione in rappresentazione. La vita ha acquistato un senso, restandone identico il contenuto' [The character who says 'I' realizes that he is a poet, and the narrative arc consists in the evolution from observation to representation. Life has acquired a meaning, with its content remaining identical] (1976: 34). The same double dimension of the 'I' can be found in Dante's *Commedia*, though in his case, it should be related to the then wide-spread practice of biblical exegesis. Contini notes two further differences between Dante and Proust. First, whereas in the *Recherche* only the narrator can be identified as an observer and legislator, in the *Commedia* narrator and protagonist are both writers. Secondly, Dante's literary identity in the *Commedia* has to be proven through an engagement with the *auctoritates* of his time, whereas Proust's narrator-protagonist can afford to have greater autonomy. The remainder of Contini's essay is then devoted to assessing whether one can gain greater insights into certain episodes of the *Commedia* if one pays particular attention to the fact that the pilgrim is a 'man of letters' (40). Contini's first case study is *Inferno* V's Francesca, whose rhetoric, he demonstrates, is none other than Dante's. Contini concludes that through the encounter with Paolo and Francesca, Dante is surpassing a courtly understanding of love which had governed his earlier poetic works, in particular the *Vita nuova*. In other words, Francesca represents a stage in Dante's development as a poet. Contini goes on to consider the reference to the poet Guido Cavalcanti in *Inferno* X, arguing that, through Guido, Dante amends for a 'theology used as a trope' (51); the encounter with the poet Forese Donati in *Purgatorio* XXIII, which marks a stylistic blunder committed by Dante in his youth; the encounter with the poet Bonagiunta in *Purgatorio* XXIV, in which Dante defines himself individually as a poet, but also notes his debt to his predecessors; and finally the encounter with the poets Guido Guinizzelli and Arnaut Daniel in *Purgatorio* XXVI, through which he expiates the eros of the Occitan tradition as well as the ethics of the *Vita nuova*. Contini thus describes each character (with the exception perhaps of Bonagiunta) as the embodiment of one of Dante's various literary identities before he became the author of the *Commedia*. Through these characters, these past identities are all rejected to make way for Dante's new identity as the poet of the *Commedia*. Indeed, Contini concludes: 'Ogni tappa e sosta del suo viaggio oltreterreno è una modalità del suo "io" antico vittoriosamente attraversata; quei suoi interlocutori sono loro, storici, e sono altro, simbolo e funzione' [Every stage of his otherworldly journey is a modality of his past self that has been overcome; his interlocutors are both historical individuals and at the same time a symbol and function] (1976: 62).

The present study follows the path opened by Contini in so far as it also considers the analogy between Dante and Proust to be a productive means to approach their texts. Moreover, I will also push further the great innovation of Contini's essay, the reunion of the two Dantes, that is, the Poet and the Pilgrim, who had been separated by early twentieth-century criticism.[2] However, Contini's essay follows the now outdated *Bildungsroman* interpretation of the *Recherche*. As a result, while Contini does connect protagonist and narrator, he preserves their separation by expressing their relationship teleologically in terms of a linear evolution from the status of protagonist to the status of narrator, which is achieved through the expurgation of the protagonist's poetic past. Despite its teleological framing, Contini's essay is however implicitly suggesting that it is reductive to only see two Dantes. Indeed, although the conclusion of the essay groups the various past identities that have been examined under the single heading of 'modalities' of one past self ('modalità del suo "io" antico'), by citing a variety of material in his analyses of Dante's literary encounters, Contini in practice has demonstrated across the essay the diversity of Dante's *œuvre* and, consequently, shown Dante's literary identity not to be monolithic, but composed of many different 'I's. In other words, Contini, in speaking of several 'modalities', is very close to speaking of several Dantes.

My reading of the *Commedia* will not neatly divide Dante's 'I' into two categories, that is, the Pilgrim making the journey and the Poet narrating the journey. Instead, I will view Dante's 'I' as the rhetorical means by which to tie together a multifaceted subject, whose history is formed of the various 'I's he constructed in different texts. These different selves, as I shall further explore in Chapter 2, are all present in the *Commedia*, which is not a sequential summary of Dante's career. While it does pursue the appearance of coherence and presents itself as its author's final word, the poem in fact leaps back and forth between the different perspectives presented in it, which coexist in unresolved tension. The necessity to divide Dante into two characters belies an unease with this multiplicity and instability of the self and the fact that the pronoun 'I' while referring to one person can imply many different perspectives since an individual changes over time.[3] The interplay between time of action and time of narration is a complex one in all first-person narratives due to the fact that a narrator-protagonist is both the subject and the object of the narration. Correcting Contini's reading of the *Recherche*, according to which the protagonist becomes the implied author of the novel, will enable us to reconsider the parallels and dissimilarities between Dante and Proust's use of the first person and, consequently, to revisit our assumptions about Dante's 'I'. This will be the first step towards a wider reconsideration of the function of first-person narration in both authors.

The division of the *Recherche*'s ambiguous *je* into protagonist and narrator, and the *telos* that is implied by this division, came under question in the 1990s. Margaret Gray refutes it persuasively in *Postmodern Proust*, in which she observes that criticism bends over backwards to divide the *Recherche*'s *je* into the category of 'erring hero' and 'masterful narrator' in order to satisfy the *Bildungsroman* reading of the novel. Gray argues that the novel collapses temporal and psychological distinctions of this kind through its refusal to stage the moment when the protagonist becomes the narrator and also by flattening temporal distinctions through its indiscriminate use of the first-person (1992: 39–42). This latter tendency of the *Recherche* is demonstrated through examples of passages in which Proust uses *je* to refer simultaneously to the protagonist, the narrator, and the implied author, such as for instance: 'je n'ai plus le temps, avant mon départ pour Balbec (où, pour mon malheur, je vais faire un second séjour qui sera aussi le dernier) de commencer des peintures du monde qui trouveront leur place bien plus tard' [I no longer have the time, before my departure for Balbec (where, to my sorrow, I am about to have a second stay which will also be the last) to begin a portrayal of high society which will find its place later on] (III, 139). Gray's reading is in explicit reaction against the precedent set by Gérard Genette, who argued for the absolute division between Proust's protagonist and narrator (1972: 259). Gray's observations resonate strongly with those made more recently by Lino Pertile (2012), who argues that Dante criticism's distinction between pilgrim and poet aims to prove that the character progresses morally and psychologically through the journey. Pertile suggests instead that the *Commedia* offers little evidence of any such spiritual growth. This goes against the traditional twentieth-century understanding of the *Commedia* as a conversion narrative, perhaps best encapsulated by John Freccero, which forms the basis for Contini's analogy between Dante and Proust's works.[4]

I read the first-person in both the *Commedia* and the *Recherche* as shifting and multivalent, able to refer within the space of a single sentence to protagonist and to narrator, and at times referring to both simultaneously. There remain instances in both works in which a distance is set out between the subject's perspective at the time of action and the time of narration.[5] In Proust this is most clearly the case in instances of prolepsis (temporal anticipation) which reveal that the protagonist will become a writer. Phrases such as 'Même plus tard, quand je commençai de composer un livre, certaines phrases dont la qualité ne suffit pas pour me décider à le continuer, j'en retrouvai l'équivalent dans Bergotte' [Even later, when I began writing a book, if the quality of certain sentences was not sufficient to determine me to continue, I would find its equivalent in Bergotte] (I, 95) point at the difference between a point in time in which the subject did not know that he would become a writer and the time of narration, when it is implied that he has become a writer. In the *Commedia*, Dante draws attention to the time of narration through addresses to the reader ('lettor'), as well as references to himself in the present tense. For example, the phrase 'Allor mi dolsi, e ora mi ridoglio' [I suffered then, and I suffer now again] (*Inf.* XXVI, 19) marks the temporal gap between time of action and time of narration through the repetition of the verb *dolere*. However, both works are also wont to use the first person in a manner that makes it impossible for readers to draw distinctions between protagonist, narrator, and, in Dante's case, author. I will account for this ambiguity by referring to the subjects of the *Commedia* and the *Recherche* as 'narrator-protagonists'.

Dante's both famous and ambiguous self-definition in *Purgatorio* XXIV is an illustrative example of the manner in which he blurs distinctions between his past and present literary identities. In this episode, the narrator-protagonist responds to the poet Bonagiunta da Lucca, who inquires after his identity by citing one of the poems of the *Vita nuova*, Dante's first book, a prosimetrum which tells the story of his falling in love with Beatrice, his discovery of a poetics of praise in order to celebrate her respectfully in his poetry, a lapse in fidelity caused by her death, and at the close of the book, a renewed commitment to writing poetry that is worthy of her. The inquiry, and Dante's answer, read as follows:

'Ma dì s'i' veggio qui colui che fore
trasse le nove rime, cominciando
"*Donne ch'avete intelletto d'amore*"'.

E io a lui: 'I' mi son un che, quando
Amor mi spira, noto, e a quel modo
ch'e' ditta dentro vo significando'. (*Purg.* XXIV, 49–54)

['But tell me if I see here the one | who drew forth the new rimes, beginning | "*Donne ch'avete intelletto d'amore*"'. | And I to him: 'I am one who, when | Love inspires me, takes note, and follows on | according to the way he dictates within me.']

Dante's reply to Bonagiunta is a clear continuation of the episode of the *Vita nuova* in which he stages the discovery of the poetics of praise ('stilo de la loda') through a moment of inspiration (*VN*, XIX, 2–3). Dante could therefore be understood here to be repeating his account of the process of being inspired by 'Amor' first given in the *Vita nuova*. Such a reading would be further suggested by the fact that the protagonist of the *Vita nuova* often dialogues with a character referred to as 'Amor', who is a personification of earthly love.[6] Following this line of argument, Dante's answer to Bonagiunta's question could be interpreted as a 'yes'. In other words: the poetics of the protagonist of the *Commedia* are those of the poet of the *Vita nuova* and he therefore still has much progress to make in order to become the narrator, who is a *scriba dei*.[7] This teleological reading would be built on the central claim that the *io* of line 52 corresponds to the protagonist of the *Commedia* ('Dante-pilgrim'), and not its narrator ('Dante-poet').

However, one could equally argue that in *Purgatorio* XXIV, 'Dante-pilgrim' is describing the process of 'Dante-poet' as *scriba dei* in the *Commedia*. There is indeed a clear parallel between 'Dante-pilgrim', who says that he is one who writes down what love tells him, and 'Dante-poet' who describes himself as a scribe writing under God's dictation (as in, for example, *Par.* X, 27). In Barolini's words: 'In this *terzina*, and within the context of love poetry, the relation between the dictator (Love) and the transcriber (Dante) is exactly analogous to the relation between God and the poet within the larger context of the *Comedy*' (1984: 90). Some readers may go so far as to suggest that 'Amor' in *Purgatorio* XXIV should therefore not be understood as the love described in lyric poetry, but as a reference to God, indeed the *Commedia* famously ends on a verse which describes God as 'l'amor che move il sole e l'altre stelle' [the love that moves the sun and the other stars] (*Par.* XXXIII,

145). Interpreted this way, the passage shows the protagonist of the *Commedia* distancing himself from the *Vita nuova*, a work which was not sufficiently Christian. The 'Amor' of *Purgatorio* XXIV has accordingly been interpreted as a reference to God and more specifically, due to the verb 'mi spira', to the Holy Spirit (Martinez 1983: 43, and Hollander 1999: 269). In such a reading, Dante's reply to Bonagiunta is understood as a 'no'. There is however an internal contradiction in such a reading of the passage, since it both presupposes that narrator and protagonist are two clearly distinct individuals, yet also suggests that the protagonist ('Dante-pilgrim') is expressing the views of the narrator ('Dante-poet', the *scriba dei*).

Ultimately, any acknowledgement that *Purg.* XXIV, 52–54, is a statement on the poetics of the *Commedia* as a whole, irrespective of the reader's understanding of the word 'Amor', collapses temporal and psychological distinctions between protagonist and narrator. These verses can therefore only be spoken by a narrator-protagonist who is both the character interacting with Bonagiunta and the implied author of the poem that we are reading. Which explains why Dante replies neither 'yes' nor 'no' and gives instead an answer that is open to interpretation. The multivalence of these lines has already been posited by scholars arguing for a more complex and inclusive understanding of the word 'Amor' in the *Commedia*. This is notably the subject of Tristan Kay's book *Dante's Lyric Redemption*, in which he argues: 'Whatever the precise valence of the term "Amor" in the famous self-definition of *Purgatorio* XXIV [...], there can be no doubt that Dante emphasizes not a rupture between his activity as the "cantor amoris" of the *Vita nova* and as the "scriba dei" of the *Commedia*, but rather a *continuity*' (2015: 153–54). In similar terms, Vittorio Montemaggi states: 'No contradiction need be seen [...]. "Amor" is accurately read here as referring not only to the love of love poetry but also to God' (2010: 71).[8] These interpretations of *Purgatorio* XXIV can be further bolstered with Regina Psaki's demonstration that earthly, sexual love is present throughout the *Commedia*, including the *Paradiso*, where it contributes to the blessed souls experience of beatitude (2003). I propose that we extend this multivalence to our understanding of the pronoun 'I'. The only way in which we can do justice to the rich allusiveness of these verses is by accepting that Dante used them to tie together his protagonist and his narrator, as well as his past and present self. The fact that this is achieved through a first-person statement in the indicative mood shows that Dante's poetics of assertiveness remains present even when he is at his most ambivalent. For although Dante's *io* is an ambiguous signifier in temporal terms, there is one aspect in which the signified remains constant and unequivocal: its reference to Dante Alighieri, the determined historical individual explicitly presented as the author of the text.

'Dante' and 'Marcel'

> 'Dante, perché Virgilio se ne vada,
> non pianger anco, non piangere ancora;
> ché pianger ti conven per altra spada'.
> [...]
> quando mi volsi al suon del nome mio,
> che di necessità qui si registra,
>
> vidi la donna che pria m'appario
> velata sotto l'angelica festa,
> drizzar li occhi ver' me di qua dal rio. (*Purg.* xxx, 55–66)

['Dante, because Virgil has left, | do not cry, do not cry yet; | for you will be crying from another sword'. | [...] | when I turned at the sound of my own name, | which by necessity is recorded here, | I saw a woman who at first appeared | veiled under the angelic celebration, | lift her eyes towards me from across the river.]

This passage contains the famous instance in which the narrator-protagonist of the *Commedia* is named, with the caveat that it is done out of necessity. As a result, this episode has been read as constituting what Philippe Lejeune calls an 'autobiographical pact', that is, an act of naming which offers the guarantee that protagonist, narrator, and author are all the same person (1975: 26).[9] But even without the clarification of *Purgatorio* xxx, the reader has already been led to believe that the narrator-protagonist is the historical individual Dante Alighieri. This is suggested first of all by the pilgrim's encounters and conversations with people whom the author of the *Commedia* knew (for example, he meets his teacher Brunetto Latini in *Inferno* xv and his friend and poetic correspondent Forese Donati in *Purgatorio* xxiii). Secondly, many characters prophesize Dante's 'future' exile from Florence. And thirdly, references are made to Dante's previous literary output, the most explicit of these being the *Commedia*'s three citations of Dante's earlier poetry.[10]

Proust stages his authorial presence in an altogether different manner from Dante, using authorial interventions not to clarify the identity of the implied author, but to further its ambiguity. Moreover, Proust and the narrator-protagonist's biographical data do not match up and this confirms that the *Recherche* is intended to be read as a work of fiction, not as an autobiography.[11] As observed by Contini, the 'personaggio-poeta' of the *Recherche* is anonymous throughout the novel except in two instances where Marcel, Proust's own first name, appears. Both are found in *La Prisonnière* and are spoken by Albertine, the protagonist's lover. The first instance is framed in a very tongue-in-cheek manner:

> Elle retrouvait la parole, elle disait: 'Mon' ou 'Mon chéri', suivis l'un ou l'autre de mon nom de baptême, ce qui, en donnant au narrateur le même prénom qu'à l'auteur de ce livre, eût fait: 'Mon Marcel', 'Mon chéri Marcel'. (iii, 583)
>
> [As soon as she was awake enough to speak, she would say: 'My' or 'My darling', followed one or the other by my first name, which, were we to give the narrator the same name as the author of this book, would sound like: 'My Marcel', 'My darling Marcel'.]

Philippe Lejeune reads this passage as an assertion of non-identity between author and narrator: the hypothetical construction tells us, implicitly, that the narrator does not have the same name as 'l'auteur de ce livre'. Lejeune observes that the comment can only be coming from the author (whom in this analysis shall be referred to as the 'implied author'), since a fictional narrator cannot know the name of his or her author. As a result, Lejeune argues, 'cette bizarre intrusion d'auteur fonctionne à la fois comme pacte romanesque et comme indice autobiographique, et installe le texte dans un espace ambigu' [this strange authorial intrusion simultaneously guarantees that this is a novel and acts as a clue that it is autobiographical, which places the text in an ambiguous space] (1975: 29).

However, in the second episode in which the name Marcel appears, we are not provided with a conditional:

> Un cycliste me porta un mot d'elle pour que je prisse patience et où il y avait de ces gentilles expressions qui lui étaient familières: 'Mon chéri et cher Marcel, j'arrive moins vite que ce cycliste dont je voudrais bien prendre la bécane pour être plus tôt près de vous. Comment pouvez-vous croire que je puisse être fâchée [...]? [...] Quelle idée vous faites-vous donc? Quel Marcel! Quel Marcel! Toute à vous, ton Albertine'. (III, 663)
>
> [A cyclist delivered a note from her encouraging me to be patient. It contained some of those sweet expressions that were common to her: 'My darling and dear Marcel, I won't arrive as fast as this cyclist, whose bike I would love to take to be close to you sooner. How could you believe that I am cross [...]? [...] Where did you get that kind of idea? What a Marcel! What a Marcel! Entirely yours, your Albertine'.]

The Pléiade edition of the *Recherche* directed by Tadié observes, on the basis of the manuscript drafts for this passage, that the name Marcel was a later addition, concluding, 'cette démarche, chez Proust, est tout le contraire d'une suppression de l'autobiographie, mais plutôt le désir de souligner à la fois la proximité et l'éloignement de l'auteur du roman par rapport à son narrateur' [Proust's process is the very opposite of a removal of autobiography, it shows rather a desire to underline both the proximity and the distance between the author of the novel and his narrator] (III, 1718). The *Recherche* therefore has both a narrator-protagonist ('le narrateur') *and* an implied author ('l'auteur'), and these are not the same person, as is made clear by metaleptic breaks in the narration, which remind us of the existence of 'l'auteur de ce livre' (III, 383).

Let us now consider two important instances of metalepsis in the *Recherche*, both of which are based on the use of proper names. The first is well known among Proustians, and has all the appearances of an authorial intervention, functioning according to Lejeune's terms as both a 'pacte romanesque' and an 'indice autobiographique':

> Dans ce livre où il n'y a pas un seul fait qui ne soit fictif, où il n'y a pas un seul personnage 'à clefs', où tout a été inventé par moi selon les besoins de ma démonstration, je dois dire [...] que seuls les parents millionnaires de Françoise [...] sont des gens réels, qui existent. Et persuadé que leur modestie ne s'en offensera pas, pour la raison qu'ils ne liront jamais ce livre, [...] je transcris ici leur nom véritable: ils s'appellent [...] Larivière. (IV, 424)

[In this book in which there is not a single fact that is not fictional, where there is not a single 'personnage à clefs', where everything has been invented by myself according to the requirements of my demonstration, I must say [...] that only Françoise's millionaire relatives [...] are real people, who exist. And convinced that I will not offend their humility, for the reason that they will never read this book, [...] I am recording here their actual name: they are called [...] Larivière.][12]

The Larivières were relatives of Proust's housekeeper, Céleste Albaret. This passage therefore simultaneously tells us that Françoise is and is not Céleste Albaret: she is Céleste, because she is related to the Larivières, and she is not her, because there is no 'personnage "à clefs"' in the *Recherche*. The passage creates a sense of disruption, as it would seem that Marcel Proust himself is speaking, letting his desire to pay moral tribute to the Larivières come before his own novelistic conventions.

An even more elaborate operation takes place when Proust confronts the nature of the character Charles Swann, whom his contemporaries believed represented one of Proust's acquaintances, Charles Haas. Proust had expressed his opposition to such a reading in a 1914 letter to Madame Strauss: 'Celui que vous appelez Swann-Haas (quoique ce ne soit pas Haas et qu'il n'y ait nulle part clés ni portraits)' [the man whom you call Swann-Haas (though he is not Haas and that there are no *clés* or portraits in the novel)] (*Corr.* XIII, 231), but he would also come to address the issue within the text of the *Recherche* itself, in the volume *La Prisonnière*:

Et pourtant, cher Charles Swann, que j'ai si peu connu quand j'étais encore si jeune et vous près du tombeau, c'est déjà parce que celui que vous deviez considérer comme un petit imbécile a fait de vous le héros d'un de ses romans, qu'on recommence à parler de vous et que peut-être vous vivrez. Si dans le tableau de Tissot représentant le balcon du Cercle de la rue Royale, où vous êtes entre Galliffet, Edmond de Polignac et Saint-Maurice, on parle tant de vous, c'est parce qu'on voit qu'il y a quelques traits de vous dans le personnage de Swann. (III, 705)

[And yet, dear Charles Swann, whom I knew so little when I was still so young and you, one step from the grave, it's actually because the person whom you thought of as a little idiot made you the hero of one of his novels that people are talking about you again and that perhaps you will live on. If in the painting of the balcony of the Cercle de la rue Royale by Tissot, where you are among Galliffet, Edmond de Polignac and Saint-Maurice, people talk so much about you, it is because they can see some of your features in the character of Swann.]

The first sentence of this passage is in keeping with the reader's expectations for the *je* of the narrator-protagonist. We can associate it with other instances of prolepsis which inform us that the protagonist will one day become a writer. We are, moreover, provided with a novel about Swann within the *Recherche*: the chapter 'Un amour de Swann'. There is no frame telling us whether we are supposed to read 'Un amour de Swann' as a book within a book, but we are told in *La Prisonnière* that the protagonist has been taking notes about Swann and Odette's love affair (III, 868) and the old Odette in *Le Temps retrouvé* is all too keen to offer him details of her relationship with Swann, in the hope that it will provide him with material to write about (IV, 597–600). However, the fiction of Proust's novel is subverted in the second sentence, which makes a reference to an extra-textual reality: the painting of the circle of the rue Royale by James Tissot. The Marquis Gaston de Galliffet, the Prince Edmond de Polignac, and the Baron Gaston de Saint-Maurice are indeed in this painting, and to their right stands Charles Haas. Suddenly, we realize that within this context 'cher Charles Swann' signifies 'cher Charles Haas' and not the fictional character Charles Swann. The second time that the name 'Swann' appears in the passage, it is used to signify the fictional character in contrast to one of the character's sources. In other words, what we are reading is: 'Dear Charles Swann, by whom I actually mean Charles Haas, there is something of you in Swann, by whom I mean Swann, the fictional character'. Of course, by choosing not to write 'Charles Haas', but using the fictional name to say two different things, Proust leads us to acknowledge simultaneously the connection and the separation between his life and his work. By the end of the passage we are no longer certain as to whether we should understand the first sentence as referring to the fictional narrator-protagonist's relationship with Swann, or to Proust's relationship with Charles Haas, or to both.

Another example of such a blurring of boundaries is the sentence ending: 'un enthousiasme qui aurait pu être fécond si j'étais resté seul, et m'aurait évité ainsi le détour de bien des années inutiles par lesquelles j'allais encore passer avant que se déclarât la vocation invisible dont cet ouvrage est l'histoire' [an enthusiasm that could have been productive, had I remained alone, and which would have consequently saved me the detour of many fruitless years which I still had to go through before the invisible vocation, of which this work is the story, would declare itself] (II, 691). The *je* seems to be that of the narrator-protagonist, considering his former actions with the benefit of hindsight, but this is problematized by the indication 'cet ouvrage' which refers to the book that we are reading. The reference to 'cet ouvrage' can therefore be read as either a metaleptic break, or as evidence that the book that we are reading is the novel that the narrator-protagonist decides to write at the end of *Le Temps retrouvé*. Whichever interpretation we choose to follow, we can see that the relationship between the implied author and the narrator-protagonist is an ambiguous one. Metaleptic breaks in the *Commedia*, in contrast, serve to assert that empirical author, implied author, and narrator-protagonist are all the same individual. This is the case for instance in the famous opening of *Paradiso* XXV, in which the *io* draws together the protagonist at the time of the otherworldly journey, the narrator (or implied author), *and* the empirical author:

> Se mai continga che 'l poema sacro
> al quale ha posto mano e cielo e terra,
> sì che m'ha fatto per molti anni macro,
>
> vinca la crudeltà che fuor mi serra
> del bello ovile ov'io dormi' agnello,
> nimico ai lupi che li danno guerra;
>
> con altra voce omai, con altro vello
> ritornerò poeta, e in sul fonte
> del mio battesmo prenderò 'l cappello;

> però che ne la fede, che fa conte
> l'anime a Dio, quivi intra' io, e poi
> Pietro per lei sì mi girò la fonte. (*Par.* XXV, 1–12)

[If it ever should come to be that the sacred poem | to which both heaven and earth have lent a hand, | so that it has for many years worn me thin, | should win over the cruelty that keeps me out | of the good sheepfold where I slept as a lamb, | enemy to the wolves that are at war there; | with another voice now, with another fleece, | I shall return a poet, and in my baptismal font | I shall take on the crown; | Since in faith, which recommends souls | to God, I entered here, and then | Peter in its name encircled my forehead.]

The canto opens with a description of the future effect that the poem we are reading might have on the fate of its implied author, who is in fact the empirical individual Dante Alighieri in exile from Florence. If the success of the *Commedia* allows his exile to end, the narrator-protagonist tells us, he will return to Florence. There, he will be crowned poet in the baptistry where he, that is, Dante Alighieri, the empirical individual, was baptized. This is because St Peter crowned him, the character undertaking the otherworldly journey recounted in the poem, a faithful Christian. (The verses come after Dante has been examined on the subject of faith by St Peter and answered the questions correctly in *Paradiso* XXIV.) Thus, the opening lines assert the equivalence of empirical author and implied author and, on top of this, the concluding lines state that the otherworldly journey was made by the empirical author.

In the *Recherche*, not only is the relationship between narrator-protagonist and implied author ambiguous, but we are also never told whether either of these correspond to Marcel Proust, the empirical author. While the *Commedia* is filled with references to Dante Alighieri's biography and literary works, Proust on the contrary only used what material from his personal life could be passed off as generic. Marcel Proust, the empirical author, was homosexual, half Jewish, and far from suffering from writer's block had been writing from a young age. When he was in his twenties, Proust was already publishing articles in a range of periodicals (*Le Mensuel*, *Le Banquet*, *La Revue blanche*) and daily newspapers (*Le Figaro*, *Le Gaulois*).[13] He also published a collection of short stories (*Les Plaisirs et les jours*, 1896) and attempted to write a first novel (*Jean Santeuil*, written between 1895 and 1897). In 1904 and 1906 he published translations of Ruskin (*La Bible d'Amiens* and *Sésame et les lys*), and in 1908 a series of pastiches of canonical French authors.[14] Later that year, he began work on the abandoned essay *Contre Sainte-Beuve*, which we shall consider in the following section. In the *Recherche,* Proust has secondary characters who are Jewish, homosexual, and writers, thereby carrying features that Proust did not pass on to his narrator-protagonist. One might think for example of Bloch, the narrator-protagonist's old school friend who is Jewish and a literary hack.

It has been argued that Proust's literary career progressed towards writing texts that were less and less autobiographical, a progression that resulted in the creation of an intangible *je*.[15] The *Recherche* thus offers us a narrator-protagonist who is more mundane than his author and, more importantly, who is *not* a novelist: 'Je ne suis pas romancier' (III, 881). However, the narrator-protagonist's neuroticism and hypersensitivity, to which we shall return, are striking features which are likely to be directly inherited from his author. Proust in a letter of 1902 dismisses any such commonalities between himself and his narrator-protagonist as nothing more than the result of a lack of imagination: 'par excès de fatigue pour des détails purement matériels, je me dispense d'inventer pour mon héros et prends des traits vrais de moi' [out of exhaustion, when it comes to purely material details, I shirk from inventing features for my hero and borrow some of my own instead] (*Corr.* XIX: 580). In other words, we should not read any ulterior motives into these similarities. Joshua Landy, one of the most passionate defenders of the fictionality of the *Recherche*, suggests that this is a case where we should take the author's word for it: 'many of the episodes in the novel have echoes in Proust's own experience; but this is only to say that Proust, like other artists, fashioned something beautiful out of that experience — not that he fashioned himself in the process' (2004: 18). Dante's literary enterprise, on the other hand, may certainly be considered an example of self-representation.

Allegory and Biographilia

The *Commedia*'s innovative stress on individuality has been most famously accounted for by Erich Auerbach, who in *Dante: Poet of the Secular World*, originally *Dante als Dichter der irdischen Welt* (1929), contrasts Dante's work with what he dismissively calls the 'vulgar spiritualism' of earlier literature: 'Dante was the first to configure [...] man [...] not as an abstract or anecdotal representative of an ethical type, but man as we know him in his living historical reality, the concrete individual in his unity and wholeness' (2001: 174–75). In a later essay entitled 'Figura', Auerbach would return to the originality of the *Commedia* and address it through the mode of biblical interpretation known as 'figuralism'. According to this method of reading, an event in the Old Testament exists in its own right, but at the same time also stands for an event in the New Testament (for example, the story of Jonah and the whale prefigures the Resurrection of Christ). So too, characters in the *Commedia* both exist as specific, historical individuals and, at the same time, carry an allegorical meaning (for example, Virgil is both the Latin poet guiding Dante and a figure for human reason). Figuralism is different from allegory because it offers both levels of meaning, whereas allegory is a non-historicized representation of abstract values. Figuralism, moreover, is an interpretative act: it relies on the reader to decipher the abstract (or general) value held by the individual character.

Auerbach's reading is a useful starting-point for a consideration of Dante's self-representation as the protagonist of an individualized journey to God. The concept of figuralism takes into account both the mode of reading employed by Dante's expected readership and the poem's innovativeness. A counter-argument to Auerbach's approach would be Leo Spitzer's 'A Note on the Poetic and the Empirical "I" in Medieval Authors'. Basing himself on the medieval horizon of expectation, Spitzer rejects the idea that Dante's highly individualized self-representation should have a bearing on our understanding of the poem which, according to him, should only be read for its allegorical value: 'Dante is not interested, poetically, in himself *qua* himself' (1946: 417). Spitzer's dismissal seems rather problematic in so far as it ignores the ground-breaking nature of Dante's use of the first-person. The Spitzerian reading of Dante's *io* has recently been critiqued by Marco Santagata in his introduction to Dante's *Opere* in the following terms:

> Pochi autori hanno parlato del mondo con la larghezza e la profondità di sguardo di Dante. Eppure questo scrittore [...] è di un egocentrismo che lascia interdetti. [...] Dante sembra incapace di immaginare un libro nel quale la sua persona, o comunque un personaggio che porta il suo nome, non abbiano una presenza di rilievo; soprattutto, non sembra concepire altra scrittura che in prima persona. E ciò anche quando l'uso dell' 'io' va contro a regole di genere o a prassi consolidate. (2011: xliii)
>
> [Few authors have spoken of the world with such breadth and depth of gaze as Dante. Yet the egocentrism of this writer [...] is stupefying. [...] Dante seems incapable of imagining a book in which his person, or at least a character bearing his name, does not hold a central role. More than anything else, he seems unable not to write in the first person. And this is the case even when the use of 'I' goes against the rules of genre or well-established praxes.]

Dante was well aware that his tendency to speak of himself could be considered transgressive, and this is made clear in his abandoned philosophical treatise the *Convivio*. In the *Convivio*, Dante tells the reader that before he can begin his exposition, he must exculpate himself of two impurities ('macule'), the first being that 'parlare alcuno di se medesimo pare non licito' ('it does not seem permissible for someone to speak of himself') (*Conv*. I, ii, 1–2). Having explained the potential pitfalls of speaking of oneself, Dante suggests two exceptional cases in which it is permissible to do so: one can talk about oneself to defend oneself against infamy, as Boethius did in the *Consolation of Philosophy*, or in order to serve others by way of example, as Augustine did in the *Confessions* (*Conv*. I, ii, 13–14). Both justifications apply in the case of the *Commedia*, but it is the latter which would have been most palpable to readers who could see in Dante's journey from sin to salvation a struggle shared by all humans and an example to be followed. Dante's need to justify himself through the citation of authoritative examples should however alert us to the unorthodoxy of his choice to favour the use of the first-person and write about himself.

Dante's textual self-representation was revolutionary. To appreciate this better we must consider that Italian vernacular literature was born from a predominantly oral culture, with the result that the first-person would be taken by audiences to refer to the performer rather than to an invisible (and consequently non-existent) author. Paul Zumthor (1975: 167) indeed describes subjectivity in medieval literature — 'Toute origine s'efface: la voix s'étouffe dans le texte qu'elle compose' [All origin is erased: the voice is muted by its own text] — with the same vocabulary with which Roland Barthes announced the death of the author: 'l'écriture est la destruction de toute voix, de toute origine' [writing is the destruction of all voice, all origin] (1968: 63). The 'pre-author age', which provides the backdrop for Dante's enterprise, and the 'post-author age', which has been seen as being announced by Proust, have thus been described in a very similar manner. What is meant by the 'age of the author' is a period of history in which biographical modes of reading literature were popular.

Such a mode of reading explains a text through the life of its author and as a result may suggest that a greater proximity between the views or events recounted in a text and the views or experiences of its author gives the text greater persuasiveness or veracity.[16] Claudio Giunta has argued that the thirteenth-century Italian lyric poetry known as *stilnovo*, which was the context for Dante's literary beginnings, differed from previous courtly models in so far as it considered personal experience to be a source of persuasiveness (2002: 355–59). We can recognize in such a belief the seeds of the *Commedia*'s claims to truthfulness, such as for example that found in *Inferno* XVI, 124–36, when the monster Geryon is introduced through an address to the reader in which Dante swears he truly saw what he is about to describe.

Duecento poetry's newfound assertion of individuality has been set into a wider context by Olivia Holmes in *Assembling the Lyric Self: Authorship from Troubadour Song to Italian Poetry Book*. Holmes explains that thirteenth-century Europe saw two innovations: first, 'a sharp increase in vernacular literacy and the widespread appearance, for the first time since classical antiquity, of a large body of secular literature for popular consumption'; and secondly, the presence in anthologies of lyric poetry of *vidas* and *razos* (2000: 1). *Vidas* were introductory biographies of the troubadours and *razos* were explanations of the circumstances in which individual songs were composed. These accounts were often entirely fictional, but they did promote the assumption that a knowledge of the life of the author was essential to a full appreciation of the work. This biographizing tendency, combined with the poetic utterance becoming frozen on the page instead of endlessly re-utilizable in the act of performance, meant that the poetic 'I' could become associated with the figure of the author. Holmes thus argues that her study traces 'the partial creation of conditions of possibility in which the Romantic concept of transparent authorship could eventually arise' (2000: 4). Dante's innovation in this context was to transfer the emerging biographizing tendencies of lyric poetry into the genre of the allegorical dream vision and to present himself as a divinely inspired poet. Relying on his medieval readers to extract the figural meaning behind his individualized journey, Dante was able to construct a narrative functioning both as a personal story carrying out an individualist agenda of 'self-authorization' and as the universal story of Everyman's journey from sin to salvation.

Dante's 'self-authorization' is the subject of Albert Russell Ascoli's *Dante and the Making of a Modern Author*, a study which examines the strategies through which Dante fashioned himself as an *auctor*, a title which in European medieval literary culture was used to describe canonical classical authors, theologians, and the human authors of the Bible.[17] The category of *auctor* should therefore have excluded Dante, who was lay, alive, and writing in the vernacular. Yet all evidence shows that Dante, through the *Commedia*, did achieve such authority: the *Commedia* began to accumulate an exegetical tradition from the moment it appeared in manuscript form, and within fifty years of Dante's death Boccaccio was called to Florence to deliver public lectures on the poem. Ascoli thus defines the subject matter of his book as follows:

> How a culture in general, in the person of one of its most remarkable members,

> can engage in a distinctly conservative attempt to maintain and embody fundamental ideological categories, but still end up radically transfiguring those categories and that ideology. (2008: 12)

Dante's authority in the *Commedia* differs from that of the traditional *auctoritates* not only in terms of genre and language, but crucially through its focus on Dante as a historicized individual. Drawing on both medieval theories of authorship and twentieth-century theories of authority and authorship (Arendt, Barthes, Foucault), Ascoli is able to demonstrate the 'proto-modern' character of Dante's authority, which includes a stress on personality and creative agency.

While Dante wrote against a backdrop in which figural readings were the norm and the figure of the *auctor* was understood as a de-personalized speaker of universal truths, Proust made his literary beginnings at a time when works of literature were interpreted in relation to their author's biography. The *Recherche* at the first stages of its conception was an essay in reaction to Charles Augustin de Sainte-Beuve, a literary critic who argued that an informed interpretation of a text required a knowledge of the life and personality of its author. These early drafts alternate between essayistic sections and narrative sketches that would later be turned into episodes of the *Recherche*. *Contre Sainte-Beuve*, a posthumously published selection of the non-narrative sections of the drafts, offers critics an insight into what Proust's motivations and concerns were when he began elaborating his future masterpiece.

In *Contre Sainte-Beuve*, Proust takes a now famous stand against biographical readings of works of literature:

> L'œuvre de Sainte-Beuve n'est pas une œuvre profonde. La fameuse méthode [...] qui consiste à ne pas séparer l'homme et l'œuvre [...] méconnaît ce qu'une fréquentation un peu profonde avec nous-mêmes nous apprend: qu'un livre est le produit d'un autre moi que celui que nous manifestons dans nos habitudes, dans la société, dans nos vices. Ce moi-là, si nous voulons essayer de le comprendre, c'est au fond de nous-même, en essayant de le recréer en nous, que nous pouvons y parvenir. (*CSB*: 221–22)
>
> [Sainte-Beuve's works have no depth. His famous method [...], which consists in not separating the man from the work, [...] ignores what any vaguely deep self-examination will tell us: that a book is the product of a different self from the one that we show in our habits, in society, in our vices. *That* self, if we are to try to understand it, can only be reached deep inside ourselves, by trying to recreate it within us.]

In other words, Sainte-Beuve's approach followed the same logic as the *vidas* and *razos* did in troubadour tradition: explaining the texts through the biography of the author. Proust in rejecting nineteenth-century 'biographilia' paved the way for the twentieth century's more problematized view of the relationship between author and text. As a result it has been said that *Contre Sainte-Beuve* foreshadows Barthes's 'Death of the Author'. This however would be inaccurate. Proust in his essay does not claim that there is no connection between the author and the work, but, on the contrary, argues that works of literature are the true expression of their creator's subjectivity. Whereas for Barthes writing is the destruction of voice and origin (1968: 63), Proust saw literature as being the only instance in which one's true voice makes itself heard. In contrast with occupations other than writing, which are deemed socially conditioned and therefore false, Proust in *Contre Sainte-Beuve* praises:

> L'occupation littéraire où, dans la solitude, faisant taire ces paroles qui sont aux autres autant qu'à nous, et avec lesquelles, même seuls, nous jugeons les choses sans être nous-mêmes [...] nous tâchons d'entendre, et de rendre, le son vrai de notre cœur. (*CSB*: 224)
>
> [Literary creation, where, in solitude, silencing those words that belong to others as much as they do to us, and through which, even alone, we judge things without being ourselves [...] we strive to hear, and render, the true sound of our heart.]

Proust thus asserts that biographical information should not have a bearing on our reading of a work of literature, because a man's work is more revelatory of his true nature than a man's life. He essentially inverts Sainte-Beuve's hierarchy: the person should be judged by the work, not the work by the person.

Proust's claim for the unity between a work of art and the individuality of its creator would remain constant throughout the elaboration of the *Recherche*, from *Contre Sainte-Beuve* — 'tout [est] dans l'individu' [everything lies in the individual] (*CSB*: 220) — to the Albertine cycle, that is the volumes that Proust was working on when he died: 'l'art [...] extériorisant dans les couleurs du spectre la composition intime de ces mondes que nous appelons les individus, et que sans l'art nous ne connaîtrions jamais' [art [...] externalizing through the colours of the spectrum the intimate composition of those worlds which we call individuals, and which, were it not for art, we would never know] (III, 762). In the *Commedia*, too, individuals are judged by the literature that they produced rather than by their lives. For example, the lyric love poets Guido Guinizzelli and Arnaut Daniel are found on Purgatory's terrace of lust, which suggests that they are being punished for the eroticism of their poetry (*Purg.* XXVI) rather than for their actions, thus rendering literal the Christian notion of retribution that Proust uses rhetorically: 'l'art est [...] le vrai Jugement dernier' [art is [...] the real Last Judgment] (IV, 458).

Proust's stress on individuality appears to be in tension with the narrator-protagonist's drive towards universalism in the concluding pages of the *Recherche*. Indeed, while many passages in the *Recherche* describe artistic creativity as the ability to express one's individuality, in *Le Temps retrouvé* the artist also becomes the person who is capable of extracting the general from the specific.[18] In both authors, therefore, there is a dialectic between the individual or historical and the universal or allegorical. This dialectic plays itself out in the choice of narrator-protagonist: a highly individualized character who speaks with the authoritative voice of a divinely inspired poet in the case of the *Commedia* and a nameless man without qualities in the case of the *Recherche*. I will end by exploring the differences between Dante's and Proust's use of the first-person and the resulting characterization of their narrator-protagonists through close readings of the openings of both works.

The Poet and the 'Unlikely Candidate'

> Nel mezzo del cammin di nostra vita
> mi ritrovai per una selva oscura,
> ché la diritta via era smarrita. (*Inf.* 1, 1–3)

[Midway through our life's journey | I found myself in a dark wood, | for the straight path was lost.]

The opening tercet of the *Commedia* comes to us with the baggage of seven centuries of commentary: most scholarly editions of the poem today will only be able to fit one single line per page, due to the lengthy exegeses that escort these lines. My aim here is not to do justice to the long history of readings of *Inferno* 1, but to consider how Dante introduces his use of the first-person and how his approach compares with Proust's in the *Recherche*. Contemporary Dante criticism associates with Charles Singleton the important observation that the juxtaposition of the first-person plural and the first-person singular ('nostra vita / mi ritrovai') informs us of the double value of Dante's journey, as both personal and universally shared (1977: 6–7). The phrase 'Nel mezzo del cammin di nostra vita', moreover, is to be understood as referring to the year 1300 when Dante, born in 1265, would have been (by the standards of the time) middle-aged. Given that this was also the year of the first Jubilee, the date gives Dante's journey greater resonance, as it is imagined to have taken place during a year when many Christians undertook a pilgrimage of their own. After the opening tercet's strong combination of the personal and the universal, the poem however rapidly focuses the reader's attention on the individual journey of the narrator-protagonist.

> Ahi quanto a dir qual era è cosa dura
> esta selva selvaggia e aspra e forte
> che nel pensier rinova la paura!
>
> Tant'è amara che poco è più morte;
> ma per trattar del ben ch'i' vi trovai,
> dirò de l'altre cose ch'i v'ho scorte. (*Inf.* 1, 4–9)

[Ah how hard it is to describe | this savage and harsh and thick forest | the thought of it alone terrifies me again! | It is so harsh, that death is barely more powerful; | but to write of the good that I found there, | I will speak of the other things that I glimpsed.]

Dante's exceptionality is suggested through the use of hyperbolic and emphatic expressions, which refer either to the unicity of the journey ('poco è più morte') or to the challenge of narrating this journey ('Ahi quanto a dir qual era è cosa dura'). Line 8 establishes that the narrator is a writer through the technical term 'trattar', which derives from the Latin *tractare* and means to 'treat' of something (as in the word 'treatise'). The second hemistich of lines 8 and 9 moreover emphasizes Dante's role as witness by repeating the same structure (first-person pronoun; adverb of place; first-person verb). The notion that the journey is not for common mortals introduced by 'Tant'è amara che poco è più morte' is further emphasized in lines 22 to 27 by the word 'mai' [never]:

E come quei che con lena affannata,
uscito fuor del pelago a la riva,
si volge a l'acqua perigliosa e guata,

così l'animo mio, ch'ancor fuggiva,
si volse a retro a rimirar lo passo
che non lasciò già mai persona viva. (*Inf.* I, 22–27)

[And as one who out of breath, | having escaped the sea, looks back | from the shore at the dangerous waters, | so my soul, which was still fleeing, | looked back again at the pass | that no person has ever yet left alive.]

These verses inform us that the narrator-protagonist is the only mortal being to have ever made this journey. While the focus in this opening passage is primarily on the uniqueness of the journey to the otherworld, as the poem develops, the unique journey will become a metaphor for the writing of an unprecedented poem and the nautical imagery of *Inferno* I will indeed be redeployed as a metapoetic metaphor: 'L'acqua ch'io prendo già mai non si corse' [The waters that I cross have never been sailed before] (*Par.* II, 7); 'non è pareggio da picciola barca' [this is no expedition for a little craft] (*Par.* XXIII, 67).[19] Literary talent will therefore become Dante's main distinguishing trait. Indeed, already in *Inferno* I, poetic identity is the key to the canto's transition from the allegorical into the historical.

Up until the arrival of Virgil, *Inferno* I stands out from the rest of the *Commedia* for being exceptionally allegorical. Rather than historical characters and detailed landscapes, we encounter beasts from Christian exegesis and an unspecified 'dark wood'. This makes the opening of the poem, with its forest that is not a forest, stand out from the rest due to its almost 'un-earthly' quality.[20] The forest satisfies the claim to universality made in 'nostra vita' because it can be read as any man's (or Everyman's) point of perdition. Virgil's introduction, beginning line 67, establishes him as the first historicized individual in the poem, by which I mean a developed character in possession of personal traits and history, rather than a figure standing for an abstract value. Virgil identifies himself by stating first where and when he lived, and, secondly, by summarizing his career:

Poeta fui, e cantai di quel giusto
figliuol d'Anchise che venne di Troia,
poi che 'l superbo Ilïòn fu combusto. (*Inf.* I, 73–75)

[I was a poet, and I sang the just | son of Anchises who came from Troy, | after the proud Ilium was set to fire.]

This allows the narrator-protagonist in turn to define himself as a historicized individual by stating his relationship to Virgil:

O de li altri poeti onore e lume,
vagliami 'l lungo studio e 'l grande amore
che m'ha fatto cercar lo tuo volume.

Tu se' lo mio maestro e 'l mio autore,
tu se' solo colui da cu' io tolsi
lo bello stilo che m'ha fatto onore. (*Inf.* I, 82–87)

[Oh glory and beacon of all other poets, | may my long study and the great love | that made me search your volume avail. | You are my master and my author, | it is from you alone that I took | the elegant style that has earned me honour.]

We thus learn not only that our narrator-protagonist is a writer (as had been suggested previously by the verb 'trattar'), but that he is an established one (line 87) and that he was highly influenced by the works of Virgil. Poetic identity therefore functions as the first step towards the protagonist's individualization. Zygmunt Barański argues that the presence of both allegory and historicity in *Inferno* I serves the proemial function of informing the reader that the rest of the *Commedia* should be read as having both of these values (Barański 1987). Within such a framework, Dante's literary vocation clearly belongs to the individualized dimension of the *Commedia* and does not contribute to its allegorical significance as Everyman's journey from sin to salvation.

The stress on poetic identity will be continued in the opening of *Inferno* II in which the Muses are invoked to assist in the narration of the poem (line 7) and Virgil is referred to as 'Poeta che mi guidi' [Poet, you who guide me] (line 10). We find again a stress on individuality with the first use of the word *io* in line 3 being couched in the emphatic terms: 'io sol uno' [I, one and alone]. Most importantly, *Inferno* II is the canto that names two predecessors for a journey to the afterworld prior to death: 'Ma io, perché venirvi? o chi 'l concede? | Io non Enëa, io non Paulo sono' [But I, why should I go there? who has permitted it? | I am no Aeneas and I am no Paul] (*Inf.* II, 31–32). Critics have wondered why the verse makes no reference to the mythical poet Orpheus, who is named elsewhere in the *Commedia* and whose journey through the underworld to reach his dead beloved offers a clear model for Dante's journey to Beatrice.[21] An explanation for this may precisely be the fact that acknowledging Orpheus would have compromised Dante's uniqueness as the 'only' poet to have made such a journey.[22] Virgil answers Dante's question by informing him that it was Beatrice who arranged for his journey to take place. This justification further establishes Dante's individuality as Beatrice's lover: 'quei che t'amò tanto, | ch'uscì per te de la volgare schiera' [the one who loved you so, | that for you he left the vulgar crowd] (*Inf.* II, 104–05), which also creates continuity between Dante's identity as narrator-protagonist of the *Commedia* and as narrator-protagonist of the *Vita nuova*.

Thus, while the *Commedia* famously opens with an inclusion of its readers through the use of the plural first person ('nostra vita'), the poem very soon strives to establish a specific identity for its *io*. The narrator-protagonist is a historicized individual (poet, reader of Virgil, and lover of Beatrice) and an exceptional character: a man who has travelled where no mortal should be allowed and is able to recount this unique journey through his poetry. His identity as a poet is therefore utilized both as a means to historicize him and as a bid for his exceptionality. The *Commedia*'s stress on Dante's poetic exceptionality indeed leads Ascoli to conclude that through this work, 'Dante shoots past the now-obvious historical implications of his program (human authorship is personal and individual *in general*) to insinuate that he and he alone impersonates, or ever could, this new figuration of the poetic author' (2008: 405). Let us now consider how Proust introduces us to the narrator-protagonist of the *Recherche*:

> Longtemps, je me suis couché de bonne heure. Parfois, à peine ma bougie éteinte, mes yeux se fermaient si vite que je n'avais pas le temps de me dire: 'Je m'endors.' Et, une demi-heure après, la pensée qu'il était temps de chercher le sommeil m'éveillait; je voulais poser le volume que je croyais avoir encore dans les mains et souffler ma lumière, je n'avais pas cessé en dormant de faire des réflexions sur ce que je venais de lire, mais ces réflexions avaient pris un tour un peu particulier; il me semblait que j'étais moi-même ce dont parlait l'ouvrage: une église, un quatuor, la rivalité de François Ier et de Charles Quint. (I, 3)
>
> [For a long time, I went to bed early. Sometimes, as soon as my candle was out, my eyes would close so fast that I would not have time to think: 'I am falling asleep.' And, half an hour later, the thought that it was time to try to get some sleep would wake me; I wanted to put down the volume that I thought I still had in my hands and blow out the light. While I was asleep, I had not stopped pondering what I had just read, but my musings had taken an unusual turn; I believed that I was what the work was about: a church, a quartet, the rivalry between Francis I and Charles V.]

The opening lines of the *Recherche* do not provide us with a 'we', but only with an 'I'. His activity, however, is one we all do every day: going to bed. The *je* from the outset is not that of an exceptional character undertaking a unique enterprise, but one recounting a mundane experience. What introduces something more individual to this first-person is the 'tour un peu particulier' taken by his thoughts: he believes he has become a church, a piece of music, or a historical relationship. While it may be normal to feel confused in the particular state of consciousness brought on by sleep, I will argue that the final sentence of this passage introduces the narrator-protagonist's most original trait: his ability to lose himself in the contemplation of characters and sensory spectacles that capture his imagination. The narrator-protagonist's malleable sense of self and his availability to strong impressions, his 'quality of awareness' to cite Edward Hughes, signal his potential as a writer throughout the narrative, even when his hopes for a literary vocation are at their lowest.[23]

The overture of the novel while ostensibly concerned with the narrator-protagonist's insomnia constantly shifts between his experience and that of other characters: an anonymous train-traveller (p. 4), a sick person (p. 4), an imaginary woman (p. 4), and a sleeping man, who comes to stand for humans in general (p. 5). The blurring of boundaries between self and other becomes more complex when the narrator-protagonist expresses his own experience in the third person: 'mon esprit' [my mind], 'mon corps' [my body], 'sa mémoire' [its memory], 'ma pensée' [my thoughts], 'mon côté' [my side] (p. 6) become the subjects of verbs as if they were acting independently. By using the third person to describe the narrator-protagonist's perceptions, Proust places them grammatically on a par with those of other characters. This stylistic choice dampens the distinction between personally lived experience and the imagined experiences of others (be they human or inanimate objects, such as the personified furniture of p. 8). These others will come to provide much of the material for the narrative, which concerns a wide cast of characters.

A key difference between Dante's and Proust's narrative styles is that Proust's narrator-protagonist is far more often an observer recording the interactions of others than an actor. This becomes most obvious if we consider both works' use of direct speech. The *io* of the *Commedia*'s narrator-protagonist frequently appears in direct speech, because most of the poem takes the form of dialogues between Dante and the characters he encounters. This is the case for instance in the opening of the *Inferno* where, as we saw, it is through his spoken interactions with Virgil that Dante is first individualized as a historical individual and a poet. The *Recherche* offers page upon page of uninterrupted dialogue, but more often than not the speakers are other characters, to whom the narrator-protagonist is quietly listening. Indeed, after the narratorial prelude that we have just been considering, the representation of the childhood memories of 'Combray' bursts into life through the polyphony of the lively individual voices of the family members and Charles Swann (I, 22–27). The child in these passages has no voice: he is silently observing and recording. These polyphonic passages are placed in alternation with the extradiegetic soliloquy of the narrative voice. Focalization varies in the extradiegetic passages and the narrative voice at times homes in on the child's perspective,[24] as is the case for example when he decides to stay up to get his goodnight kiss:

> Quand j'irais me mettre sur le chemin de ma mère au moment où elle monterait se coucher, et qu'elle verrait que j'étais resté levé pour lui redire bonsoir dans le couloir, on ne me laisserait plus rester à la maison, on me mettrait au collège le lendemain, c'était certain. Eh bien! dussé-je me jeter par la fenêtre cinq minutes après, j'aimais encore mieux cela. (I, 33)
>
> [When I would go and stand in the path of my mother on her way to bed, and she would see that I had stayed up to say goodnight to her again in the corridor, I would no longer be allowed to live at home: they would send me to boarding school the next day, it was certain. Well! Were I to throw myself out of the window five minutes after, it would still be worth it.]

The child's perspective is expressed through the language of an adult (as signalled for instance by the past subjunctive), resulting in a comical contrast between the gravity of the style and the nature of the situation.

When he does speak, the protagonist's voice is frequently dampened through the use of reported speech. A clear example of this process may be found in the episode of a dinner party during which the Guermantes and the protagonist discuss Elstir (II, 790). The Guermantes' words are rendered through direct speech, yet the protagonist's responses are rendered, within the very same dialogue, through lengthy paraphrases. This representational double-standard makes him a voice-less participant, as well as an anonymous one, and contributes to his insubstantiality.[25] Dante on the contrary presents himself, through the use of direct speech, as an actor as well as an observer and consequently as a worthy subject of representation. The *Recherche*'s narrator-protagonist's observing and available nature will betray his artistic potential throughout the narrative. His *je* is available in two senses: first, within the fiction of the *Recherche* it is receptive to the experiences of other characters which the narrator-protagonist observes and describes in minute detail; secondly, the *je* is open to the readers of the *Recherche* because it refers to a face-less and anonymous man. In Jean-Yves Tadié's eloquent words: 'nous passons au travers et ne le voyons pas, comme pour nous-mêmes' [we go through him without seeing him, as we do for ourselves] (2003: 30).

While the *Commedia,* as we saw, opens with a 'we' ('nostra vita') before then devoting itself to the individualization of the 'I', the *Recherche* opens with an 'I', but very soon after introduces a 'we' (in French *nous* or *on*) that will be used throughout the novel. The *nous* is first introduced tentatively through a rhetorical question (I, 6). The pronouns *nous* and *on* are then interlaced with the *je* on the following page:

> Ces évocations tournoyantes et confuses ne duraient jamais que quelques secondes; souvent, ma brève incertitude du lieu où je me trouvais ne distinguait pas mieux les unes des autres les diverses suppositions dont elle était faite, que nous n'isolons, en voyant un cheval courir, les positions successives que nous montre le kinétoscope. Mais j'avais revu tantôt l'une, tantôt l'autre des chambres que j'avais habitées dans ma vie, et je finissais par me les rappeler toutes dans les longues rêveries qui suivaient mon réveil; chambres d'hiver où quand on est couché, on se blottit la tête dans un nid qu'on se tresse avec les choses les plus disparates: un coin d'oreiller, le haut des couvertures, un bout de châle, le bord du lit, et un numéro des *Débats roses* [...] chambres d'été où l'on aime être uni à la nuit tiède, [...] où on dort presque en plein air [...] parfois la chambre Louis XVI, si gaie que même le premier soir je n'y avais pas été trop malheureux [The sentence continues with 'je']. (I, 7–8)
>
> [The flitter of these vague evocations never lasted more than a few seconds. In my brief uncertainty of where I was, I often could not tell the various possibilities apart from each other, just as we are not able to isolate, when we watch a running horse, the succession of positions displayed by the kinetoscope. But I had glimpsed now one, now another of the bedrooms in which I had stayed during my life, and I would end up reminiscing about them all during the long reveries that followed my awakening: winter bedrooms in which one lies snuggled in a nest that one has made out of the most heterogeneous items: the corner of a pillow, the top of the blankets, a bit of shawl, the edge of the bed, a copy of the *Débats roses* [...] summer bedrooms where one enjoys being united with the warm night, [...] where one sleeps almost out in the open [...] sometimes the Louis XVI bedroom, so cheerful that even on my first night there, I had not been too sad [The sentence continues with 'I'].]

Collective pronouns create an association between the narrator-protagonist and the other characters in the novel, as well as with the reader, and, by extension, humanity itself. The pronoun *nous* in particular often allows the narration to transition seamlessly from the experiences of the narrator-protagonist and other individual characters to general pronouncements on human experience. The use of *nous* in the first sentence of this passage includes the reader in an analogy that assumes that he or she has seen images from a 'kinétoscope'. It is the use of *on* which makes the paragraph take a more unexpected turn. The narrator-protagonist is speaking of *his* life and *his* personal memories, which as the paragraph advances become increasingly specific, and therefore less likely to be shared experiences, but he uses a pronoun suggesting the very contrary, in other words, that we all have made a nest using 'un coin d'oreiller, le haut des couvertures, un bout de châle, le bord du lit, et un numéro des *Débats roses*'. Paradoxically, it is the very process of specification, of lavishing upon the reader rich sensual detail, that makes the experience become shared. It is this literary strategy that forms the basis of George Steiner's comparison of Dante with Proust: 'precise trivia gather to a formidable persuasion. [...] The text is timeless, universal, because utterly dated and placed. Dante and Proust, like no others, give us the gossip of eternity' (1978: 171–72).

By replacing the 'I' with a 'we', the opening of the *Recherche* undertakes the operation that Dante expects his readers to undertake for themselves through a figural reading of the *Commedia* as the story of Everyman. Dante's introductory 'nostra vita' and Proust's consistent use of *nous* and *on* state that the highly historicized story of a specific individual can be universal. The use of the French pronoun *on* is perfect for this end because it is both a synonym for *nous* and also the impersonal form: grammatically it corresponds to the third person — in English it may be translated as 'one'. Dante's readership, meanwhile, would inevitably have sought an allegorical interpretation of his poem. Taking the universal aspect of his narrative as a given, Dante focused on the individualization of his narrator-protagonist, which was a necessary step towards his self-authorization. Faced with a readership who would seek in his literature the individual, not to say the anecdotal, Proust's use of 'we' and his removal of key personal traits (religion, sexual orientation, and literary career) seem to form part of an attempt to bring the narrator-protagonist closer to the reader, as opposed to closer to the author. Indeed, the *Recherche* may be read (and has been read) as figuring the universal story of a man's journey from meaninglessness to salvation through art.[26]

However, Proust's very efforts to create a faceless narrator-protagonist result in another form of characterization in so far as they create an observant and impressionable character. Moreover, the narrator-protagonist's inability to write is described as arising from a lack of will power (see for instance II, 447–48, from 'Si, au moins, j'avais pu commencer à écrire!'), a characteristic which is personal to him. His 'maladie de la volonté' [sickness of the will] is the first individual trait that we are offered, making him different from other children (I, 11, 33). From the perspective of the novel's ending, his neurotic nature is ultimately part of a latent artistic sensitivity. Proust's narrator-protagonist thus falls within the late nineteenth-century and early twentieth-century tradition of the antihero, that is, a character who calls into question traditional models of heroic figures by turning what may have hitherto been considered a weakness into a strength (Brombert 1999). But he is also at times reminiscent of a Romantic type: the misunderstood artist (Shroder 1961). Proust's narrator-protagonist's neurotic eccentricities are often a source of comedy. For instance, as a boy his disproportionate fascination with Charles Swann can manifest itself in a grotesquely literal way: 'pour tâcher de lui ressembler, je passais tout mon temps à table, à me tirer sur le nez et à me frotter les yeux. Mon père disait: "Cet enfant est idiot, il deviendra affreux"' [In order to look more like him, I would spend all my time at the dinner table, pulling my nose and rubbing my eyes. My father would say: 'This child is stupid, he will become hideous'] (I, 406). And in other cases through the juxtaposition of his lyrical expansiveness and its pedestrian cause, revealed only at the end of the sentence as a punchline: 'Quelle mélancolique volupté, d'apprendre que cet après-midi-là, profilant dans la foule sa forme surnaturelle, Swann avait été acheter un parapluie' [What a melancholy pleasure it was to discover that on that afternoon, cutting his supernatural figure through the crowd, Swann had bought an umbrella] (I, 407). At the very same time, while it is an overstatement to call the family friend Charles Swann 'supernatural', the youth's strange fascination also shows his ability to find beauty in the everyday. Such hypersensitivity will later be revealed to be the goal of the artist (IV, 474–75).

The most important example of the clash between social norms and the writer's development of his sensitivity is staged in the encounter with his father's colleague, the diplomat Norpois, in *À l'ombre des jeunes filles en fleurs* (I, 444–66). Norpois shames the adolescent protagonist by criticizing his writing as well as the writing of his favourite author, Bergotte, concluding that their main sin is that they privilege formal intricacy when their priority should be relevance to current affairs:

> Dans un temps comme le nôtre où la complexité croissante de la vie laisse à peine le temps de lire, où la carte de l'Europe a subi des remaniements profonds et est à la veille d'en subir de plus grands encore peut-être, où tant de problèmes menaçants et nouveaux se posent partout, vous m'accorderez qu'on a le droit de demander à un écrivain d'être autre chose qu'un bel esprit qui nous fait oublier dans des discussions oiseuses et byzantines sur des mérites de pure forme, que nous pouvons être envahis d'un instant à l'autre par un double flot de Barbares, ceux du dehors et ceux du dedans. (I, 464–65)
>
> [In a time like ours, when the growing complexity of life barely leaves any time for reading, when the map of Europe has been profoundly reorganized and is perhaps about to suffer even greater changes, when so many menacing new problems are arising everywhere, you must admit that one has the right to ask of writers to be something more than witty characters who make us forget in pointless byzantine discussions, whose only merit is form, that we could at any moment be invaded by a double flood of Barbarians: those from without and those from within.]

Norpois becomes the emblem of the social expectations against which the young protagonist measures himself with great distress: 'je sentis une fois de plus ma nullité intellectuelle et que je n'étais pas né pour la littérature' [I felt yet again my intellectual uselessness and sensed that I was not born to write literature] (I, 466). Later on, when he experiences an involuntary memory caused by the damp smell of the Champs Elysées's public lavatories, he concludes that he truly deserves to be despised, for 'j'avais préféré jusqu'ici à tous les écrivains celui qu'il appelait un simple "joueur de flûte" et une véritable exaltation m'avait été communiquée, non par quelque idée importante, mais par une odeur de moisi' [among all writers, I had chosen as my favourite the one whom he called a mere 'flute player' and a true exaltation had been communicated to me, not by a meaningful idea, but by a mouldy smell] (I, 485). Involuntary memory will ultimately be elevated to a privileged position, so that this 'exaltation' is retrospectively justified as being caused by a return of the past. What was originally experienced as an inadequacy becomes valuable as an example of the 'impressions vraies' towards which artists are supposed to work (IV, 475). Moreover, the narrator-protagonist in *Le Temps retrouvé* explicitly criticizes those who judge literature in terms of its sociopolitical content (IV, 466, 471–72), observing: 'On préférait à Bergotte, dont les plus jolies phrases avaient exigé en réalité un bien plus profond repli sur soi-même, des écrivains qui semblaient plus profonds simplement parce qu'ils écrivaient moins bien' [Bergotte, whose prettiest sentences had in fact required a far more profound retreat into himself, had been left aside in favour of authors who seemed more profound simply because they wrote less well] (IV, 472).[27]

That said, there is also a degree of ambiguity in terms of the narrator-protagonist's future success as a writer. As we know, the moment of writing is projected and not enacted. Consequently, examples cited in defence of the value of art are drawn from the work of other artist characters and not that of the narrator-protagonist. The only reason why the reader is led to believe in the narrator-protagonist's potential is the act of narration itself, that is, the literary talent displayed by Proust's style. Indeed, while examples of direct speech *in medias res* are extremely rare in the *Recherche*, this paucity is more than compensated for by the narrator-protagonist's extradiegetic words. As has been observed by Genette, one of the paradoxes of the *Recherche* is that although the narrative is organized as a series of 'scenes', the presence of the narrative voice remains constant and intense, and plays the role of 'source, garant et organisateur du récit, comme analyste et commentateur, comme styliste [...] et particulièrement — on le sait de reste — comme producteur de métaphores' [source, guarantor and organizer of the narrative, as analyst and commentator, as stylist [...] and most particularly — as is well-known — as producer of metaphors] (1972: 188). This highly individual use of language offers us the most interesting aspect of the narrator-protagonist's characterization.

To use Tadié's concise words, 'Proust s'est donné tous les styles' [Proust has used every style] (1998: 24): in the *Recherche* alone we might think of the linguistic tics characterizing Odette, Mme Verdurin, or Oriane de Guermantes, and even the pastiche of the Goncourt brothers. Yet in spite of this, readers will still speak of 'le style de Proust', by which they mean the narrative passages that form only one third of the whole work. Polyphony is staged and the narrator-protagonist, passive in the scenes depicted, yet present in the act of depiction, emerges victorious as the one who crafts the French language with greatest skill. An example of this process, through which the text imparts greater authority to the narrator-protagonist than to other characters, is the contrast between Norpois's direct speech, which is full of clichés, and the razor-sharp analogies used by the pithy narrator to account for it (I, 444–45): we are told that Norpois speaks of literature 'comme d'une personne vénérable et charmante du cercle choisi de laquelle, à Rome ou à Dresde, on a gardé le meilleur souvenir et qu'on regrette par suite des nécessités de la vie de retrouver si rarement' [as a venerable and charming person, of whose select circle, in Rome or Dresden, one has kept the best of memories and whom one regrets, due to the necessities of life, not having the opportunity to see more often], and that he uses 'le même ton rassurant que si elles avaient été des dispositions non pas à la littérature, mais au rhumatisme' [the same reassuring tone as if he were speaking not of a leaning towards literature, but of a tendency towards rheumatism].

Dante also gives his characters a variety of voices, using even different languages and dialects to this purpose, and this aspect of the *Commedia* has been described as 'plurilingualism'. The term 'plurilingualism' was coined in Contini's essay 'Preliminari sulla lingua del Petrarca' (1951), which contrasts Petrarch's 'monolinguismo', that is, the rarefied use of language in Petrarch's *Rerum vulgarium fragmenta*, with the 'plurilinguismo' of the *Commedia*, that is, the poem's linguistic and stylistic diversity, but the notion of plurilingualism is already present in Auerbach's analysis of the style and genre of the *Commedia* in *Mimesis* (2000: 184–90).[28] Auerbach notes that the designation of Dante's poem as a comedy rather than a tragedy derives in great part from its use of the vernacular language and lower registers of speech. In practice, however, the *Commedia* defies both categories: 'Themes which cannot possibly be considered sublime in the antique sense turn out to be just that by virtue of his way of molding and ordering them' (2000: 84). Dante's plurilingualism is more generous than what I have called Proust's polyphony in so far as Dante does not necessarily make use of it to highlight his narrator-protagonist's linguistic superiority. Indeed, although Dante as narrator-protagonist and *scriba dei* invests himself with the highest poetic authority, the most beautiful and memorable lines of the *Commedia* are delivered by a wide range of characters, including sinners. Two important factors contribute to creating a greater proximity between the narrator-protagonist's style and the speech of other characters. First, as noted by Contini (1976), in some cases characters function as alter egos of Dante, and therefore their use of language is intentionally close to that of the narrator-protagonist. Secondly, due to the form of the *Commedia*, all characters, be they represented as eloquent or inarticulate, are inevitably expressing themselves in hendecasyllables arranged in terza rima (the verse scheme of the *Commedia*); as a result, if they are expressing themselves in the Italian vernacular, rhyme and metre can alleviate the difference between their voice and Dante's. As a result, while readers speaking of 'le style de Proust' have the narrative voice in mind, readers speaking of Dante's style are drawing from passages spoken by a variety of characters and are thus just as likely to have Ulysses's oration or St Bernard's prayer in mind as the words spoken by the narrator-protagonist.

Narration in the *Recherche* relies on what are known as the Proustian 'périodes', that is lengthy sentences of elaborate construction, which would sound unnatural in direct speech. The form of the 'périodes' contributes to the narrator-protagonist's characterization by illustrating his attention to detail, his nature as an observer rather than an actor. The sentences' frequent open-endedness also speaks of a character who wanders and is not able to focus on one single goal, yet, who due to this ability to observe and wander, possesses the necessary qualities for literary creation.[29] While anonymous, the narrator-protagonist therefore is a strongly defined character by virtue of his unique voice. There is a tension between form and plot as the *Recherche*'s insightful, eloquent, and original narrative style works against our understanding of the narrator-protagonist as an 'unlikely candidate for greatness'.[30] To quote Adam Watt, 'The ordinary, that which is mundane, everyday or run-of-the-mill, is everywhere in Proust's book. But nowhere is his writing, or his thinking, plain *ordinary*' (2011: 97). The construction of the narrator-protagonist in Proust's novel thus relies on a combination of self-deprecation and irony, the greatest irony being that the narrator-protagonist tells us in exquisite literary form that he has no talent for writing. There is no such place for irony in Dante's poetics of self-assertiveness: the narrator-protagonist of the *Commedia* establishes his authority by being the author of a poem which could only have been written by an exceptional individual, and he is not afraid to state it.

In conclusion, although both the *Commedia* and the *Recherche* are narratives centred on a narrator-protagonist in pursuit of his literary vocation, they present important differences in terms of narration, characterization, and the treatment of literary authority. These differences can be related to the different literary cultures in which they were written, against which both authors reacted. Dante, by presenting himself as the narrator and protagonist within the text and by using his literary identity to provide an individual story outside of the scope of allegory, contributed to the creation of the modern figure of the author. Proust was explicitly against biographical readings of literature, yet inscribed himself into his text through at times playful, and at times disruptive, references to extra-textual reality, which as a result make the 'I' of the *Recherche* ambiguous and slippery. Though the narrator-protagonist's literary vocation will retrospectively invest his existence with meaning, Proust does not idealize his main character, who is passive, awkward, and insecure, and spends most of the novel not writing anything at all. At the same time, the form of the narrative passages contradicts the suggestion that the protagonist is devoid of talent. Dante's poetics of assertiveness create a sharply defined narrator-protagonist, whose writing is invested with a great level of authority. Though Dante was mainly concerned with his own poetry and self-presentation, his operation in the *Commedia* led to a broader change in the status of vernacular poetry, which for the first time was given the authority to approach issues which had hitherto been confined to the realm of philosophy and theology. Proust's poetics of self-effacement and ambiguity undermine the narrator's authority and in so doing create an ambivalence around the status of art and literature in his novel, as well as in society more broadly.

Notes to Chapter 1

1. Contini's analysis is cited as seminal by such distinguished critics as Barolini 1984: 3, n. 1, and Picone 2000.
2. For a concise overview of early twentieth-century Dante scholarship see Picone 2000: 13–14. Contini observes that the commentators of the Trecento often interchanged *agens* and *auctor* (1976: 40).
3. Representing humans in time is precisely the proclaimed goal of the protagonist's future novel in the conclusion of the *Recherche* which ends with the words 'dans le Temps' (IV, 625). On the inextricability of identity and change, see Bynum 2001.

4. 'As in all spiritual autobiographies, so in the *Confessions* and in the *Divine Comedy* there is a radical division between the protagonist and the author who tells his story' (Freccero 1986: 25). We can find a clear parallel here between Freccero's and Genette's readings, since Genette too bolsters his argument with a reference to St Augustine's *Confessions* (1972: 259).
5. By 'time of narration' I refer to what is called by German critics 'Erzählzeit' and by Genette 'temps du récit' (1972: 77).
6. This poetic device is exposed in *Vita nuova* XXV.
7. This corresponds for instance to Giuseppe Mazzotta's reading: 'As Dante formulates his poetics of love he dramatizes both his desire to be a *poeta-theologus* and his awareness that his poetry, like Guinizzelli's, falls short of this desire' (1979: 226).
8. Gragnolati (2012) conceptualizes this multivalence of 'Amor' through the analogy of the multistable image (such as Wittgenstein's duck-rabbit).
9. Lejeune's definition has been applied to Dante by Giuseppe Ledda (2002: 13–14).
10. The self-citations of the *Commedia* are 'Amor che ne la mente mi ragiona' in *Purgatorio* II, originally from the *Convivio*; 'Donne ch'avete intelletto d'amore' in *Purgatorio* XXIV, originally from the *Vita nuova*; and 'Voi che 'ntendendo il terzo ciel movete' in *Paradiso* VIII, originally from the *Convivio*. The episode of *Purgatorio* II will be analyzed in Chapter 2. For a detailed analysis of the individual implications of these three self-citations, see Barolini 1984: 3–84.
11. One should note that by drawing this distinction between Dante and Proust, I am not suggesting that the *Commedia* offers us an accurate picture of Dante's biography, but only that it presents itself as doing so.
12. In French a 'roman à clefs' is a novel in which the characters are real, but their names have been altered.
13. A selection of Proust's articles can be found in Proust, *CSB*: 338–677.
14. The pastiches are collected under 'L'Affaire Lemoine', *CSB*: 7–59.
15. Tadié 2003: 17–33.
16. This mode of reading would eventually lead in the mid- to late-twentieth century to a backlash against the figure of the author and of literary subjectivity. For a thorough debunking of Barthes, Foucault, and Derrida's rejection of subjectivity and authorship see Burke 1992. For an insightful re-appraisal of the last century of literary discourse on the figure of the author see Talamo 2013. Talamo proposes a mode of reading which places intentionality in the text, not the moment of composition, and thus allows us to speak of authorial intentionality without biographizing or psychologizing implications.
17. The term *auctor* is defined in Ascoli 2008: 3–12, and in Minnis 1988, especially p. 10.
18. I return to this in the section 'Transcending the Individual' in Chapter 4.
19. This imagery is analyzed in Chapter 2.
20. I translate Benedetto Croce's phrase 'selva che non è selva'. Croce finds the allegorism of *Inferno* I forced, and as a result deems it the poem's weakest canto (1921: 73). On the earthly character of Dante's afterworld, particularly in terms of imagery, see Auerbach 2001: 153–54.
21. See Hollander 1980: 88, n. 100, and Giorgio Padoan's entry for 'Orfeo' in the *Enciclopedia dantesca* (Bosco 1970–78: IV, 192).
22. See Barański 1999 and Frisardi 2009.
23. Hughes takes the phrase from Susan Sontag's essay 'The Pornographic Imagination': 'The question is not *whether* consciousness or *whether* knowledge, but the quality of the consciousness and of the knowledge. And that invites consideration of the quality or fineness of the human subject — the most problematic standard of all' (cited in Hughes 1983: 4). Hughes's book 'takes as its mandate Proust's own view that multiple ways of feeling and reflection form a source of artistic potential' (1983: 5). Hughes's study is thus germane to this chapter in its definition of Proust's protagonists (both in *Jean Santeuil* and the *Recherche*) in terms of their 'hyperawareness' or 'hypersensitivity'.
24. Focalization is intended in the Genettian sense of the perspective from which information is given in a narrative. See Genette 1972: 203.
25. An exception to this general rule would be the extended conversation with Albertine in *La Prisonnière* (III, 877–83).

26. Bales argues that 'both the *Commedia* and *A la recherche* are histories of a struggle on an uphill path to a final illumination which sets all that has gone before into its proper context. And the manner in which illumination is achieved is presented to the reader as a profitable path to follow' (1975: 137). On this subject, see Chapter 4.
27. On descent imagery and artistic creation, see Chapter 2.
28. For a more recent exploration of Dante's theories of language as they relate to his poetics, see Fortuna, Gragnolati and Trabant 2010.
29. This will be further explored in Chapter 2. The 'périodes' also allow, through contrast, shorter more axiomatic pronouncements to stand out as definitive. An example of this would be the declaration 'Chaque personne est bien seule', coming after the description of the dying grandmother's futile visits to doctors (II, 614).
30. The expression 'unlikely candidate for greatness' is taken from William C. Carter (1992: 213).

CHAPTER 2

Journeys to Writing

The Figure of Ulysses

The *Commedia* and the *Recherche* both draw on the metaphor of the journey to describe the process of artistic creation. In Proust the journey to writing is to be found in the frequent metaphors employed by the narrative voice.[1] In Dante it is present not only at the narrative level, but also at an allegorical level: the 'literal' journey through Hell, Purgatory, and Paradise stands for Dante's spiritual and poetic development.[2] Both authors describe a two-step journey, beginning with a descent into the underworld, which is then followed by an upward flight. But though they use similar imagery, Proust and Dante ultimately have two different destinations in mind when they describe where art can take us. In order to introduce the significance of the journey as a metaphor for artistic progress, I will begin by comparing Dante's and Proust's use of the figure of Ulysses, the most famous traveller of Western literature.[3]

In the *Commedia*, Ulysses is encountered among the fraudulent counsellors of *Inferno* XXVI, where he recounts his death in one of the most famous monologues of the *Commedia*. Dante's Ulysses did not settle back in Ithaca, for neither the love of his son, nor his father, nor Penelope could overcome in him:

> l'ardore
> ch'i' ebbi a divenir del mondo esperto
> e de li vizi umani e del valore. (*Inf.* XXVI, 94–99)

> [my passion | for gaining experience of the world | and of mankind's vices and worth.]

Ulysses leads his now old and weary crew on the most ambitious of all journeys: out of the Mediterranean, beyond the Straits of Gibraltar, which were then considered an impassable limit for mortal men. To do this, he spurs his men on to make 'wings of their oars' for their 'mad flight' ('de' remi facemmo ali al folle volo', *Inf.* XXVI, 125) through impassioned rhetoric on man's desire for experience and knowledge ('fatti non foste a viver come bruti, | ma per seguir virtute e canoscenza' [you were not made to live as brutes, | but to pursue virtue and knowledge], *Inf.* XXVI, 119–20). God punishes him for his *hubristic* 'mad flight' by sinking the ship. It is well accepted among Dante scholars that Ulysses functions as an alter ego whose failed journey shows the potential pitfalls of Dante's own journey.[4] Ulysses's role has been most convincingly studied in relation to the lexical field of aeronautics (that is, the combination of sailing imagery and flight imagery) by Teodolinda Barolini, who stresses the similarity between Dante's self-portrayal as author of a poem covering uncharted territory and the portrayal of the intrepid Ulysses (1992: 48–73). Observing that Ulysses's presence is maintained across the poem through his naming in each canticle, the 'surrogate' figures of Phaeton and Icarus, the use of the adjective 'folle', and the use of flight and sailing imagery, Barolini suggests that Ulysses serves the function of a 'lightning rod': we, as readers, are expected to think of Ulysses as the most *hubristic* character in the *Commedia*, when in fact one of the most presumptuous events in the *Commedia* is Dante's self-anointment as *scriba dei* (1992: 52–54).

Ulysses is metapoetically associated with the risky enterprise of representing the divine, as is suggested by Ulyssean passages such as the opening of *Paradiso* II:

> O voi che siete in piccioletta barca,
> desiderosi d'ascoltar, seguiti
> dietro al mio legno che cantando varca,
>
> tornate a riveder li vostri liti:
> non vi mettete in pelago, ché forse,
> perdendo me, rimarreste smarriti.
>
> L'acqua ch'io prendo già mai non si corse. (*Par.* II, 1–7)

[O you, who in a fragile little raft, | filled with the desire to listen, sail behind | my ship, which breaks the waves singing, | go back to your own shores: | do not set forth, for perhaps, losing sight of me, | you may remain lost at sea. | The waters that I sail have never been sailed before.]

As observed by Ernst Robert Curtius in his rich and concise survey, the nautical voyage was used as a metaphor for the composition of a work of literature by Latin authors such as Virgil, Horace, and Statius, and was a commonplace by the time Dante was writing these verses (1953: 128–30). Metapoetic passages of this ilk are most frequent in the *Paradiso*, where 'it is the poet who struggles while the pilgrim is safe' (Marguerite Mills Chiarenza, quoted in Barolini 1992: 54). The religiously and poetically transgressive nature of the third canticle leads Barolini to conclude her reading of the relationship between Dante and Ulysses in terms of the traditional Pilgrim versus Poet binary: Dante-Pilgrim is an anti-Ulysses, whereas Dante-Poet is a Ulysses (1992: 52, 73). Although Barolini resolves the relationship between Dante and Ulysses by emphasizing the poet/pilgrim distinction, it is important to bear in mind its ambivalence: Dante both is and is not Ulysses, with whom he shares a desire for knowledge, a way with words, and the language of aeronautics, which is used both to describe the upwards spiritual voyage to God and the process of writing the *Commedia*.[5]

In the *Recherche*, exploration is often used metaphorically to express the quest for experience, often of a sexual nature: this is the case for instance in the masturbation scene in 'Combray' (I, 156) or when the narrator-protagonist is spying on Charlus and Jupien's first sexual encounter (III, 10). As well as this playful use of the image, which is symptomatic of Proust's expert handling of analogy not only for depth but also for comedy, the *Recherche* also uses the semantic field of the journey beyond mortal limits to describe the experience of art. Exploration, journey, and aeronautics in Proust are not semantic tags for Ulysses, as they are in Dante's poem. But Proust did cast Ulysses as an alter ego for himself as a writer in his correspondence. I refer to a text often cited in discussions of the genesis of the *Recherche*, the letter to Antoine Bibesco of 20 December 1902:

> Tout ce que je fais n'est pas du vrai travail [...]. Cela suffit à réveiller ma soif de réalisations, sans naturellement l'assouvir en rien. Du moment que [...] j'ai pour la première fois tourné mon regard à l'intérieur, vers ma pensée, je sens tout le néant de ma vie, cent personnages de romans, mille idées me demandent de leur donner un corps comme ces ombres qui demandent dans *L'Odyssée* à Ulysse de leur faire boire un peu de sang pour les mener à la vie et que le héros écarte de son épée. J'ai réveillé l'abeille endormie et je sens bien plus son cruel aiguillon que ses impuissantes ailes. (*Corr.* III, 196)
>
> [Nothing of what I do is real work [...]. It is enough to awake my thirst for realization, without satisfying it in any shape or form. Ever since [...] I have turned for the first time my gaze inward, towards my thoughts, I feel just how empty my life is. A hundred novel characters, a thousand ideas are asking me to give them body, just like those shadows in the *Odyssey* ask Ulysses to let them drink a little blood so that they may return to life, while the hero pushes them aside with his sword. I have awoken the sleeping bee and I feel its sharp sting more acutely than its powerless wings.]

Proust speaks of a burning desire to write literature, which is metaphorically rendered as a thirst ('soif de réalisations') and stinging ('cruel aiguillon'), and is frustrated by his incapacity for flight ('impuissantes ailes').[6] Ulysses here is drawn on not as a figure for the explorer, but in terms of the specific episode of the nekyia, or summoning of the dead, in *Odyssey* XI.

In the *Recherche*, Proust draws on two classical sources when he speaks of descents to the underworld: Homer's *Odyssey* XI and Virgil's *Aeneid* VI. In *Odyssey* XI, Ulysses and his men sail to the entrance to the underworld to consult the seer Tiresias. They do not enter the underworld, but summon the dead to the surface. This is done through drink offerings and prayers, and an animal sacrifice. Once the blood has filled a trench, the dead come trooping up to drink it. Ulysses holds the dead back with his sword so that the blood is saved for Tiresias, who needs to drink it in order to make his prophecy. (This leads to sorrow as the first two dead people to emerge are a lost comrade and Ulysses's mother.) Aeneas, on the other hand, instead of summoning the dead to the surface, undertakes a descent into the underworld guided by the Sybil (a prophetess). He is ferried across the Styx and travels through various subterranean locations, making his encounter with the underworld more active and exploratory than that of Ulysses. As is well known, *Aeneid* VI is the putative historical model for Dante's *Inferno*, which is also a guided descent into the world of the dead. The term for Aeneas's and Dante's physical voyage into the underworld is katabasis, whereas Proust's summoning of characters and ideas can be compared to the Homeric nekyia.[7]

Proust's use of the nekyia as a metaphor for the artist's enterprise has been explored by Luc Fraisse and Françoise Létoublon, who also associate the nekyia to

Proust's exploration of the world of sleep: 'L'ouverture de la *Recherche*, tout enrobée d'obscurité, constitue donc le premier pas dans cette Nekuia, chaque apparition de souvenir et de rêve se formant aussitôt en récit' [The opening of the *Recherche*, which is shrouded in darkness, is thus the first step in this nekyia, every apparition of a memory or dream instantly coming together as narrative] (1997: 1077–78).[8] These two threads of their analysis can be tied together and pushed further if we consider that the opening of 'Combray', in which the narrator-protagonist suffers from insomnia in Mme de Saint-Loup's countryside home, offers a frame for the narration of the protagonist's childhood, adolescence, and younger adult years. The *enchâssement* of the narrative thus begins with:

> Le branle était donné à ma mémoire; généralement je ne cherchais pas à me rendormir tout de suite; je passais la plus grande partie de la nuit à me rappeler notre vie d'autrefois, à Combray chez ma grand-tante, à Balbec, à Paris, à Doncières, à Venise, ailleurs encore, à me rappeler les lieux, les personnes que j'y avais connues, ce que j'avais vu d'elles, ce qu'on m'en avait raconté. (I, 9)
>
> [My memory had been jigged; usually I would not try to go back to sleep right away; I would spend most of the night remembering our old life, at Combray at my great-aunt's, at Balbec, in Paris, at Doncières, in Venice, and other places still, remembering the locations, the people I had known there, what I had seen of them, what I had been told of them.]

The following paragraph, beginning 'À Combray, tous les jours dès la fin de l'après-midi' [At Combray, every day, from the late afternoon onwards], introduces the first of the summoned memories. The frame of Mme de Saint-Loup's countryside home is only returned to six volumes later in the opening of *Le Temps retrouvé* (IV, 275), after which the narrative progresses chronologically describing Paris during the First World War, then skipping ahead (IV, 433) in order to set the scene for the Matinée which will lead to the final revelation that the narrator-protagonist can give meaning to his life through art. The entirety of the narration taking place between the framing passages (I, 9– IV, 275) can therefore be called a nekyia: a summoning of the past, specifically under the form of 'les personnes que j'[...]avais connues' [the people I had known].

Dante's Ulysses embodies the intrepid explorer, who risks his life and soul in the pursuit of knowledge. Proust instead homes in on Ulysses as a human confronted with the memory of those he has lost. In their different uses of Ulysses as an alter ego, Dante and Proust demonstrate a rather different vision of the writer, which also corresponds to the characterization of their narrator-protagonists: Dante's writer-traveller is active and looks out towards the places he has never been to, Proust's writer-traveller is passive and introspective, preoccupied with the things he has already seen.

Descent into the Underworld

Proust draws on the Ulyssean nekyia in the most famous passage of the *Recherche*: the madeleine scene, where the sense of taste is able to conjure long-forgotten memories of the narrator-protagonist's childhood. A draft of the passage, which the Pléiade edition entitles: 'Esquisse XIII [La biscotte trempée dans le thé]' (I, 695–97), explicitly compares the summoning of forgotten memories to the summoning of the dead that takes place in Odyssey XI, which Proust mistakenly remembers as a scene in the *Aeneid*: 'Et je sentais des morts que je ne reconnaissais pas qui comme les morts de l'Érèbe quand passe Énée disent: "Rends-nous le sang qui va nous ressusciter." Et j'écartais leur foule importune' [And I could sense, without recognizing them dead people, who like the dead of the Erebus say to Aeneas as he passes them said 'Give us the blood that will bring us back to life.' And I pushed aside the bothersome crowd] (I, 696–97). This comparison comes as a conclusion to a passage which was already rich with the imagery of the descent into the self:

> Je cherchais en moi, au fond de moi, car il semblait que mon être avait pris une sorte de profondeur infinie. Et je sentais quelque chose qui réveillé sans doute par ce goût de thé, se détachait, cherchait à monter à la lumière de ma conscience, s'élevait, traversait des espaces anciens dont elle me rendait la sensation comme une ancre qui a traversé toute la profondeur de l'eau avant d'apparaître. (I, 696)
>
> [And I searched within myself, in the depths of my self, for it seemed that my being had taken on a kind of endless depth. And I could feel something which, having probably been awoken by the taste of the tea, was detaching itself and trying to come up to the light of my conscience, travelling up, crossing ancient spaces of which it brought along the sensation, like an anchor that has had to cross the full depth of the water before appearing.]

The final version of the madeleine episode preserves the initial image of the submerged past becoming unanchored and travelling up a vertical axis, and replaces the reference to Aeneas/Ulysses with a paragraph which expands on the image of the summoning of memories through strata of the past:

> Arrivera-t-il jusqu'à la surface de ma claire conscience, ce souvenir, l'instant ancien que l'attraction d'un instant identique est venue de si loin solliciter, émouvoir, soulever tout au fond de moi? Je ne sais. Maintenant je ne sens plus rien, il est arrêté, redescendu peut-être; qui sait s'il remontera jamais de sa nuit? (I, 46)
>
> [Will it reach the surface of my clear conscience, this memory, this old moment that has been attracted by an identical moment and has come from such a distance to call on me, move me, lifting everything from the depths of my self? I do not know. Now I no longer feel anything, it has stopped, gone back down perhaps; who knows if it will ever rise again from its darkness?]

The image of human existence taking place through quasi-geological layers of time used in the madeleine passage and its draft, is brought home in the conclusion of the *Recherche*. Indeed, in the final sentence of *Le Temps retrouvé*, the narrator-protagonist proposes to write a novel in which each individual will be shown to occupy 'une place [...] prolongée sans mesure' [a place [...] extending beyond measure], because he or she is in contact with the most distant layers of time: 'puisqu'ils touchent simultanément, comme des géants plongés dans les années à des époques, vécues par eux si distantes, entre lesquelles tant de jours sont venus se placer' [since they touch simultaneously, like giants submerged in years, periods which they have experienced so far apart from one another — periods of their lives between which so many days have come] (IV, 625).

The *Recherche*'s use of images of exploration and excavation to describe the process of descending into the self in pursuit of the past resonates with early accounts of the process of psychoanalysis, a field that was emerging even as Proust was writing.[9] As has been analyzed by Malcolm Bowie, Sigmund Freud compared himself to an archaeologist, because both archeologists and psychoanalysts are interested in the study of 'anterior states' and excavating a 'previously lost past' (1987: 18–19).[10] Carl Gustav Jung (1968: 7) too understood the exploration of the unconscious as a journey into a subterranean area. Proust and the early psychoanalysts' accounts of the exploration of the human self in terms of a journey through an underworld can prove illuminating for an interpretation of Dante's journey in the *Inferno*. Such an interpretation is in fact anticipated by Jung, who went so far as to argue that all myths of descent *ad inferos* stood for the conscious mind's foray 'into the deeper layers of the unconscious psyche' (1968: 41),[11] as well as by Wallace Fowlie's reading of Dante's *Inferno*. According to Fowlie:

> In a general sense, it is not difficult to make the transition from the dead in the underworld regions of Homer and Virgil, and the damned souls in Dante's *Inferno*, to the descent into the subterranean cosmos of personality which one can achieve today [...] to consult [...] the dead figures of our own personality who desire to return to the living self and resume an interrupted existence. (1981: 6)[12]

Such a psychological understanding of the descent into Hell finds expression in Giorgio Pressburger's twenty-first-century rewriting of Dante's *Inferno*, *Nel regno oscuro* (2008), in which the protagonist is guided in his descent by none other than Sigmund Freud himself. This understanding of the journey into the world of the dead as a metaphor for the journey into the hidden recesses of the self allows us better to understand the extremely personal dimension of Dante's journey.

Although the *Commedia* does not contain introspective passages of the kind we would find in Proust, Dante's journey does stage several encounters with his past identities, which are materialized as characters. Both the *Commedia* and the *Recherche* in this sense can be read as 'studies of anterior states', to use Bowie's term (1987: 18). Fowlie, by speaking of 'the dead figures of our own personality who desire to return to the living self and resume an interrupted existence' (1981: 2), is drawing on a deeply Proustian understanding of identity.[13] Indeed, the *Recherche* suggests that the human self is composed over time of a series of separate *moi* (selves). While our bodily presence gives us the illusion of continuity, the different habits and desires that we have in different periods of our lives make us different persons, each *moi* dying when we change.[14] As was shown in Chapter 1, Contini draws on a similarly fragmented understanding of identity, but reframes it in teleological terms, by arguing that every stage of Dante's journey stands for an 'overcome' past self (1976: 62). Thus, although Dante's and Proust's works present important formal and structural differences, they both explore the problematic relationship that individuals have with their past by staging the difficulties of reconciling the different people that we are during our time on earth. Proust does this explicitly when the narrative voice theorizes the fragmented nature of the self, whereas in Dante this is done allegorically through the embodiment of different stages of his life by different characters.

The most famous Dantean example of this process is the character of Francesca da Rimini in *Inferno* v. Ever since Contini's suggestion that Francesca's rhetoric is none other than Dante's own rhetoric, and that in analyzing her discourse on love, we are really analyzing Dante through 'interposte persone' (1976: 42–48), it has been widely accepted that Francesca stands for Dante's past as a writer and reader of erotic poetry.[15] Francesca's literary allusions range from courtly literature (the Lancelot) to the classics (she refers to Boethius as Dante's 'dottore' in line 123). They also include a reference to the poetry of the stilnovists (line 100), a school of lyric poets with whom Dante was associated, and through her linking of love and death Francesca also alludes to the poetry of Guido Cavalcanti, a poet whom Dante greatly admired and sought to emulate at the beginning of his career.[16] Francesca presents Dante with his own literary background, so that when he looks at her he sees himself — an unlikely candidate for divinely sanctioned writing. It is no surprise that he faints (*Inf.* v, 144). Another alter ego, as we saw, is Ulysses, who in his quest for knowledge is generally seen as embodying Dante's pursuit of philosophy in the *Convivio.* The motif of the encounter with a past self continues beyond the *Inferno*, playing an important role in the *Purgatorio* which revisits Dante's poetic history through self-citation and encounters with friends and fellow poets. *Paradiso*, depicting as it does a realm in which earthly conceptions of selfhood are transcended, does not lend itself to this motif, but it does nonetheless engage with Dante's history through a self-citation (*Par.* viii, 37), three canti devoted to Dante's putative ancestry (*Par.* xv–xvii), and the choice of Dante's beloved Beatrice as guide. In the final section of this chapter, I shall consider the implications of Dante's embodied encounters with his past by analyzing the meeting with Casella in *Purgatorio* ii.

Up until now we have considered Dante's journey and Proust's imagery from the perspective of the descent into the self. There is however a second aspect that we must not ignore. The descent into the underworld also stands for a harrowing confrontation with what were considered the most objectionable aspects of human nature. This is where Dante's descent comes into its own, offering a more fruitful intertext with the *Recherche* than the classical descents. More than an elegiac meditation on our relationship with the dead, Dante's underworld offers a confrontation with human sin.[17] That is why Proust wants us to think of Dante, rather than Ulysses or Aeneas, when he stages his narrator-protagonist's difficulty in recounting the Baron de Charlus's lust-driven loss of control. This is done through a comparison between the efforts of a twentieth-century poet seeking to write about homosexuality and Dante's encounter with the sodomites:

> Le poète est à plaindre, et qui n'est guidé par aucun Virgile, d'avoir à traverser les cercles d'un enfer de soufre et de poix, de se jeter dans le feu qui tombe du ciel pour en ramener quelques habitants de Sodome. (III, 711)
>
> [One must lament the task of the poet who, with no Virgil to guide him, must cross the circles of a hell of sulphur and pitch, to throw himself into the fire falling from the sky and bring back a few inhabitants of Sodom.]

The 'pluie de feu' shows Proust's familiarity with the *contrapasso* (punishment) of *Inferno* XV, in which the sodomites run naked under a rain of fire. (And though the passage's tone condemns homosexuality, one may draw autobiographical inferences from Proust's poet's participation in the *contrapasso*: rather than merely observing the sinners as Dante does in the *Commedia*, he is throwing *himself* into the rain of fire.) This narratorial complaint finds a parallel in the opening of *Inferno* XXXII, where Dante laments the poetic challenge that he is faced with in attempting to describe the horror of the very lowest circle of Hell:

> S'ïo avessi le rime aspre e chiocce,
> come si converebbe al tristo buco
> [...]
> io premerei di mio concetto il suco
> più pienamente; ma perch'io non l'abbo
> non sanza tema a dicer mi conduco;
>
> ché non è impresa da pigliare a gabbo
> discriver fondo a tutto l'universo,
> né da lingua che chiami mamma o babbo. (*Inf.* XXXII, 1–9)
>
> [If I had the harsh and twisted rhymes | that befit such a sorrowful hole | [...] | I would squeeze the essence of my thoughts out | to the full; but because I do not have them | it is not without fear that I begin to speak; | for it is no enterprise to laugh at | describing the bottom of the entire universe, | nor for a language that still calls 'mum' and 'dad'.]

While Proust's narrator-protagonist laments not having the assistance of a (literary) guide such as Virgil, which makes observing and representing the sodomites more challenging, Dante here laments the insufficiency of his own poetry to describe the Traitors of Kin. The use of the adjective 'aspre' [harsh] calls to mind Dante's youthful lyric poems collectively known as the *rime petrose*, in which the poetic subject describes his unrequited love for a cold woman metaphorized as a stone ('petra'). One of these poems in particular opens with the subject saying he will make his language as harsh as the woman's actions: 'Così nel mio parlar voglio esser aspro | com'è ne li atti questa bella petra' ('I want to be as harsh in my speech as this fair stone is in her behaviour') (Dante 1967: I, 170–71).[18] While the opening of the *rima petrosa* is announcing what follows, the opening of *Inferno* XXXII is describing the 'rime aspre e chiocce' as an unattainable goal: the conditional 'S'ïo avessi' informs us that no verse that Dante can write will ever equal the horror of what he saw. The third terzina of the quoted extract however points at Dante's literary talent: by stating that describing the bottom of the universe is a great challenge (lines 7–8) which requires linguistic prowess (line 9), and then going on to carry out such a description, Dante is ultimately attracting attention to his achievement.

We cannot know for certain whether Proust would have been familiar with this particular passage of the *Commedia*. What is clear, however, is that while he draws on classical descents for his account of the process of introspection, when it comes to describing the challenges that come with being a writer, it is Dante's journey that Proust wishes to call to mind. Dante provides a valuable intertext to this purpose for two reasons: first, his Christian Hell in its representation of punished human sin offers a dimension that is absent from classical visions of the underworld, and, secondly, the struggles of Dante's literal journey through the afterworld are mirrored by the metapoetic struggles of Dante as explicit author of the poem. As will become all the more apparent through an analysis of Dante's use of flight imagery, the *Commedia* successfully intertwines the Christian journey to God with the literary journey to the poem.

Aeronautics

Julian Barnes in his autobiographical work *Levels of Life* puts his finger on three sources of flight: 'We live on the flat, on the level, and yet — and so — we aspire. Groundlings, we can sometimes reach as far as the gods. Some soar with art, others with religion; most with love' (2013: 36). Barnes's account of human flight is very close to Dante's in the *Commedia*, where love for Beatrice enables the ascent to God, who in turn is described as the first lover ('primo amante', *Par.* IV, 118) and 'l'amor che move il sole e l'altre stelle' [the love that moves the sun and the other stars] (*Par.* XXXIII, 145). Love plays a central role in Dante's poetry. As we saw in the previous chapter, in *Purgatorio* XXIV (52–54) Dante defines the first step in his poetic practice as taking dictation from love. And in the same passage, the composition of poetry is expressed through flight imagery (*Purg.* XXIV, 58–60). In Dante's poem therefore we soar through art, religion, and love, and these three sources of flight are inextricably linked. In contrast, in the world-vision of the *Recherche*, one only soars through art. As we shall see, Dante's use of flight imagery interweaves the Christian notion of spiritual ascent, lyric poetry's metaphorization of poets as birds, and classical literature's metapoetic use of nautical imagery, whereas Proust's draws on the technological advances of the early twentieth century.

Flight imagery in Dante is related first and foremost to desire. Desire, as observed by Lino Pertile, is the psychological correlative to the metaphor of the journey, and this is the case both in Dante's *Commedia* and in Christian life: 'nei riti della Chiesa i cristiani pregano perché, affrancata da tutte le concupiscenze terrene, la loro mente s'innalzi ai desideri celesti' [in religious rites, Christians pray for their mind to be freed from earthly concupiscence, so that it may elevate itself towards heavenly desires] (2005: 35–36). The metaphor of life as pilgrimage was ubiquitous in medieval culture, mainly through Augustine's formulation in *Confessions* I, xix, and *On Christian Doctrine* I, iii, 3–4, though it is also found in earlier texts such as the Epistle to Diognetus in which it said of Christians that 'They dwell on earth, but they are citizens in heaven' (Ladner 1967: 236). In his unfinished philosophical treatise the *Convivio*, Dante argues that all men desire to return to God (*Conv.* IV, xii, 14) and draws on the Augustinian image of the pilgrimage of desire in a passage which has been called by Barolini a 'virtual blueprint' for the *Commedia* (1992: 99–121):

> E sì come peregrino che va per una via per la quale mai non fue, che ogni casa che da lungi vede crede che sia l'albergo, e non trovando ciò essere, dirizza la credenza all'altra, e così di casa in casa, tanto che all'albergo viene; così l'anima nostra, incontanente che nel nuovo e mai non fatto cammino di questa vita entra, dirizza li occhi al termine del suo sommo bene, e però, qualunque cosa vede che paia in sé avere alcuno bene, crede che sia esso. (*Conv.* iv, xii, 15)
>
> [And just as the pilgrim who walks along a road on which he has never traveled before believes that every house which he sees from afar is an inn, and finding it not so fixes his expectations on the next one, and so moves from house to house until he comes to the inn, so our soul, as soon as it enters upon this new and never traveled road of life, fixes its eyes on the goal of its supreme good, and therefore believes that everything it sees which seems to possess some good in it is that supreme good.]

Augustine's influence is most clearly present in the *Purgatorio* in which the souls purge their attachments to earthly objects of love and redirect their desire upwards towards God.

The *Commedia* frequently refers to the 'wings' ('ali', or by synecdoche 'penne') of desire bearing the pilgrim upwards, as has been studied in an article by Hugh Shankland, who reads Dante's surname, Alighieri, as 'wing bearing'. Shankland observes that Dante, in the course of the *Purgatorio*, 'will be cunningly represented as developing "the swift wings and plumage" of his *gran disio*, an elaborate serial metaphor for the maturing process whereby the loving mind raises itself to the level of God' (1975: 766). The image of the wings of desire and the flight to God is present all the way to the final canto of *Paradiso*, where we encounter it in Bernard's prayer to the Virgin (*Par.* xxxiii, 15). Bernard's prayer reminds us of the difference between Ulysses's horizontal journey — his oars attempted to be wings, but did not lead to flight — and Dante's aided Christian ascent. Flight imagery in the *Commedia* is the lexical means by which the Christian and the poetic journey are made inextricable, for it is used interchangeably to speak of both Christian aspiration and poetic vocation. The final flight metaphor of the *Commedia*, 'ma non eran da ciò le proprie penne' [but my quills were not capable of as much] (*Par.* xxxiii, 139), refers to the protagonist's inability to withstand the vision of the Godhead, but also implies Dante's inability to write of it.[19] Indeed, the poem often uses the word 'penne' ('quills') as a pun, seeing as it can be understood both as 'feathers' and as 'pens'.

Bird imagery played an important part in Italian thirteenth-century poetry and featured in a prominent poetic exchange of the time between the poets Guido Guinizzelli and Bonagiunta da Lucca.[20] Guinizzelli, who had been criticized for his poetic innovations by Bonagiunta in the sonnet 'Voi, ch'avete mutata la mainera', responded with 'Omo ch'è saggio non corre leggero'.[21] In lines 9–11 of this sonnet, Guinizzelli allegedly responds to Bonagiunta's attack on his poetic innovations by using a bird metaphor:

Volan ausel' per air di straine guise
ed han diversi loro operamenti,
né tutti d'un volar né d'un ardire.

[Different birds fly through the air | and they all have different ways of being, | neither do they all fly in the same way, neither are they all bold in the same way.]

Dante stages encounters with these two poets in *Purgatorio* XXIV and XXVI, thereby continuing the debate on the criteria that make great vernacular lyric poetry. In the episode of *Purgatorio* XXIV referred to in Chapter 1, Bonagiunta reacts to Dante's answer by acknowledging Dante and his peers' poetic superiority through bird imagery:

Io veggio ben come *le vostre penne*
di retro al dittator sen vanno strette,
che de le nostre certo non avvenne.
(*Purg.* XXIV, 52–60; my emphasis)

[I see clearly how *your quills follow* | *closely the one who dictates,* | which certainly did not happen in our case.]

Beatrice uses a similar language to Bonagiunta when she critiques Dante's failures as a poet and as a Christian:

Ben ti dovevi, per lo primo strale,
de le cose fallaci, *levar suso*
di retro a me che non era più tale.

Non ti dovea *gravar le penne in giuso,*
ad aspettar più colpo, o pargoletta,
o altra novità con sì breve uso.
(*Purg.* XXXI, 55–60; my emphasis)

[You should have, at the very first arrow | of deceitful things, *followed me upwards* | since I was no longer one of them. | You shouldn't have *turned your quills downwards,* | waiting to be struck again, by some young girl, | or other novelty of equally brief use.]

As shall be further examined in Chapter 4, Beatrice's intervention plays a key role in linking Dante's spiritual redemption to his poetic output. This could not be achieved as vividly without the language of flight, which allows her to combine the bird imagery of vernacular lyric poetry and the ascent imagery of the Bible and the exegetical tradition.

The repetition of the expression 'di retro' in Beatrice and Bonagiunta's description of Dante's poetic activity as a flight towards something higher can in turn be connected to the oration that Ulysses gives his men in order to spur them on to undertake the 'folle volo', which like Bonagiunta's speech, also uses the term *frate* [brother]:

'O frati,' dissi, 'che per cento milia
perigli siete giunti a l'occidente,
a questa tanto picciola vigilia

d'i nostri sensi ch'è del rimanente
non vogliate negar l'esperïenza,
di retro al sol, del mondo sanza gente.

Considerate la vostra semenza:
fatti non foste a viver come bruti,
ma per seguir virtute e canoscenza'.
(*Inf.* XXVI, 112–20; my emphasis)

['O brothers,' I said, 'who despite a hundred thousand | perils have reached the West, | now that but our short vigil | is all that is left for our senses | do not deny yourselves the experience, | *following the sun*, of a world without people. | Consider your birth: | you were not made to live as brutes, | but to pursue virtue and knowledge.]

In all three cases, the preposition 'di retro a' (which I have translated as 'following') opens a verse and is syntactically followed by the motor of the movement it describes. In *Purgatorio* XXIV it refers to the much debated 'dittator' who leads to the composition of poetry, in *Purgatorio* XXXI it refers to Beatrice and the spiritual elevation attained through love for her, and in *Inferno* XXVI to the Icarian attraction of the unknown. This intertextual echo is consistent with the metapoetic relevance of Ulysses's journey to Dante's poetic enterprise. While the image of writing as sailing was a classical commonplace, Ulysses's attempt to 'fly by boat' creates the more original image of the aeronautical journey, an image which becomes the hallmark of Dante's metapoetic discourse. Barolini has indeed shown that the aeronautical imagery associated with Ulysses is also present in the encounter with Geryon (*Inferno* XVI–XVII), an infernal monster who combines the face of a kind man with a hideous and fascinating body composed of animal parts, knots, and cogwheels. Geryon embodies the sin of fraud ('quella sozza imagine di froda', *Inf.* XVII, 7) and can be understood as a metaphor for the deceitful power of language (Barolini 1992: 63–65).[22] The monster rises up to meet and transport Dante and Virgil in a motion resembling swimming, but which is in fact flying; he is thus implicated in the poem's use of the image of aeronautical travel. By merging the nautical imagery of classical literature with the bird imagery of lyric poetry and the ascent imagery of Christian discourse, Dante thus creates a rich metaphorical discourse which both innovates and incorporates three important traditions.

While air travel for Dante was but a fantasy, a felicitous image for his ambitious poem, Proust was writing at the time of the invention of the aeroplane. The technological developments of the dawn of the twentieth century were to have a tremendous effect on his novel, as has been studied by William C. Carter in *The Proustian Quest*. Carter observes that 'there is scarcely an invention, new at the time, that was not put to good metaphorical use by the writer; obvious examples would include the telephone, X-ray machine, and camera' (1992: 184). In the context of artistic creation, Proust's most notable technological metaphor is that of the aeroplane, its journey on a vertical axis providing an eloquent contrast with the automobile's journey on a horizontal axis.[23] This creates an important parallel with the journey imagery of the *Commedia* in which Dante's ascent to God and Ulysses's negative journey also take place on opposite axes. The analogy between the artist and the aviator, to which Carter devotes a chapter (1992: 187–205), is made explicit in the passage of *À l'ombre des jeunes filles en fleurs* explaining the nature of Bergotte's genius, and by extension offering a general definition of artistic genius.

> Mais le génie, même le grand talent, vient moins d'éléments intellectuels et d'affinement social supérieurs à ceux d'autrui, que de la faculté de les transformer, de les transposer. [...] Pour se promener dans les airs, il n'est pas nécessaire d'avoir l'automobile la plus puissante, mais une automobile qui, ne continuant pas de courir à terre et coupant d'une verticale la ligne qu'elle suivait, soit capable de convertir en force ascensionnelle sa vitesse horizontale. De même ceux qui produisent des œuvres géniales ne sont pas ceux qui vivent dans le milieu le plus délicat, qui ont la conversation la plus brillante, la culture la plus étendue, mais ceux qui ont eu le pouvoir, cessant brusquement de vivre pour eux-mêmes, de rendre leur personnalité pareille à un miroir, de telle sorte que leur vie si médiocre d'ailleurs qu'elle pouvait être [...] s'y reflète, le génie consistant dans le pouvoir réfléchissant et non dans la qualité intrinsèque du spectacle reflété. Le jour où le jeune Bergotte put montrer au monde de ses lecteurs le salon de mauvais goût où il avait passé son enfance et les causeries pas très drôles qu'il y tenait avec ses frères, ce jour-là il monta plus haut que les amis de sa famille, plus spirituels et plus distingués: ceux-ci dans leurs belles Rolls-Royce pourraient rentrer chez eux en témoignant un peu de mépris pour la vulgarité des Bergotte; mais lui, de son modeste appareil qui venait enfin de 'décoller', il les survolait. (I, 544–45)

> [But genius, even great talent, come less from intellectual elements or superior social refinements than from the ability to transform them, to transpose them. [...] In order to roam the heavens, one does not require the most powerful automobile, but an automobile which, instead of running on the ground, cuts vertically the line it had been following, and is able to convert its horizontal speed into an ascending force. Similarly, those who produce brilliant works are not those who live in the most delicate milieu, whose conversation is the most dazzling or knowledge the most vast, but those who had the power, ceasing suddenly to live for themselves, to make their personality similar to a mirror, so that their life, however mediocre it may have been [...] might be reflected. Genius consists in the power to mirror and not in the intrinsic quality of the spectacle being mirrored. The day when the young Bergotte was able to show his readers the vulgar drawing room in which he had spent his childhood and the rather dull conversations he had had there with his brothers, that day he soared higher than their wittier and more distinguished family friends: they may have travelled home in their elegant Rolls-Royces looking down on the uncouth Bergottes; but Bergotte, in his modest machine which was just 'taking off', was flying high above them.]

One may hear in the concluding sentence an echo of Charles Baudelaire's poem 'L'Albatros', in which the great bird serves as an analogy for the poet: when the 'prince des nuées' is placed on the horizontal axis he becomes 'gauche' and is despised, just as Bergotte is by the family friends (Baudelaire 1975–76: I, 9–10). Proust's great innovation however is that he combines the Romantic figure of the misunderstood artist with imagery taken from technological development, including specialized vocabulary such as 'décoller'. Through his references to scientific progress, Proust is able to bring new nuance to the well-worn conceits of art as alchemy and the process of spiritual or intellectual enlightenment as ascent.[24] Artistic abilities are also metaphorized in terms of flight in the passage of *Le Temps retrouvé* describing the 'célibataires de l'art', individuals who express a hyperbolic enthusiasm for art because they failed to be artists themselves. Proust combines both natural and technological imagery, comparing them to the first attempts at flying machines and to chicks that have not yet grown their wings. The narrator concludes: 'Ces amateurs velléitaires et stériles doivent nous toucher comme ces premiers appareils qui ne purent quitter la terre mais où résidait, non encore le moyen secret et qui restait à découvrir, mais le désir du vol' [These uncommitted and sterile amateurs should move us, like those first machines that could not yet leave the ground, but in which there resided, not the secret means which had yet to be discovered, but the desire for flight] (IV, 471). Both the *Commedia* and the *Recherche* thus make important use of aeronautical imagery to describe a journey towards a detachment from earthly concerns and an enlightened perspective. The analogy between medieval Christian flight iconography and the twentieth-century development of aeronautics is in fact drawn by Proust himself when he describes the angels of Giotto's Arena as 'mettant la plus grande aisance à exécuter des loopings' [looping the loop with the greatest of ease], calling to mind 'de jeunes élèves de Fonck s'exerçant au vol plané' [young students of Fonck's, practicing gliding] (IV, 227).[25] However, while in Dante's poem ascension is enabled by love and religion, in Proust it is powered entirely by art.

The *Recherche*'s most famous passage on the journey made possible by art comes in a context of suffocating jealousy and loss of artistic aspiration, when the protagonist goes to a concert hosted by the up-and-coming Verdurins. His true motivation for attending is the hope of seeing the composer's daughter, whom he suspects of being a former lover of his mistress Albertine. This is symptomatic of the blinkered world-view that love causes in Proust's novel: from an Augustinian perspective, one would describe love for Albertine as concupiscence, an earthly appetite holding him back from ascent.[26] Music is contrasted with this horizontal concern during the day of the concert, when expecting Albertine to arrive home soon, the narrator-protagonist finds himself momentarily calm enough to study Vinteuil's sonata: 'je pouvais disposer de ma pensée, la détacher un moment d'Albertine, l'appliquer à la Sonate' [I had my thoughts at my disposal and could detach them from Albertine for a moment to apply them to the Sonata] (III, 664), and then Wagner's *Tristan*:

> La musique bien différente en cela de la société d'Albertine, m'aidait à descendre en moi-même, à y découvrir du nouveau [...]. Comme le spectre extériorise pour nous la composition de la lumière, l'harmonie d'un Wagner, la couleur d'un Elstir nous permettent de connaître cette essence qualitative des sensations d'un autre où l'amour pour un autre être ne nous fait pas pénétrer. Puis, diversité au sein de l'œuvre même, par le seul moyen qu'il y a d'être effectivement divers: réunir diverses individualités. (III, 665)
>
> [Music, which in this regard was very different to Albertine's company, would help me descend into myself and discover something new [...]. Just as the spectrum exteriorizes for us the composition of light, the harmony of a Wagner and the colour of an Elstir allow us to encounter the qualitative essence of the

sensations of an other, an essence that we cannot penetrate through love for an other. Then, diversity within one same work, through the only means there is to effectively be diverse: by bringing together different individualities.]

His thoughts will then take a different turn, so that by the time he is heading to the concert he believes that:

> L'Art [...] n'était pas quelque chose qui valût la peine d'un sacrifice, quelque chose d'en dehors de la vie, ne participant pas à sa vanité et son néant, l'apparence d'individualité réelle obtenue dans les œuvres n'étant due qu'au trompe-l'œil de l'habileté technique. (III, 702–03)
>
> [Art [...] was not something that warranted a sacrifice, something outside of life, independent from its futility and emptiness, because the appearance of real individuality in works of art was nothing more than a trompe l'oeil obtained through technical ability.]

But this downturn only prepares the ground for a far better-known passage. The audition of Vinteuil's posthumous masterpiece provides irrefutable evidence that there is such a thing as individuality and that art alone can communicate it:

> Cette patrie perdue, les musiciens ne se la rappellent pas, mais chacun d'eux reste toujours inconsciemment accordé en un certain unisson avec elle [...] ce chant singulier dont la monotonie [...] prouve chez le musicien la fixité des éléments composants de son âme. Mais alors, n'est-ce pas que [...] cet ineffable qui différencie qualitativement ce que chacun a senti et qu'il est obligé de laisser au seuil des phrases où il ne peut communiquer avec autrui qu'en se limitant à des points extérieurs communs à tous et sans intérêt, l'art, l'art d'un Vinteuil comme celui d'un Elstir, le fait apparaître, extériorisant dans les couleurs du spectre la composition intime de ces mondes que nous appelons les individus, et que sans l'art nous ne connaîtrions jamais? Des ailes, un autre appareil respiratoire, et qui nous permissent de traverser l'immensité, ne nous serviraient à rien. Car si nous allions dans Mars et dans Vénus en gardant les mêmes sens, ils revêtiraient du même aspect que les choses de la Terre tout ce que nous pourrions voir. Le seul véritable voyage [...] ce ne serait pas d'aller vers de nouveaux paysages, mais d'avoir d'autres yeux, de voir l'univers avec les yeux d'un autre, de cent autres, de voir les cent univers que chacun d'eux voit, que chacun d'eux est; et cela, nous le pouvons avec un Elstir, avec un Vinteuil; avec leurs pareils, nous volons vraiment d'étoiles en étoiles. (III, 761–62)
>
> [This lost homeland, musicians do not remember it, but every one of them always remains unconsciously in tune with it [...] the unique song whose monotony [...] proves the fixity of the elements composing the musician's soul. But then, is it not true that [...] this ineffable qualitative difference between what every person feels, that one must leave outside of the sentences in which one can only communicate with others by limiting oneself to external points that are common to everyone and of no interest, art, the art of a Vinteuil like the art of an Elstir, can bring it to light, exteriorizing through the colours of the spectrum the intimate composition of those worlds which we call individuals, and which, were it not for art, we would never know? Wings, another respiratory apparatus, allowing us to traverse infinite spaces, would be of no use at all. For if we went to Mars or Venus with the same senses, everything we would see would take on the same aspect as that which we encounter on Earth.

> The only true journey [...] would not be to see new landscapes, but to have other eyes, to see the universe with the eyes of an other, of a hundred others, to see the one hundred universes that each one of them sees, which each one of them *is*. And that, that can be done with an Elstir, with a Vinteuil — with their equals, we truly fly from star to star.]

There are clear lexical signals that these two passages are part of one same discursive thread: the use of the indefinite article in 'un Vinteuil [...] un Elstir' picks up from 'un Wagner, [...] un Elstir', as well as the reference to exteriorizing the 'spectrum' of colour. Read as a diptych, these two extracts present us with a dual vertical movement: a descent into the self ('descendre en moi-même') followed by a spiritual ascent. While the first passage speaks of the disappointments of 'le voyage', the second passage contrasts literal travel with metaphorical travel, the latter being 'le seul véritable voyage'. Wings are here said to be useless since the true journey is the change taking place in one's perceptions as a result of embracing another individual's sensitivies, and consequently, a different worldview. Both passages stress the intersubjective value of art, making Proust's journey through art the opposite of Ulysses's sinful journey away from people (*Inf.* XXVI, 117). But Proust's artistic flight is not Christian either: the spectator is not flying towards God, but towards other human individuals — artists. The image of the artist's 'patrie perdue' subverts the *topos* of Christians as citizens of Heaven, living in exile on earth. While Dante believed that all individuals were travelling back to their common origin, God (*Conv.* IV, xii, 14), Proust stresses the journey to the self, which is unique, and therefore gives every artist a different homeland: 'Chaque artiste semble ainsi comme le citoyen d'une patrie inconnue [...] différente de celle d'où viendra, appareillant pour la terre, un autre grand artiste' [Every great artist can thus be seen as the citizen of an unknown land [...] which is different to the one from which will land another great artist] (III, 761).

Although the *Recherche*, like the *Commedia*, describes artistic enterprise through the image of the aeronautical journey, the metaphor is brought to different fruition. In the *Commedia* we find a continuation of the Christian topos of the journey upwards towards God, which Dante, through the metaphor of aeronautics, successfully combines with the journey of poetic creation. In the *Recherche*, we find the imagery of aeronautics and astronautics, but Proust does not sustain the analogy between aviator and writer beyond a certain point. Bergotte is compared to an aeroplane in terms of an ability for the conversion of forces and astronautical travel is used as a contrast to offset the far more valuable journey allowed by art, which takes place through interior change. Thus, while I agree with Carter's emphasis on the aviator as a symbol for the artist, I find it important to note that in contrast with the sustained engagement with aeronautics present in the *Commedia*'s metapoetic passages, Proust ultimately places most emphasis on the journey inwards, not upwards. This is all the more explicit in the section of the novel known as 'L'Adoration perpétuelle',[27] where the protagonist repeatedly uses images implying that the truth that will form the basis of his work of art is to be found not by ascending upwards, but by plumbing the depths of the self: 'J'avais trop expérimenté l'impossibilité d'atteindre dans la réalité ce qui était *au fond* de moi-même' [I had too often experienced the impossibility of reaching through reality what was *deep within* myself] (IV, 455; my emphasis); 'La réalité à exprimer résidait, je le comprenais maintenant, non dans l'apparence du sujet mais à une *profondeur* où cette apparence importait peu' [The reality that I had to express resided, I could now see, not in the subject's appearance, but at a *depth* where this appareance mattered little] (IV, 461; my emphasis); and:

> Ce travail qu'avaient fait notre amour-propre, notre passion, notre esprit d'imitation, notre intelligence abstraite, nos habitudes, c'est ce travail que l'art défera, c'est la marche en sens contraire, le *retour aux profondeurs* où ce qui a existé réellement *gît* inconnu de nous, qu'il nous fera suivre. (IV, 475; my emphasis)
>
> [This joint effort of our pride, our passion, our spirit of imitation, our abstract intelligence, our habits, it is this effort that art will undo. It is a march in the reverse direction, a *return to the depths* where what did truly exist *lies* unknown to us, that we will have to undertake.]

Dante's and Proust's different conceptions of subjectivity are thus also expressed through their different uses of the journey metaphor: in Dante the poet travels upwards, towards God, serving as a model for his readers; in Proust the ultimate destination for both the writer and the reader is down into the depths of their own unique self.[28]

Deviations and Returns

So far we have considered linear journeys towards determined points of arrival: down towards the self and the past, and up towards God and artistic creation, but we did not take into account the important deviations and circular movements that are also present in these texts. The word 'deviation' implies the existence of a point of arrival which is momentarily not being pursued. A deviation can involve an actual detour, that is taking a route from A to B which is not the most direct one, or a stepping-aside from the way, a pause for loitering. Loitering and deviating have negative connotations to this day and their rhetorical manifestation is the digression, which etymologically is also a stepping aside from the way (*gradi* [to step, walk, go] is combined with the negative prefix *dis-*). In the Christian narrative the point of arrival is God, and I cited *Convivio* IV, xii, 14–15 in this regard. The same section of the *Convivio* sets out an analogy connecting the direct roads between cities to a correct way of life, and longer routes to more or less erroneous ways of life:

> Ché, sì come d'una cittade a un'altra di necessitade è una ottima e dirittissima via, e un'altra che sempre se ne dilunga (cioè quella che va nell'altra parte), e molte altre, quale meno alungandosi, quale meno appressandosi: così nella vita umana sono diversi cammini, delli quali uno è veracissimo e un altro è fallacissimo, e certi meno fallaci e certi meno veraci. (*Conv.* IV, xii, 18)
>
> [For just as from one city to another there is only one road which is of necessity the best and most direct, and another which leads completely away (namely the one which goes in the opposite direction), and many others, some leading away from it and some moving toward it, so in human life there are different paths, among which only one is the truest way and another the falsest, and some less true and some less false.]

Dante contrasts 'lo buono camminatore', who goes straight to the city, and 'lo erroneo' who never arrives there because he is always looking around himself, greedily taking in his surroundings, instead of focusing on the destination (*Conv.* IV, xii, 19).[29] This end-orientated depiction of life as pilgrimage could not be further from the syntax of the *Recherche*. Perhaps more surprisingly, it is also resisted by the *Commedia*. The narrative structure of Dante's poem can be interpreted teleologically, pointing forwards to its own writing (the summit of Dante's poetic career) and the vision of the Godhead (the climax of Dante's experience of the otherworld); so too Proust's novel points forward to the narrator-protagonist's transformation into a writer. But both works also actively resist such a reading through their use of non-linear forms (Dante's terza rima and Proust's meandering sentences), which contribute to both works' staging of a complex temporality made of returns and revisitations.

It is precisely in terms of non-linear movement that the *Recherche* formulates its most explicit comparison between its protagonist and that of the *Commedia*:

> Bientôt le cours de la Vivonne s'obstrue de plantes d'eau. Il y en a d'abord d'isolées comme tel nénuphar à qui le courant au travers duquel il était placé d'une façon malheureuse laissait si peu de repos que comme un bac actionné mécaniquement il n'abordait une rive que pour retourner à celle d'où il était venu, refaisant éternellement la double traversée. [...] Je [le] retrouvais de promenade en promenade, toujours dans la même situation, faisant penser à certains neurasthéniques au nombre desquels mon grand-père comptait ma tante Léonie, qui nous offrent sans changement au cours des années le spectacle des habitudes bizarres qu'ils se croient chaque fois à la veille de secouer et qu'ils gardent toujours [...]. Tel était ce nénuphar, pareil aussi à quelqu'un de ces malheureux dont le tourment singulier, qui se répète indéfiniment durant l'éternité, excitait la curiosité de Dante et dont il se serait fait raconter plus longuement les particularités et la cause par le supplicié lui-même si Virgile, s'éloignant à grands pas, ne l'avait forcé à le rattraper au plus vite, comme moi mes parents. (I, 166–67)

> [Soon the course of the Vivonne is obstructed by water plants. At first they are isolated, like one water lily, the current in the path of which it was unfortunately placed giving it so little respite that, like a mechanically actioned ferry, it would approach one shore only to return to the one it had come from, eternally repeating the double crossing. [...] I would find [it] there walk after walk, always in the same situation, reminding me of certain neurasthenics, among whose number my grandfather counted my aunt Léonie, who offer us over the years the unchanging spectacle of their bizarre habits, which they keep thinking they are about to quit and that they always keep up [...]. Such was this water lily, which also resembled one of those unfortunate souls whose singular torment, indefinitely repeated throughout eternity, would excite the curiosity of Dante, and the particularities and cause of whose punishment he would have been happy to hear more about from the tortured soul, had Virgil, pressing on swiftly, not forced him to hurry after him, as I did after my parents.]

This passage describes both a negative and a positive form of non-linear movement. The negative form is that of the 'nénuphar', tante Léonie, and the sinners of Dante's *Inferno*, who are condemned to the circles of endless and fruitless repetition.[30]

Proust here shows himself very perceptive to the nature of the stasis of Dante's Hell, which has been read as a physical manifestation of the sinners' fixation on their sins or 'monomania' (Hawkins 2006: 40). The child-protagonist instead offers us a positive of non-linear movement: loitering followed by return (implied by the *re-* prefix of *rattraper*). The child's movement is reflected by the text, which lingers on its description of plants, digresses by connecting one of them to tante Léonie, returns to the water lily, digresses again through a comparison with Dante's *Inferno*, and finally returns to the child and his parents. The child's deviations assert from an early stage the main characteristic of the novel and its narrator-protagonist: a propensity for digressiveness, fuelled by attention to detail, humour, and a flair for analogies. Moreover, the concluding sentence of the passage is constructed in such a manner as to make it impossible for the reader to skip any clause, as this would result in a loss of meaning. The reader is forced to take the longer way, going, along with the narrator-protagonist, through every step of the *Inferno* analogy, which goes from the water lily to Dante's *Inferno* and then from Dante's *Inferno* back to the *Recherche*'s narrator-protagonist and his parents. The very form of Proust's meandering sentences and its effect on the reader mirrors the character of the narrator-protagonist who, as we saw in Chapter 1, is observant, hypersensitive, and receptive to otherness.[31] The rectilinear outlook on life is associated with the character of Norpois, whom we also considered in Chapter 1. As well as criticizing the narrator-protagonist and Bergotte's writing, Norpois describes a young man who possesses the qualities which according to him make a successful writer: single-mindedness and official recognition. While Bergotte is critiqued for his 'chinoiseries de forme' [intricacies of form] (I, 465), this young writer is praised as one who takes a direct route and does not loiter: 'il n'est pas homme à s'arrêter en route' [he is not the kind of man who will stop along the way] (I, 445).

The journey of the *Commedia*, though ostensibly orientated to the end of redeeming Dante, is also a work full of digressions, in so far as the journey narrative is used as a frame for many shorter narratives, which interrupt the journey every time that an encountered soul recounts its personal story to Dante. This is precisely the aspect that Proust picks up on in the water lily analogy, when he compares Dante's desire to loiter to that of the child. The entire structure of the *Commedia*, divided as it is into three equally long canticles devoted to Hell, Purgatory, and Paradise, rests upon the fact that Dante takes the longest route possible. In *Inferno* I, Dante attempts to climb away from the dark forest, but finds his way barred. He is told by Virgil that he will instead have to make another journey (*Inf.* I, 91). As a result, he travels through the entirety of Hell before beginning the ascent of Mount Purgatory. His itinerary is made even longer by the fact that he goes down Hell and then up Mount Purgatory not in a straight line, but in a spiral.[32] Dante's *Paradiso*, finally, is a supreme example of digression. As is made explicit by Beatrice, the souls of the blessed in reality are all together; they are not separated into different circles as Dante is seeing them (*Par.* IV, 37–48). Within the fiction of the *Commedia*, the souls are showing themselves to Dante in this manner because as a mortal he cannot conceive of a realm beyond space and time. Of course, Dante is setting out this fiction because, as observed by Barolini, 'without the temporal/spatial/narrative continuum to which text and voyage subscribe in the first two canticles, the poet is [...] at a representational loss' (1992: 188). Narrative relies on a before and an after, on difference: it is the journey between the beginning and the end. Moreover, the route between beginning and end must be long and winding, because narrative, as has been studied by Peter Brooks, is made precisely of the digressive movement of detours and postponements:

> Plot is a kind of arabesque or squiggle toward the end. It is like that arabesque from *Tristram Shandy*, retraced by Balzac, that suggests the arbitrary, transgressive, gratuitous line of narrative, its deviance from the straight line, the shortest distance between beginning and end — which would be the collapse of one into the other, of life into immediate death. (1984: 104)

The existence of the *Commedia* depends on Dante's 'cammino' [path] not being 'diritto' [direct] but going through every circle of Hell, every terrace of Purgatory, and every metaphorical region of Paradise, with frequent pauses to take in the surroundings and engage with the inhabitants of the otherworld.

Proust's novel also offers an important case study for Brooks's definition of the narratable. In terms of its very composition, Proust began by writing the beginning and the ending of the *Recherche*, before expanding the novel from the middle (Finch 1977). This has led Margaret Topping to note that 'one might provocatively argue that the 3000-page, seven-volume novel into which these initial two volumes organically evolved in the period until Proust's death in 1922 is largely composed of digressions from this teleological frame' (2011: 106).[33] Proust's digressiveness ranges from the structure of the *Recherche* to its very fabric, as we saw above by looking at the syntax of the sentence comparing the water lily to a damned soul in Dante's *Inferno*. Digression offers an aesthetic of multiplicity: a single Proustian sentence may fork out down several avenues, some of which are pursued, while others are abandoned and left to the reader's imagination — a dizzyingly succinct example of Proustian accumulation can be found for instance in the description of the Grand-Hôtel's lift-operator's behaviour: 'Mais il ne me répondit pas, soit étonnement de mes paroles, attention à son travail, souci de l'étiquette, dureté de son ouïe, respect du lieu, crainte du danger, paresse d'intelligence ou consigne du directeur' [But he did not answer, either because he was surprised at my words, or focused on his job, or conscious of etiquette, or deaf of hearing, or respectful of the setting, or fearful, or intellectually lazy, or instructed to by the hotel manager] (II, 26). These avenues can also lead to one of the novel's broader thematic threads, which wind their way through the novel, crossing (and at times even converging with) others. This is why there are different, and equally valid, possible interpretations of the *Recherche*, the most common example being the seeming contradiction of the triumph of art and the inescapability of death in *Le Temps retrouvé*. All different threads are equally present within the single body of the novel. The *Recherche* in this respect corresponds to Chambers's definition of 'loiterly literature':

> More in tune with the complexity of things and the tangled relations that join them. [...] For the end-directedness of suspense and the goal-oriented consistency of single-mindedness, it substitutes a kind of relaxed openness, an

> endless availability to otherness that means one can never *arrive*, since no point can ever be 'the' point. (1999: 31–32)

In Dante the teleological journey to God provides a dominant narrative thread. The stories of the encountered souls can be seen as digressions from the journey in so far as by pausing to converse with characters Dante is, quite literally, loitering — which is precisely the subject of the guardian of Purgatory, Cato's rebuke: 'Che è ciò, spiriti lenti? | qual negligenza, quale stare è questo?' [What is this, you dawdling spirits? | what negligence, what loitering is this?] (*Purg.* II, 120–21), an episode to which I shall return. However, Dante's otherworldly encounters are also incorporated into the linear narrative of salvation, in so far as by conversing with the souls, Dante is gaining a greater spiritual understanding and this, we are told, is the reason why his journey was ordained. The linear temporality of Christian narrative, which foreshadows the modern notion of progress, has been opposed by John Freccero to the circular temporality of antiquity. Freccero argues that linear temporality finds expression in the genre of the novel, where the reader is often tempted to 'skip ahead' in order to reach the conclusion, which is 'awaited with anxiety and suspense'; circular temporality, in contrast, finds expression in the genre of the epic, in which 'gem-like episodes are strung together as on a necklace, one set of events succeeding another quite independently' (1986: 137–38). We can see how Dante combines both temporalities by further developing Freccero's image of the necklace: the journey to God provides a linear narrative thread (as per the temporality of the novel); the encounters with the souls are the gems that are threaded on to this linear narrative (as per the unrelated episodes of epic). The *Recherche*, though a novel, also draws heavily on what Freccero identifies as the circular temporality of the epic. Proust's combination of linear and circular temporalities however differs from Dante's: rather than the necklace formed by a series of gems united by one main thread, the *Recherche* is an elaborate braid formed by the interweaving of many threads of equal importance.

The narrator-protagonist of the *Recherche* explicitly claims that the novel that we are reading follows a main thread or, to use Dante's image, a direct path that has been deviated from: the story of his literary vocation. As a result, all other episodes in his life are to be regarded as a pointless detour ('le détour de bien des années inutiles' [the detour of many pointless years], II, 691). In practice, however, only a minority of passages in the *Recherche* can be described as telling the story of his vocation. And, moreover, the narrator-protagonist observes in *Le Temps retrouvé* that it cannot be said that literature played a major role in his life:

> Ainsi toute ma vie jusqu'à ce jour aurait pu et n'aurait pas pu être résumée sous ce titre: Une vocation. Elle ne l'aurait pas pu en ce sens que la littérature n'avait joué aucun rôle dans ma vie. Elle l'aurait pu en ce que cette vie, les souvenirs de ses tristesses, de ses joies, formaient une réserve pareille à cet albumen qui est logé dans l'ovule des plantes [...] lequel est [...] le lieu de phénomènes chimiques et respiratoires secrets mais très actifs. (IV, 478)

> [Thus my entire life until this day may have been and may not have been summarized under the heading: A vocation. It may *not* have in so far as

> literature had played no role in my life. It *may* have in so far as this life, the memories of its sorrows and its joys, formed a reserve similar to the albumen which is located in the ovule of plants [...] in which secret, yet very active, chemical and respiratory phenomena are taking place.]

This passage plays a corrective role in relation to the previous one, suggesting that there is no such thing as a 'détour de bien des années inutiles', given that all his lived experiences have been nourishing his future work. In doing so, the passage also explains what the narrator might have meant by 'vocation invisible' (II, 691). The promise of the future work reframes all that has come before, making the novel, post hoc, the story of a literary vocation. This however means that the *Recherche* can only be summarized as 'the story of a vocation' if we read it teleologically from the perspective of its ending. If it were not for the final pages of *Le Temps retrouvé*, such a summary would not be justified.

Rather than arguing that the *Recherche* has one main thread (i.e. the story of a vocation) that is being digressed from, I find it more productive to consider the *Recherche* as interweaving several threads. As in a braid, different strands appear intermittently, coming to the fore and disappearing under the surface, crossing each other, and offering various combinations.[34] This is the reason why the genre of the *Recherche* has been challenging to classify. An important contribution in this respect is Hannah Freed-Thall's suggestion that the text of the *Recherche* can be compared to that of belle époque newspapers, and in particular *Le Figaro*, the cover of which would juxtapose such diverse items as international news, avant-garde manifestos (including Baudelaire's 'Le Peintre de la vie moderne', Jean Moréas's Symbolist manifesto and Marinetti's Futurist manifesto), weather forecasts, and gossip columns. Freed-Thall observes that the *Recherche*, like *Le Figaro* c.1908, is a patchwork text, drawing together a range of points of view, oscillating between gossip and philosophy, and generally covering a broad range of topics (2015: 31–40).

As with Chambers's definition of 'loiterly literature', none of the threads of Proust's novel is presented as 'the point', that is, the dominant discourse that is being deviated from. However, this form of narration is making a point in itself. It further establishes the narrator-protagonist's characterization as someone who does not make a beeline, but on the contrary is willing to 's'arrêter en route' [stop along the way] (I, 445). And it makes a statement about the relationship between art and life through what Chambers has called 'the transvaluation of the trivial':

> By insisting on the importance of that which is thought to be unworthy of attention, loiterature implies [...] not only the unexpected otherness of the ordinary but also the generalized ordinariness of all others [...]. If the familiar other is only a digression away from our daily beelines, and if one digression leads inevitably to others, then the exotic itself may in turn be only a digression or two away from home and so, potentially familiar too. (1999: 34–35)[35]

The notion of the 'transvaluation of the trivial' offers us an exegesis of the digressive analogies of the water lily passage, where something as trivial as a plant is connected to something as ordinary as a hypochondriac elderly relative, which are related in turn to that 'other' that is art, in this case, Dante's *Commedia*. The multiple analogies made possible by Proust's dilatory style are thus related to a poetics of equalization, which can also be found in the *Commedia*'s developed similes.[36]

For a case study of Proustian interweaving, let us take one of the threads which we considered earlier in this chapter: the voyage made possible by music (III, 665, 761–62). What happens in the ninety-six pages that interrupt this thread? The protagonist witnesses Morel mistreat his fiancée; Albertine and the protagonist go out to the Bois de Boulogne by car, where the sight of other women leads him to ponder on what his life with Albertine is depriving him of — not only other women, but also journeys abroad — but also to consider the similar disappointments he would experience with travel and other women; they dine and the protagonist suspects Albertine to be telling many lies; we learn of Bergotte's death, which leads to a shift in focalization on to Bergotte's last hours, and then leads the narrator to wonder whether art guarantees a form of afterlife; we return to Albertine's lies; on his way to the Vinteuil concert the protagonist runs into Morel who regrets having insulted his fiancée; the protagonist then encounters Brichot and they discuss Swann's death, which leads the narrator to consider the afterlife he has brought Swann by making him a character in his novel; Brichot mentions the beginning of Swann and Odette's relationship; they are joined by Charlus, this leads to a consideration of his love affair with Morel, who is one of the musicians performing the septet; Charlus mentions that Mlle Vinteuil will be coming, which leads to a fit of jealousy from the protagonist; with Mme Verdurin we reach considerations on the nature of her callous worldly relations, but that she is also a patron of art. Once the concert begins, the description of the septet is in turn interwoven with observations on the musicians and thoughts of Albertine, before the protagonist turns his full concentration to the music.

Two main threads already come to the fore: the question of whether art provides an afterlife and the jealousy-ridden nature of romantic relationships. The latter thread is approached through various couplings, both heterosexual and homosexual: the protagonist and Albertine; Morel and his fiancée; Swann and Odette; Charlus and Morel; Albertine and Mlle Vinteuil. The former thread poses a question through Bergotte's death which is returned to through the consideration of Swann's afterlife and answered in the positive by Vinteuil's septet. These two threads however cross over at many points and at times even converge. The clearest example of their convergence is the contrast made between literal horizontal voyages and aero- or astro-nautical voyages in our two framing passages, which resurfaces in Albertine and the protagonist's excursion by car. This automobile, moreover, echoes the analogy made earlier in the novel between Bergotte and an aeroplane. Albertine and the protagonist's car journey is both horizontal and circular, it does not lead to anywhere new, nor to an understanding of the other. Another example of convergence is Morel, who is one of the most sexually fluid and active characters of the *Recherche*, and, at the same time, an artist. The object of Charlus's monomaniacal jealousy performs the music which will allow the equally jealous protagonist to detach himself for a moment from thoughts of his mistress and reach something higher.

The discussion of the voyage made possible by art therefore is not interrupted on p. 665 to be picked up again on p. 761: it is truly interwoven with the novel's other threads, in particular here with its exploration of jealousy. The concept of digression is therefore insufficient to account for Proust's text, in which there is no dominant thread being deviated from and, moreover, in which the various threads are interlaced. This is why the image of the braid is useful: the 'journey through art' thread runs on throughout those one hundred pages, at times coming to the fore, at others appearing obliquely, and at others hiding under the surface. Our cursory summary will also have shown that as well as interweaving themes, the *Recherche* interweaves different levels of plot (one thread being provided by the protagonist's life, and many others being drawn from what he hears or speculates of the lives of others) and more general musings, which often depart from an observed event in order to reach more general pronouncements on human nature. The narrative voice occasionally highlights this interweaving of different levels of narration with playful metaleptic interjections. For instance, in the section of the novel that we have been considering, we read:

> On verra, en effet, dans le dernier volume de cet ouvrage, M. de Charlus en train de faire des choses qui eussent encore plus stupéfié les personnes de sa famille et ses amis [...].
>
> Mais il est temps de rattraper le baron qui s'avance, avec Brichot et moi, vers la porte des Verdurin. (III, 722)

> [We shall indeed see, in the final volume of this book, M. de Charlus doing things which would have shocked even further the members of his family and his friends [...].
>
> But it is now time to catch up with the baron who walks on, alongside Brichot and me, towards the front door of the Verdurins.]

The notion of interweaving can be further enriched if we relate it to the narrator's observations on the mysterious threads that connect various aspects and parts of a human being's existence. The reflection is triggered by the introduction of Mlle de Saint-Loup in *Le Temps retrouvé*: as the daughter of Gilberte Swann (which makes her the granddaughter of the middle-class family friend Charles Swann) and Robert de Saint-Loup (which makes her directly related to the aristocratic Guermantes family), she embodies the coming-together not only of two social worlds, but of many events and relationships which had an important effect on the narrator-protagonist's life. This leads him to use two metaphors to describe her place in his life. The first is that of a road, comparing her to 'les "étoiles" des carrefours où viennent converger des routes venues [...] des points les plus différents' [the 'stars' of crossroads, where roads originating at the most distant points [...] come together] (IV, 606). Having developed the road analogy by listing the innumerable 'transversales' connecting different parts of his life to Mlle de Saint-Loup, the narrator then turns to a weaving metaphor:

> Certes, s'il s'agit uniquement de nos cœurs, le poète a eu raison de parler des 'fils mystérieux' que la vie brise. Mais il est encore plus vrai qu'elle en tisse sans cesse entre les êtres, les évènements, qu'elle entre-croise ces fils, qu'elle

> les redouble pour épaissir la trame, si bien qu'entre le moindre point de notre passé et tous les autres un riche réseau de souvenirs ne laisse que le choix des communications. (IV, 607)
>
> [Of course, if we are only considering our hearts, the poet was right to speak of the 'mysterious threads' that life breaks. But it is even truer that life endlessly weaves threads between people and events, that it crosses these threads over each other, that it doubles them in order to thicken the fabric, so that even between the smallest point in our past and the rest of it, a rich network of memories offers us a wide array of connections.]

Therefore, if it can be said that the digressions of the Proustian 'périodes' mirror the observing and loitering nature of the narrator-protagonist, it can equally be argued that the narrative's interweaving of various threads mirrors the complex temporality of human life as described in *Le Temps retrouvé*.

Interweaving is also present in the *Commedia*, and most noticeably so in the form of the terza rima which Freccero has described as an '*entrelacement*' (1986: 258–71). Dante in the *Commedia* created a new rhyme scheme, in which the rhyme appears three times, first at the heart of the terzina (three-line stanza) which introduces it and then returning in the framing two verses of the following terzina. This results in each rhyme being interwoven both with the previous and with the successive rhyme: ABA BCB CDC DED and so forth, *ad libitum*. As observed by Freccero, 'the rules for closure are not inherent in the form: the terzina as a metric pattern could theoretically go on forever and must be arbitrarily ended' (1986: 261). Terza rima can thus be compared to the movement of digression in two ways: first because it progresses by association, each stanza is connected to the following stanza through its central verse; and secondly, because it could potentially go on forever. Moreover, the fact that the framing verses of Dante's stanzas point back to the central verse of the previous stanza generates, as observed by Freccero, a 'forward movement, whose progress is also a recapitulation' (1986: 261). Barolini builds on Freccero's insights by arguing that terza rima therefore 'mimics the voyage of life by providing both unceasing forward motion and recurrent backward glances' (1992: 24). Barolini and Freccero (1986: 263) suggest that the pattern that best encompasses the contradiction of forward motion which is at the same time recapitulatory is the spiral.[37] The motion of the *Recherche* has also been described as spiral-like by Julia Kristeva (1994: 14), in so far as the novel ends by pointing back to its own beginning, and Clive Scott has described the temporality of terza rima in Proustian terms: 'Terza rima balances on the very cusp of time lost and time regained, time regained within time lost, losing as an inevitable consequence of regaining' (2000: 115–16). It is with this idea of a movement which is circular but not static, in which every return is a revisitation (and not a repetition, as is the case with infernal circles), that I wish to conclude this chapter.

The experience of the return of the past is explored in two poignant passages which put into play 'cet anachronisme qui empêche si souvent le calendrier des faits de coïncider avec celui des sentiments' [the anachronism which so often stops the calendar of facts from coinciding with the calendar of emotions] (III, 153): the encounter with Casella in *Purgatorio* II and the section of *Sodome et Gomorrhe* entitled

'Les Intermittences du cœur' (III, 152–55). In *Purgatorio* II Dante, newly arrived on the shores of Mount Purgatory, is spotted by an old friend, the singer Casella. As he sees this friendly figure rush forwards to hug him, Dante opens his arms, only to enclose them around thin air, for Casella is no longer made of flesh and bone. To console Dante who regrets his friend's lost physical presence, Casella sings one of Dante's earlier poems. All of the other souls gather round to listen 'come a nessun toccasse altro la mente' [as if nothing else were on anyone's mind] (*Purg.* II, 117) until Cato, the guardian of Purgatory, interrupts the performance with angry admonishments, making the souls resume their penitential journey. In Proust's case, the episode pivots on an instance of involuntary memory. The protagonist has just settled into his room at the Grand-Hôtel of Balbec for the first time since his grandmother's death. The physical act of unbuttoning his boots suddenly triggers a reaction which is described in one of Proust's briefest sentences: 'Bouleversement de toute ma personne' [Upheaval of my entire person] (III, 152). The remembered presence of his grandmother, who had been with him when he had last stayed in the room, suddenly manifests itself. Both episodes tell us of a failed embrace with a lost loved person: 'tre volte dietro a lei le mani avvinsi, | e tante mi tornai con esse al petto' [three times I closed my arms behind him | and each time found them against my own chest] (*Purg.* II, 79–81); and :

> Je venais d'apercevoir, dans ma mémoire, penché sur ma fatigue, le visage tendre, préoccupé et déçu de ma grand-mère [...] et ainsi, dans un désir fou de me précipiter dans ses bras, ce n'était qu'à l'instant [...] que je venais d'apprendre qu'elle était morte. (III, 153)
>
> [I had just caught sight, in my memory, leaning over my fatigue, of the sweet, worried, and disappointed face of my grandmother [...] and thus, in a mad desire to throw myself into her arms, it was only in that moment [...] that I had learned that she was dead.]

This failed embrace forces each protagonist to face the contradiction between presence and absence that is the essence of mourning: 'Ohi ombre vane, fuor che ne l'aspetto!' [Oh shades, non-existent but for your appearance!] (*Purg.* II, 79); 'cette contradiction: d'une part, une existence, une tendresse, survivantes en moi [...] et d'autre part, [...] un néant' [this contradiction: on the one hand an existence, a sweetness, surviving inside of me [...] and on the other hand, nothing] (III, 155). Both protagonists are then described as moving on from these encounters: Dante moves up Mount Purgatory, after having been rebuffed by Cato for loitering, and Proust's protagonist moves towards an acceptance of his loss and an assuaging of his guilt, made possible by 'l'instinct de conservation' [the instinct of self-preservation] (III, 157). The fact that the protagonists travel onwards allows these episodes to be read teleologically, in Proust's case as a process of mourning and in Dante's case as an abandonment of earthly love in favour of God.[38]

The fact that Casella sings a poem from Dante's abandoned philosophical treatise the *Convivio* has led critics to argue that Dante through this episode distances himself from his literary past. Freccero, for instance, suggests: 'In such a linear evolution, a glance backward to a previous poetic achievement is more likely to be a sign of transcendence rather than of return' (1986: 186).[39] I too interpret Casella as the embodiment of one of Dante's past identities, but I disagree with the suggestion that Dante introduces the figure of Casella solely in order to distance himself from his past. As has been demonstrated by Gragnolati (2013: 91–110), the Virgilian intertext of the failed embraces of *Purgatorio* II imbues the episode with nostalgia for the corporeal aspect of individuality and human affection, a nostalgia also experienced by the blessed souls of the *Paradiso* (see *Par.* XIV, 61–66). Such a reading allows us to see that the affection felt for Casella is part of the protagonist's subjectivity, which indeed is not left behind. The episode reveals that the forces driving Dante's journey cannot be reduced to the desire to reach God. Moreover, by having Casella sing his former poetry, as well as showing the enduring importance of his earthly relationship with Casella, Dante is also showing his enduring relationship with his literary past. 'Les Intermittences du cœur' too makes clear that the relationship with the grandmother is part of the narrator-protagonist's identity. Her return is nothing other than the return of the person that he was: 'L'être qui venait [...] c'était celui qui [...] dans un moment où je n'avais plus rien de moi [...] m'avait rendu à moi-même, car il était moi et plus que moi' [The being who came to me [...] was the one who [...] at a time when I had lost everything of myself [...] had brought me back to myself, for she was me and also more than me]; 'Le moi que j'étais alors et qui avait disparu si longtemps, était de nouveau si près de moi' [The person I was then and who had disappeared for so long, was once again right beside me] (III, 153, 154).

The encounter with Casella and 'Les Intermittences du cœur' offer us a complex negotiation of the relationship between past and present. The different phases of one's life, the different persons that one has been, are interrelated and collaborate in forming one's identity, which is neither stable nor monolithic: 'À n'importe quel moment que nous la considérions, notre âme totale n'a qu'une valeur presque fictive, malgré le nombreux bilan de ses richesses, car tantôt les unes, tantôt les autres sont indisponibles' [At any one time that we consider it, the sum total of our soul is almost a matter of fiction, despite our high estimate of its assets, since different parts of it will always be alternatively unavailable] (III, 153). Dante and Proust through their narrative use of digressions and returns portray identity as intermittent and suggest that human progression through time is always laced with backward glances. Despite their pauses and detours, both narratives do however spiral towards an ending. Dante's teleology as we have seen is Christian, with redemption and the vision of the Godhead as its end, whereas Proust's teleology is projected towards the book to be written. But both works also make a final push against linearity by giving us an ending which is also a return to a beginning. Indeed, to reach God according to Dante is to reach the beginning of all things, including our selves (*Conv.* IV, xii, 14). In the chronology of autobiography, narrative moves towards its source: the point at which it is being written, a paradoxical logic which forms the basis for Contini's comparison of the *Commedia* and the *Recherche*.[40] The final pages of the *Recherche* point back to the work that we have just read when they inform us that the narrator-protagonist's future book will be drawn from the life experiences that we have just read about. Proust's ending in this respect seems the extreme manifestation of what Brooks perceives as a general tendency of literary fiction: 'It is the role of fictional plots to impose an end which yet suggests a return, a new beginning: a rereading' (1984: 109).

The present that is informed by the past and the beginning that treads on already covered ground find their lexical expression in the prefix *re-* in French and *ri-* in Italian.[41] These prefixes abound in the opening lines of both works, and are most famously recognizable in the first verb of the *Commedia*, 'Nel mezzo del cammin di nostra vita | mi ritrovai per una selva oscura' (*Inf.* I, 1–2), and in the title of the final volume of Proust's novel: *Le Temps retrouvé* [Time Regained].[42] Dante's and Proust's journeys are more than straight lines downwards into the past and upwards to a transcendent state: they are also full of deviations and returns, tracing squiggles and spirals, and in Proust's case interweaving all of the different threads that make up the human experience of time, memory, and identity. We should not forget, moreover, that the circularity of the spiral allows for an important form of epistemological progression, in that returns and revisitations allow for an accretion of meaning. So it is that Proust's hundred pages of 'digression' in the middle of his discussion of the voyage made possible by art (III, 665–761) allow this thread to have new implications when it re-emerges, and that Dante can make a transformative journey, which is also a return to his point of departure: 'Casella mio, per tornar altra volta | là dov'io son, fo io questo vïaggio' [My dear Casella, I make this journey to return again | to the place where I am] (*Purg.* II, 91–92).

Notes to Chapter 2

1. Literal travelling also takes place in the novel, but this does not dramatize literary development.
2. On the allegorical see the section 'Allegory and Biographilia' in Chapter 1.
3. For a rich overview of the figure of Ulysses in Western literature, from Homer to Modernism, see Boitani 1994.
4. See for instance: Thompson 1967; Mario Fubini's entry for 'Ulisse' in the *Enciclopedia dantesca* (Bosco 1970–78: v, 803–09); Scott 1977; and Hawkins 1980.
5. As has been argued in Hawkins 1980: 10–11, '[t]he Ulysses episode has been convincingly presented as a palinode on the philosophical enterprise, an exposure of the fatal presumption of genius which owns no heavenly guide. [...] Yet from the context of *Inferno* XXVI, it would seem that the "ingegno" in question is more the power of language than of philosophy'.
6. These are all key metaphors for Dante's treatment of desire in the *Commedia*. See Pertile 2005.
7. On the Orpheic katabasis in Dante and Proust see Rushworth 2016.
8. On Proust and Homer see also Fraisse 2011: 55–92.
9. On Proust and Freud see Baudry 1984, Tadié 2012, Rushworth 2016, and Elsner 2017.
10. Freud also identified with the figure of the conquistador, thereby expressing the same desire for knowledge embodied by Dante's Ulysses: 'In Freud's narrative, travel and theory, conquest and cognition, reconnaissance and recognition, are counter-pointed to form a complete portrait of scientific desire' (Bowie 1987: 31).
11. Fraisse & Létoublon (1997: 1075), without referring to Jung, also interpret the Homeric nekyia in psychological terms.
12. Carter also draws the comparison between the quest for self-knowledge in modern literature and the descent into the underworld in classical and medieval literature (1992: 94).
13. Fowlie had worked on Proust before he approached Dante and saw his reading of the *Inferno* as complementing and offsetting his reading of Proust.

14. The theory is exposed in the context of the protagonist's two arrivals at the Grand Hôtel de Balbec (II, 31–32, and III, 152–55) and will be further explored in this chapter's section 'Deviations and Returns' below.
15. See Lombardi 2012 for both a re-appraisal of the critical tradition and new insights into what is one of Dante's most studied cantos.
16. On Dante's relationship with Cavalcanti see the section 'The Forerunner' in Chapter 3.
17. This is rather the subject of *Purgatorio* II, which rewrites the failed embraces of *Odyssey* XI and *Aeneid* VI.
18. On Dante's *rime petrose* see Durling & Martinez 1990.
19. On the enterprise of writing *Paradiso* XXXIII, see Boitani 1989, Barolini 1992: 218–56, and Pertile 2005: 265–81.
20. Pertile in his article on *Purgatorio* XXIV (1994: 62–66) provides an even wider context, giving several examples of poetic exchanges which make use of the words *penne*, *ali*, and *volo*, adding that in the *Commedia*, the poets as birds metaphor is used as early as in *Inferno* IV's presentation of Homer as an eagle (95–96).
21. The poems can be found in Contini 1960: II, 481–83. These sonnets are read in dialogue with each other on the basis of their ordering in the 'Vaticano 3793' manuscript.
22. Geryon, as a metapoetic figure for 'beauty that hides ugliness', has also been related to the figure of the 'femmina balba' [stuttering woman] in *Purgatorio* XIX. See Lombardi, 2012: 242–43.
23. The aeroplane was to gain the most personal relevance to Proust through the death of his lover, Alfred Agostinelli. Heedless of warnings, the enthusiastic and reckless young aviator died an Icarian death, drowning after crashing his aeroplane in the Bay of Angels (Carter 1992: 159).
24. On Proust's use of alchemical imagery see Topping 2006.
25. Certain manuscripts carry the name Garros rather than Fonck. On this see Proust 1987–89: IV, 1125, n. 1.
26. Albertine in this respect plays the opposite role of Beatrice, who leads Dante upwards (see Chapter 3).
27. For my position on 'L'Adoration perpétuelle' see the opening section of Chapter 4, 'The Redemption Narrative'.
28. This will be further explored in the section 'Transcending the Individual' in Chapter 4.
29. The 'unsettling' contradiction of the curious pilgrim was an important theological question, from the writings of Augustine to the late Middle Ages. As is explained by Christian Zacher, 'theologians looked on *curiositas* as a phase of original sin, which made all men wanderers in the fallen world; curiosity about this inferior world would prevent a man from reaching that other land of the Father. As a form of religious worship, pilgrimage allowed men to journey through this present world visiting sacral landscapes as long as they kept their gaze permanently fixed on the invisible world beyond' (1976: 4).
30. One should note that in the *Paradiso* circular motion is instead the sign of a positive form of repetition: desire endlessly satisfied and rekindled.
31. Ross Chambers in his engaging account of digressive literature explores the negative implications of 'making a beeline', that is taking the most direct route, as it is symptomatic of an unwillingness to engage with otherness, exemplified by the colonial outlook of Phileas Fogg in *Around the World in Eighty Days* (1999: 26–35).
32. On circular motion in Dante's journey see Freccero 1986: 70–92.
33. Jennifer Rushworth in her Freudian reading of the *Recherche* has argued that 'by endlessly deferring the end (goal) of the novel, the protagonist's unending desire to write is allowed to survive' (2013: 162).
34. Pierre Bayard has drawn the connection between digressiveness and the Proustian concept of intermittence, to which I shall return. Bayard's work makes the important contribution of suggesting that digression is in the eye of the beholder (1996: 171–72). I do however hold reservations about certain aspects of his study, namely, his tendency to conflate author and narrator (see for instance pp. 43, 178, 181). This puts him in a position where he needs to reject the Proustian notion of the 'moi profond' because it does not serve his reading of the *Recherche* as 'cette perpétuelle échappée de soi-même dont le texte est à la fois l'histoire et la forme' (1996:

181). I accept instead the multistability of Proust's text, which theorizes both a fragmented and a unified understanding of the self (see for instance III, 761–62).

35. *Loiterature*'s 'transvaluation of the trivial' corresponds to what Freed-Thall calls, drawing on Bourdieu and Rancière, the 'spoiled distinctions' of French modernism (2015).
36. On the equalizing potential of Dante and Proust's analogies see Hartley 2017.
37. Barolini goes so far as to suggest that 'Dante's spires of poetic life — terza rima — bear a resemblance to modern science's spires of biological life, DNA' (1992: ix).
38. 'No episode in *Inferno* or *Paradiso* captures the essence of the earthly pilgrimage like the Casella episode at the beginning of *Purgatorio*, whose structure faithfully replicates life's — and terza rima's — continual dialectic between forward motion and backward glance, voyage and repose, illicit curiosity and necessary desire' (Barolini 1992: 101). On the parallels between the process of detachment in *Purgatorio* and the work of mourning in Freud's 'Mourning and Melancholia', see Rushworth 2016.
39. See also Contini 1976: 62 and Hollander 1975.
40. Contini speaks of 'la sutura dei due "io"' [the converging of the two 'I's] (1976: 34). Freccero relates this 'paradoxical' movement of autobiography to terza rima (1986: 263–64).
41. Barolini has observed that 'the prefix *ri-* in the poem's first verb, "ritrovai," echoes the form of the spiral, in which no conversion is final' (1992: 25–26).
42. In *Inferno* I we find 'mi ritrovai' (2), 'ridir' (10), 'si volse a retro a rimirar' (26), 'i' fui per ritornar più volte vòlto' (36), 'ripigneva' (60), 'rispuosemi' (67), 'perché ritorni a tanta noia?' (76), 'rispuos'io lui' (81), 'rispuose, poi' (92); and in the opening pages of 'Combray' we find 'réveil', 'recouvrais', 'reposante', 'retour', 'réveillé', 'réjouit', 'rendormais', 'retournais', 'rejoint', 'révolu', 'retrouvé', 'retrouvais', 'retourner', 'rejoindre', 'retrouver', 'reculer' (I, 3–5).

CHAPTER 3

❖

Guide Figures

The Forerunner

The most famous character of the *Commedia* after Dante is his guide Virgil, without whom the journey through Hell and Purgatory could not take place, and without whom, Dante informs him, he would not have found his poetic voice (*Inf.* 1, 85–87). The relationship between Virgil and Dante is one of the most enduring in Western literature. As well as being the poet whom Dante admires the most, Virgil is his literal guide through the afterworld, his spiritual guide (though he defers to Beatrice's greater understanding of theological matters), and a father figure. The deeply affectionate nature of their bond has perhaps best been captured by Botticelli in his detailed illustrations (1480–95, Staatliche Museen zu Berlin), where we find the pair conversing with vivid expressions and gestures, Virgil often imperious and Dante coyly attentive and, in the more frightening encounters, the Latin poet protectively putting his arm around his charge. When comparing Dante's and Proust's treatment of literary vocation, one is therefore brought to ask whether there is in Proust's novel a character who plays such a significant role as Virgil does in the *Commedia*. Considering the role of mentors in the *Recherche* and the *Commedia* will also lead us to the question of gender: how do the male narrator-protagonists' relationships with their female mentors differ from those with their male mentors? And is having literary authority ultimately a male privilege?

Samuel Borton assigns a Virgilian role to the narrator-protagonist's friend Robert de Saint-Loup, who through his social status grants the narrator-protagonist access to the most exclusive social circles (1958: 39). While Borton's article draws pertinent analogies, in this instance the parallel between social circles and infernal circles is rather superficial.[1] Dante's otherworld is not an exclusive club to which certain people are granted access through the fluctuating whims of the rich and the fashionable, nor do its hierarchies re-arrange with every sociopolitical shift: the souls encountered in the *Commedia* have reached their ultimate fate, which conveys the essence of their character (Auerbach 1961: 86–88). Moreover, though it can be said that the adolescent protagonist looks up to him, Saint-Loup is a friend and peer, and not a paternal figure. In this chapter I argue that the *Recherche*'s Virgil can only be the character of Charles Swann, who also shares important parallels with the characters of Guido Cavalcanti (a real poet and friend of Dante) and Ulysses.[2] The differences between the roles played by Swann and Virgil also illuminate Proust's and Dante's respective treatments of literary vocation.

If Virgil enters the stage to save a desperate protagonist, he is not infallible. As has been studied by Barolini in her work *Dante's Poets*, as the *Commedia* unfolds, there is an inverse relationship between Virgil's authority and our attachment to him (1984: 201–56). The further we read, the more frequently we encounter affective expressions, the most important kind being the references to Dante as 'figlio', as in, 'portandosene me sovra 'l suo petto, | come suo figlio, non come compagno' [carrying me in his arms | as though I were his son, not his companion] (*Inf.* XXIII, 50–51), and to Virgil as a mother or father, the most charged example of the latter being the moment at which Virgil disappears from the narrative: 'Ma Virgilio n'avea lasciati scemi | di sé, Virgilio dolcissimo patre' [But Virgil had left us deprived | of him, Virgil the sweetest of fathers] (*Purg.* XXX, 49–50). Virgil's authority, however, is steadily undermined, until finally the pilgrim overtakes his guide and proceeds to travel on without him. As the poem progresses, moreover, intertextual references to the *Aeneid* decrease and are overtaken by biblical intertexts. What happens on a narrative and on a textual level functions as a metaphor for the poet-characters' literary output: Dante's poetry (according to the poem) is ultimately superior to Virgil's because it is vernacular and Christian. Dante further emphasizes the religious dimension of Virgil's inadequacy by showing him being overtaken by a minor Latin poet, Statius, who we are told was secretly Christian, and is therefore saved. Statius famously compares his illustrious predecessor to one who carries a light behind him, showing the way to others, but not profiting from it himself:

> Facesti come quei che va di notte,
> che porta il lume dietro e sé non giova,
> ma dopo sé fa le persone dotte. (*Purg.* XXII, 67–69)

> [You were as one who goes by night, | carrying a light behind him without benefiting from it, | but enlightening those who come after.]

This is not the first time that Dante constructs a narrative of artistic surpassing. Such a displacement also takes place in the *Vita nuova*, Dante's first narrative work. The little book, or *libello*, alternates between narrative prose passages describing the story of Dante's love for Beatrice, her death, and the discovery of his poetic vocation; poems he claims to have written during this period; and prose commentaries on these poems. In the *Vita nuova*, Dante, who here too is poet, protagonist, and narrator, overtakes his first friend, the older and more experienced poet Guido Cavalcanti. This overtaking is however more subtle than in the case of Virgil. The most important episode of the process takes place in Chapter XXIV of the *Vita nuova*, in which Beatrice is described as walking behind Cavalcanti's beloved, who is called Giovanna and nicknamed 'Primavera'. Dante tells us that this is because Primavera stands for 'prima verrà' [she will come first] and Giovanna is named after John the Baptist 'lo quale precedette la verace luce' ('who preceded the True Light') (*VN*, XXIV, 4). This therefore creates an association between Cavalcanti, his beloved, and John the Baptist, all figures of the 'forerunner', and an association between Dante, Beatrice, and Christ.[3]

By the time we reach the *Commedia*, Cavalcanti is absent as a character. In narrative terms, this is a necessity in so far as Cavalcanti was still alive at the time when the fictional journey is set, but it is still a noticeable absence in so far as Dante in the *Commedia* names vernacular poets who had far less influence on his writing than Cavalcanti did. Moreover, when in *Inferno* x Dante encounters Guido Cavalcanti's father, Cavalcante, it is unclear whether it is suggested that Guido will ultimately be damned or saved. Seeing Dante travelling through Hell while still alive, Cavalcante asks:

> Se per questo cieco
> carcere vai per altezza d'ingegno,
> mio figlio ov'è? e perché non è teco? (*Inf.* x, 58–60)

> [If it's due to the worthiness of your genius | that you walk through this blind prison, | where is my son? why is he not with you?]

Dante answers that he is not undertaking the journey independently, but is being led by one whom 'forse cui Guido vostro ebbe a didesgno' [perhaps your Guido held no regard for] (*Inf.* x, 63), a line which is generally understood as referring to Beatrice. Cavalcante is thus shown to be mistaken in thinking that the journey through the otherworld is a matter of individual talent ('ingegno'). This allows Dante to highlight the preordained nature of his journey, but also, if we understand the ambiguous line as referring to Beatrice, the key role played by his love for a woman in making his journey to salvation possible. This path to salvation would not have been available to Guido Cavalcanti, who was renowned for understanding love as an irrational and destructive force, a view most forcefully captured in his poem 'Donna me prega'.[4] As well as disagreeing about matters of love, the two poets also had theological divergences: Cavalcanti was known for his interest in the work of Averroes, which by the standards of the time was tantamount to courting heresy, given that the Islamic philosopher was condemned by the Catholic church (Barański 2004). Averroes is explicitly rejected by Dante in *Purgatorio* xxv through the mouthpiece of Statius, who in his exposition of the generation of the soul throws in the following aside:

> quest'è tal punto,
> che più savio di te fé già errante,
> sì che per sua dottrina fé disgiunto
> da l'anima il possibile intelletto,
> perché da lui non vide organo assunto. (*Purg.* xxv, 62–66)

> [This is a point, | that has already eluded a wiser man than you, | so much so that his doctrine separated | the soul from the possible intellect, | because he could not find an organ for it to reside in.]

Dante's surpassing of Cavalcanti is thus of a double nature: he is both a better poet and a better Christian than his former 'primo amico' [first friend]. Moreover, Dante's love for Beatrice is instrumental in both aspects of this surpassing, given that for Dante love inspires not only poetry, but also virtue.

Charles Swann, an alter ego from the parents' generation who is greatly admired by the young protagonist and prefigures his experiences in love and society, but is ultimately a forerunner who never 'saw the light', shows many parallels with both the characters of Guido Cavalcanti and Virgil. He has indeed been described as a John the Baptist figure: 'Le récit comporte, outre "Marcel" le narrateur, un autre protagoniste qui le préfigure et l'annonce comme Jean-Baptiste "prophétise" Jésus [...] Swann est la doublure et la contre-épreuve de Marcel, celui qui manque le salut' [Beyond 'Marcel' the narrator, the narrative provides us with another protagonist who prefigures and announces him, like John the Baptist 'prophetized' Jesus [...] Swann is the double and the foil of Marcel, the one who does not reach salvation] (Claude Edmonde Magny, quoted in Muller 1979: 10). Moreover, he too is surrounded by an eternal question:

> Était-ce cela, ce bonheur proposé par la petite phrase de la sonate à Swann qui s'était trompé en l'assimilant au plaisir de l'amour et n'avait pas su le trouver dans la création artistique; [...] l'appel rouge et mystérieux de ce septuor que Swann n'avait pu connaître, étant mort comme tant d'autres avant que la vérité faite pour eux eût été révélée? (IV, 456)

> [Was this it, the happiness offered to Swann by the sonata's little phrase, which he had mistakenly assimilated to the pleasure of love and failed to find in artistic creation; [...] the red and mysterious calling of this septet which Swann was never able to hear, having died like many others before the truth that was made for them had been revealed?]

But while the fate of Cavalcanti remains one of the open mysteries of Dante studies, the speculation of the *Recherche* is immediately undercut: 'D'ailleurs, elle n'eût pu lui servir, car cette phrase pouvait bien symboliser un appel, mais non créer des forces et faire de Swann l'écrivain qu'il n'était pas' [And indeed, it could not have served him, for while this phrase could symbolize a calling, it could not create new strength and make Swann the writer he was not] (IV, 456). Swann, like Virgil in the *Commedia*, cannot be saved. Thus, it appears that Barolini's key observations on the character of Virgil can just as well be applied to Charles Swann:

> Vergil resides within this limbo of perpetual tension, of simultaneously positive and negative significance [...]. It is therefore not so much theologically vain as poetically unrealistic to speculate about Vergil's possible salvation, since it is an essential condition of his existence in the poem that he shall also cease to exist. (1984: 200)

The text of the *Recherche* itself establishes a connection between Charles Swann and Virgil. Dante, Virgil, and their works of literature are referred to several times in the novel and the first reference made to either of them coincides with Swann's first appearance in the narrative. His double identity and the fact that he moves seamlessly from the narrator-protagonist's family's bourgeois milieu to the most exclusive aristocratic salons is compared to Aristaeus magically entering 'un empire soustrait aux yeux des mortels et où Virgile nous le montre reçu à bras ouverts' [an empire unreachable to mortals, where Virgil shows him being welcomed with open arms] (I, 17–18). Moreover, Swann's entrance has much in common with Virgil's arrival in the *Inferno*. Swann arrives at night through the garden and is only recognizable by his voice: 'mon grand-père disait: "Je reconnais la voix de Swann." On ne le reconnaissait en effet qu'à la voix [...] parce que nous gardions le moins de lumière possible au jardin' [my grandfather would say: 'I recognize Swann's voice.'

Indeed, he could only be recognized by his voice [...] since we kept as little light as possible on in the garden] (I, 14). These traits are emphasized by being reformulated shortly after the reference to Virgil, with the added detail that he is leading the way: 'l'obscur et incertain personnage qui se détachait, suivi de ma grand-mère, sur un fond de ténèbres, et qu'on reconnaissait à la voix' [the obscure and uncertain character, who would appear, followed by my grandmother, against a backdrop of darkness, and whom we recognized by his voice] (I, 18). Virgil's first appearance in the *Commedia* is described as follows: 'dinanzi a li occhi mi si fu offerto | chi per lungo silenzio parea fioco' [before my eyes appeared | he who appeared faint from the long silence] (*Inf.* I, 62–63). The pilgrim cries for help, calling him 'qual che tu sii, od ombra od omo certo!' [be you a shade or a real living man] (line 66). Virgil introduces himself to Dante and offers to guide him, the last words of the canto being: 'Allor si mosse, e io li tenni dietro' [Then he moved forward, and I followed him] (line 136). Proust's 'obscur et incertain personnage' seems to echo Dante's uncertainty in line 66, just as 'suivi de' [followed by] echoes the motion in line 136. The act of speaking in both cases is what identifies the figure in the dark: Swann is recognized by his voice and Virgil identifies himself by speaking to Dante. Finally, both characters are introduced through a description of their descendance, with several lines devoted to Swann's father (I, 14–15) and Virgil introducing himself by saying: 'li parenti miei furon lombardi' [my parents were from Lombardy] (line 68).

While we cannot know for certain whether the intertextual connections between Swann's introduction and Virgil's introduction were intentional, it is undeniable that Swann and Virgil present strong parallels from a narrative perspective. Indeed, both are the most developed characters in the narrative after the protagonist; both disappear from the narrative before the protagonist's final revelations (Virgil cannot follow Dante up to Paradise, Swann dies long before the epiphanies of *Le Temps retrouvé*); both lead the protagonist to the promised land but cannot enter it themselves; both are the products of a religion that pre-dates Christianity; both fail to transcend their limited world-view even if art gives them the opportunity to do so (Swann refuses to appreciate Vinteuil's music limiting instead its significance to his relationship with Odette, Virgil cannot see the prophetic value of his own literature); both had great potential as insightful and creative individuals and failed due to one tragic flaw (paganism in Virgil's case, and a fear of movement on the vertical axis of descent and flight in Swann's case).

While they share a similar role, Virgil and Swann are very different in terms of the guidance that they offer. The first difference between the two is that Proust's protagonist's quest is ultimately a solitary one. While Virgil does not leave Dante's side until the arrival of Beatrice and is there to answer his charge's questions, Swann comes and goes, and although in 'Combray' he performs an educational role by bringing the protagonist photographs of artworks from Italy (I, 18) and acting as a mediator for Bergotte (I, 96), he is unaware of the strong influence that he exerts on the child. At one point in the narrative, as Gilberte's protective father, Swann will even become estranged from the protagonist (I, 481–82). Swann and the narrator-protagonist are extremely close, yet extremely distant. In this sense, their relationship can be seen as contributing to the *Recherche*'s demonstration of the impossibility of true communication between individuals. Thus, ironically, Swann, who is the cause of the 'drame du coucher' (the opening episode of 'Combray', in which the child protagonist is refused his customary bedtime kiss), is the only person who would have understood the young protagonist: 'L'angoisse que je venais d'éprouver, je pensais que Swann s'en serait bien moqué [...] or, au contraire, comme je l'ai appris plus tard, une angoisse semblable fut le tourment de longues années de sa vie et personne' [I thought that Swann would have laughed at the anguish that I had just experienced [...] yet, on the contrary, as I would learn later on, a similar anguish had been the torment of his life and his person for many years] (I, 30). Neither of them knows this and instead it is the protagonist who will have to attempt to guide himself, to be his own Virgil: 'je tâchais de [...] m'attacher à des idées d'avenir qui auraient dû *me conduire au-delà de l'abîme prochain qui m'effrayait*' [I did my best [...] to focus my mind on the future, so that I might *lead myself beyond the imminent abyss that so terrified me*] (I, 24; my emphasis). As a result of the solitary nature of his search, the narrator will explicitly declare himself guide-less in *Sodome et Gomorrhe*:

> Le poète est à plaindre, et qui n'est guidé par aucun Virgile, d'avoir à traverser les cercles d'un enfer de soufre et de poix, de se jeter dans le feu qui tombe du ciel pour en ramener quelques habitants de Sodome. (III, 711)
>
> [One must lament the task of the poet who, with no Virgil to guide him, must cross the circles of a hell of sulphur and pitch, to throw himself into the fire falling from the sky and bring back a few inhabitants of Sodom.]

The second important difference between the two couples is that the line of demarcation between Swann and the protagonist is not as clear-cut as that between Dante and Virgil. Swann is an alter ego as well as a guide. Kristeva in her psychoanalytical reading argues that '"narrateur" et "Swann" sont souvent difficilement "opérables", je veux dire séparables' [the 'narrator' and 'Swann' are often hard to 'operate on', by which I mean, to separate] (1994: 39). Their interchangeability is suggested by early drafts such as the Cahier 25, and the genesis of the character has been described as 'un processus de démarcation comme d'identification' [as much a process of demarcation as identification] (Hassine 1994: 14).

The final and most crucial difference is that Swann's influence in the *Recherche* is not a literary or stylistic one. In contrast, Virgil, not as the character in the *Commedia* but as an extra-textual entity, actually inspired and influenced Dante as an author. The *Commedia,* as has been well documented by scholars, is a text that owes much to Virgil's writings.[5] Therefore while Dante's dialogue with Virgil is fictional, he is in fact close to extra-textual reality when he declares:

> Tu se' lo mio maestro e 'l mio autore,
> tu se' solo colui da cu' io tolsi
> lo bello stilo che m'ha fatto onore. (*Inf.* I, 85–87)

[You are my master and my author, | it is from you alone that I took | the elegant style that has earned me honour.]

The only character who comes close to the title 'my author' in the *Recherche* is Bergotte, who is introduced in 'Combray' as the protagonist's favourite writer. We are proleptically informed that the protagonist will later measure the quality of his own writing by comparing it to that of Bergotte (I, 95), just as Virgil's style is claimed as Dante's main point of reference in *Inferno* I.[6]

Returning to Virgil and Swann, the key difference in their respective status can be considered as follows: while Virgil is Dante's author, in the *Recherche* it is the protagonist who is Swann's author. This is made clear in the metaleptic passage that we considered in Chapter 1: 'Et pourtant, cher Charles Swann, [...] c'est déjà parce que celui que vous deviez considérer comme un petit imbécile a fait de vous le héros d'un de ses romans [...] que peut-être vous vivrez' [And yet, dear Charles Swann, [...] it's actually because the person whom you thought of as a little idiot made you the hero of one of his novels [...] that perhaps you will live on] (III, 705). Swann does play a crucial role in determining the protagonist's life experiences. His influence (though not literary or stylistic) is therefore undeniable as it provides the coarse material that the protagonist will turn into art: 'la matière de mon expérience, laquelle serait la matière de mon livre, me venait de Swann' [the material that built my experiences, which would become the material of my book, came from Swann] (IV, 493–94). Swann could not lead the protagonist to a final illumination, but he was instrumental in this process. In this respect, his role in the *Recherche* is extremely close to Virgil's in the *Commedia*. Virgil could not enlighten Dante when it came to theological intricacies because he lacked faith, but his guidance remained a necessary step both in terms of Dante's journey to salvation and of his development as a poet.

The differences between Virgil's and Swann's roles in their respective narratives stand for the different nature of the artistic surpassing enacted by Dante's narrator-protagonist and that enacted by Proust's narrator-protagonist. The former redeems himself because he is illuminated by Christianity and expresses himself in the vernacular, while the latter redeems himself because he is illuminated by a power for introspection and observation which enables him to become an artist. Therefore, a comparative analysis of Virgil and Swann suggests that whereas in the *Commedia* Dante must measure his poetic success according to the criteria of Christian faith and mastery of the vernacular, in the *Recherche* the only failure is that of not producing art. Indeed, Swann is not an artist, whereas one cannot stress enough that Dante's guide is a celebrated poet. Dante could have chosen a philosopher or a theologian as the character guiding the pilgrim. By choosing to have a literary guide, he was clearly establishing that this narrative is one of poetic development, in Franco Ferrucci's words: 'Sarai Enea e sarai Paolo, a patto che tu scriva' [You will be Eneas and you will be Paul, as long as you write] (1990: 274). What is the purpose then of having someone who is not an artist as an alter ego in the *Recherche*?

Swann's Failed Conversion

While Virgil's predicament is caused by the fact that he was born 'nel tempo de li dèi falsi e bugiardi' [in the times of false and lying gods] (*Inf.* I, 72), in Swann's case we are offered the detailed narrative of a failed 'conversion' which could have been the narrator-protagonist's: 'Un amour de Swann'. An initial opportunity to take on a meaningful existence was offered Swann when he first heard Vinteuil's sonata. The second opportunity is double: when he hears in Odette's presence an extract of the sonata which features his favourite musical phrase of the piece, he is offered another opportunity to pursue the higher truths of music or, by focusing on his feelings for Odette rather than music, he could ultimately extract truths from the painful experience of love. But he does neither of these things. The passage describing the first of these missed opportunities provides us with a key to Swann's character and I therefore quote it at length:

> Cet amour pour une phrase musicale sembla un instant devoir *amorcer* chez Swann la possibilité d'*une sorte de rajeunissement.* Depuis si longtemps il avait renoncé à *appliquer sa vie à un but idéal* et la bornait à la poursuite de satisfactions quotidiennes, qu'il croyait, sans jamais se le dire formellement, que cela ne *changerait* plus jusqu'à sa mort; bien plus, ne se sentant plus d'idées élevées dans l'esprit, *il avait cessé de croire* à leur réalité, sans pouvoir non plus la nier tout à fait. Aussi avait-il pris l'habitude de se réfugier dans des pensées sans importance qui lui permettaient de laisser de côté le fond des choses. De même qu'il ne se demandait pas s'il n'eût pas mieux fait de ne pas aller dans le monde, [...] de même dans sa conversation il s'efforçait de ne jamais exprimer avec cœur une opinion intime sur les choses, mais de fournir des détails matériels qui valaient en quelque sorte par eux-mêmes et lui permettaient de ne pas donner sa mesure. [...] Parfois malgré tout il se laissait aller à émettre un jugement sur une œuvre, sur une manière de comprendre la vie, mais il donnait alors à ses paroles un ton ironique comme s'il n'adhérait pas tout entier à ce qu'il disait. Or, comme certains valétudinaires [...] qui [...] commencent à envisager la possibilité inespérée de *commencer sur le tard une vie toute différente*, Swann trouvait en lui [...] la présence d'une de ces *réalités invisibles auxquelles il avait cessé de croire* et auxquelles, comme si la musique avait eu sur *la sécheresse morale dont il souffrait* une sorte d'influence élective, il se sentait de nouveau *le désir et presque la force de consacrer sa vie.* Mais n'étant pas arrivé à savoir de qui était l'œuvre qu'il avait entendue, il n'avait pu se la procurer et avait fini par l'oublier. (I, 207–08; my emphasis)

> [This love for a musical phrase seemed for a moment to *trigger* for Swann the possibility of *a kind of rejuvenation.* He had for such a long time now given up on *devoting his life to an ideal goal* and limited himself to the pursuit of everyday satisfactions, that he believed [...] that this would not *change* until his death. More than that, because he did not feel that his mind had any elevated thoughts, *he had ceased to believe* in their reality, without being able to completely deny it. Thus he had formed the habit of taking refuge in unimportant thoughts that allowed him to leave aside the deeper meaning of things. Just as he would not ask himself whether it would have been better for him not to spend his time in high society, [...] in conversation he forced himself to never full-heartedly express a personal opinion, but to offer instead material details, which were somehow worthwhile in themselves and allowed him not to give his take on

things. Despite this, he would sometimes allow himself to express a judgment on a work of art or a way of seeing life. But he would then give his words a sarcastic tone, as if to suggest that he did not completely endorse what he was saying. Yet, like some valetudinarians [...] who [...] begin to envisage the — as of yet unhoped for — possibility of *beginning a completely new life in their later years*, Swann found that there resided in him [...] one of those *invisible realities in which he had ceased to believe* and to which, as though music had had a kind of elective influence on *his moral dryness*, he could feel again a *desire and even the strength to devote his life*. But not having been able to find out who the piece he had heard was by, he was not able to get hold of it and had ended up forgetting it.]

As highlighted by my emphasis, the lexical field of conversion permeates this passage. But there will be no new life for Swann. The long-standing renouncement to devote himself to higher things referred to in this passage is the renouncement of an artistic vocation, and consequently, of contact with his inner self.[7] As a result Swann lacks depth, as made clear by the use of images on a vertical axis: 'idées élevées' and 'le fond des choses', which as we saw in Chapter 2, are part of the metaphorical expression of the journey towards artistic creation. While Dante resolved the love lyric's tension between divine and earthly love by making love for Beatrice lead upwards to God and investing his poetry with a religious dimension, Swann remains on the ground caught in a tug of war between Odette and Vinteuil's music, foreshadowing the narrator-protagonist's predicament with Albertine. By complying when Odette asks him never to have the full sonata played and thus ensuring that the music holds no other purpose than to signify their affair, he is confining the music, and consequently himself, to the horizontal plane of metonymy (I, 215).

The fact that Swann leans towards the woman rather than the music is not necessarily an artistic death sentence: within the philosophy of the *Recherche* love, and particularly the suffering it provokes, can be an effective means to reach personal enlightenment, as well as an excellent source for artistic material (II, 189–90; IV, 484–86). Swann's feelings for Odette are just as much of an antidote to his 'sécheresse morale' as Vinteuil's music is. Indeed, his love affair is described as 'cette période nouvelle de la vie de Swann où à la sécheresse, à la dépression des années antérieures avait succédé une sorte de trop-plein spirituel' [this new epoch in Swann's life, where the dryness and the depression of the previous years had been replaced by a kind of spiritual overflow] (I, 299). The problem is that Swann does not exploit this mine of new feelings by extracting the truths it could offer him. On the contrary, he turns away from the task. This is the case for example when he almost realizes that the fact that he regularly sends Odette considerable amounts of money makes her a kept woman:

> Il ne put approfondir cette idée, car un accès de paresse [...] vint à ce moment éteindre toute lumière dans son intelligence, aussi brusquement que, plus tard, quand on eut installé partout l'éclairage électrique, on put couper l'électricité dans une maison. (I, 264)
>
> [He was not able to further develop this thought, for an attack of laziness [...] in that very instant turned off the light of his intelligence, as suddenly as, later,

when electrical lighting had been installed everywhere, one could cut off a house's electricity.]

We saw in Chapter 2 the importance of the developed metaphor of aeronautics, which connects and differentiates Ulysses's horizontal nautical journey towards knowledge and Dante's aeronautical journey upwards towards God. The *Recherche*'s negative alter ego does not err by undertaking a transgressive journey. On the contrary, the spiritual confinement which results from Swann's love is expressed on a literal level by the fact that since falling in love with Odette he cannot leave Paris. He is tied to the same spot, just like the monomaniacal souls in Dante's *Inferno* whose physical condition of confinement is a manifestation of their spiritual condition. Unable to travel to Holland or even Combray, Swann becomes even more of an anti-Ulysses when it is his lover's travels that limit his movements: he is not allowed to travel anywhere Odette goes (I, 289), all he can do therefore is wait for her return. This Ulysses-Penelope subversion is most clear when Odette finally takes to sea on an endless Mediterranean cruise with the 'petit clan', leaving Swann in Paris. If artistic creation is a metaphorical voyage beyond limits, it is no surprise that Swann, who never fights against his limits, fails to create.

If Swann's narrative is that of a failed conversion, he is the one to be blamed since he did not have the courage, ambition, or will power necessary to reach self-knowledge — qualities that are expressed in their negative form by Dante's Ulysses: recklessness and hubris. While Ulysses stands for what would happen if Dante went 'too far', Swann stands for what would happen if Proust's narrator-protagonist never went anywhere at all. Adam Watt (2005) has explored the intertextual relationship between Stéphane Mallarmé's sonnet 'Le Vierge, le vivace, et le bel aujourd'hui' and the *Recherche*, linking Mallarmé's image of the trapped swan unable to take flight to Albertine, the protagonist's imprisoned mistress, who is often compared to a swan and who admires Mallarmé's sonnet. I would further add that through his choice of surname, Proust also wanted to connect the figure of Charles Swann to Mallarmé's swan with trapped wings. Indeed, Swann, along with the Baron de Charlus, is considered one of what *Le Temps retrouvé* names the 'célibataires de l'art', individuals 'qui n'extraient rien de leur impression' [who do not extract anything from their impressions] and lead a dissatisfied existence because they fail to realize their artistic potential (IV, 470). As we saw in Chapter 2, the 'célibataires de l'art' are described in terms of an inability to fly. They are compared to the first attempts at flying machines and to 'l'oison qui n'a pas résolu le problème des ailes et cependant est travaillé du désir de planer' [the gosling who has not yet resolved the issue of its wings and yet burns with the desire to fly] (IV, 471). Swann does not quite fit the account of the 'célibataires de l'art' in so far as he lacks their desire to fly and their (over-)excitement about art. Indeed, whereas these characters are described in almost grotesque terms, bellowing 'Bravo, bravo' at concerts and making 'de grands gestes, des grimaces, des hochements de tête quand ils parlent d'art' [big gestures, grimaces, and vigorous nods when they talk about art] (IV, 470), Swann is always restrained. When he allows himself to express a personal opinion on art, he does so in a dispassionate manner. Though his detachment is criticized, by his dignified silence Swann appears more elegant and refined than the 'célibataires', who are called 'risibles' [laughable]. As with Virgil and even to a certain extent Ulysses, everything about Swann has a 'simultaneously positive and negative significance' (Barolini 1984: 200).

One of Swann's functions as an alter ego is that he puts the threat of the narrator-protagonist's lack of will power into greater relief. Indeed, the narrator-protagonist in some situations acts and speaks so very much like Swann that it does appear that history repeats itself. Some examples of déjà vu are his interactions over tea with Gilberte which echo Swann and Odette's (I, 497, 218), his jealousy for Albertine which parallels Swann's jealousy for Odette, and his social success with the Guermantes. After Swann's death he has effectively become Oriane de Guermantes's new Charles, amusing her with precious descriptions of her outfits in an exchange (III, 547) which echoes her interaction with Swann at the Sainte-Euverte soirée in 'Un amour de Swann' (I, 335). Therefore, when we read that Swann has 'une nature d'artiste' (I, 220) and as an adolescent had fancied himself an artist (I, 235), were it not for the novel's proleptic narratorial interventions, we might expect Swann's failure to prefigure that of the narrator-protagonist. However, though weak willed, the protagonist does not suffer from Swann's fear of intellectual heights (I, 26), and is shocked by Swann's superficial attitude (I, 97).

While flight comes with a cautionary warning in Dante, hubris does not enter the picture in the *Recherche* where the desire to fly is shown as entirely positive. It has indeed been argued by Stéphane Chaudier that when it comes to art, Proust's work draws on classical virtues and aesthetics which counterbalance the Christian influences present in the novel (2004: 141). In Proust we therefore do not have character dynamics equivalent to Ulysses who, though admirable in certain respects, is confined to Hell for undertaking the wrong journey, or Virgil and Cavalcanti, who are great poets, but not (good) Christians. Swann functions as a negative alter ego in so far as, unlike the narrator-protagonist in *Le Temps retrouvé*, he fails to move 'vers une vie nouvelle' [towards a new life] (IV, 496). Combined with art's presentation as the 'seul véritable voyage' [only true journey] (III, 762), Swann's character would suggest that all journeys to art and to the self should be undertaken. In Dante on the other hand, the poet also faces the pressure of undertaking the right kind of journey: one in accordance with divine will. With important differences, Dante and Proust both represent their narrator-protagonists' journeys to literary creation through the oedipal surpassing of a paternal figure.[8] The gendered nature of the journey to literary creation becomes all the more apparent if we contrast the function of these male guides with that of female guides. These female guides are a model for virtue and offer a standard against which the narrator-protagonists are to measure their behaviour and their literary output. More than poetic muses, they are judges whose presence in the narrative imbues literary creation with a moral dimension. These characters are Dante's Beatrice and Proust's Bathilde, better known as 'grand-mère'.

Beatrice: A True 'cosa nova'

The character of Beatrice, who plays a central role in the *Vita nuova* as well as the *Commedia*, is both a continuation of the duecento lyric tradition of the 'donna angelo' or salvific woman, and a radically new creation.[9] This section takes its title from the *Vita nuova*'s poem 'Donne ch'avete intelletto d'amore', in which we read:

> Dice di lei Amor: 'Cosa mortale
> come esser pò sì adorna e sì pura?'.
> Poi la reguarda, e fra se stesso giura
> che Dio ne 'ntenda di far cosa nova. (*VN*, XIX, 11)

> [Love says of her: 'How can a mortal body achieve such beauty and such purity?' He looks again and swears it must be true: God does have something new in mind for earth.]

In the *Vita nuova* Beatrice is an unattainable young woman whose beauty and virtue inspire others, and in particular Dante, to lead a more virtuous life. After a first phase in which he desires his love to be requited, Dante discovers the 'stilo de la loda' [the style of praise], which consists in finding beatitude in the act of praising the beloved without expecting anything in return (*VN*, XVIII, 6–9). As argued by Joan Ferrante in her work *Woman as Image in Medieval Literature*, in courtly literature woman could symbolize either a positive value, when love for her 'awakens man to a new sense of himself, to higher aspirations', or a negative value, when desire for her is carnal and distracts man from higher aspirations (1975: 2). The *Vita nuova* follows this model in so far as love for Beatrice only becomes unequivocally virtuous after the epiphany that the poet should not want anything from her in return for his love. The selfless love inspired by Beatrice is contrasted with the feelings Dante develops for another woman after Beatrice's death, referred to as the 'donna gentile' (*VN*, XXXV–XXXVIII).[10] In both cases, women are not characters with their own subjectivity, but rather a screen on which the male character can express his potential for virtue or for sin. Ferrante observes that in the later Middle Ages women came to symbolize man's negative potential rather than a force for good, with the exception of lyric poetry and mystic writings where 'no longer a symbol of something in man', they have become 'an intermediary between man and God' (1975: 3). Ferrante's account of the evolving image of women in medieval literature also fits the development of Beatrice's character from the *Vita nuova* to the *Commedia*. While in the *Vita nuova* she led Dante to God through the feelings she inspired, in the *Commedia* she becomes an active intermediary. We are told at the beginning of the journey that she is the one who sent Virgil to guide Dante (*Inf.* II, 52–74). When they meet in the earthly paradise at the top of Mount Purgatory, she forces Dante to confess his sins and to repent, so that he can be worthy of travelling to Paradise. Finally, she guides him through Paradise to the Empyrean.[11] And it is by giving her this active role that Dante in the *Commedia* radically reinvents the figure of the angelic beloved.

Beatrice in the *Commedia* is still the Beatrice of the *Vita nuova* in so far as she is the beautiful Florentine woman with whom Dante fell in love. The continuity is marked both in *Purgatorio*, 'conosco i segni de l'antica fiamma' [I recognize the signs of the ancient flame] (*Purg.* XXX, 48), and in Paradiso:

> Io dissi: 'Al suo piacere e tosto e tardo
> vegna remedio a li occhi, che fuor porte
> quand'ella entrò col foco ond'io sempr'ardo'.
> (*Par.* XXVI, 13–15)

[I said: 'As soon or as late as pleases her | may a remedy come for my eyes, which were the doors | through which she entered, bringing the fire that still blazes in me'.]

> Dal primo giorno ch'i' vidi il suo viso
> in questa vita, infino a questa vista,
> non m'è il seguire al mio cantar preciso.
> (*Par.* XXX, 28–30)

[From the first day that I saw her face | in this life, until the sight of her now, | I never ceased singing her praise.]

Beatrice's past as the beloved of the *Vita nuova* invests her with a historicity that makes her more than an allegorical figure standing for Faith or Grace, just as Virgil is more than an allegory for Reason.[12] She lived a human life and the poem explicitly acknowledges that physical desire is an important part of Dante's love for her, Beatrice herself stating that:

> Mai non t'appresentò natura o arte
> piacer, quanto le belle membra in ch'io
> rinchiusa fui. (*Purg.* XXXI, 49–51)[13]

[Never did nature or art present you with | any pleasure equal to the beautiful limbs in which | I was contained.]

Beatrice's new status as spiritual guide does not stop Dante from calling her 'la mia donna' or 'la donna mia' [my lady] and references are frequently made to her beautiful eyes or beautiful smile, which 'nel foco faria l'uom felice' [would make a man happy even if he were burned alive] (*Par.* VII, 18). At times, Dante is so much more enthralled by the vision of Beatrice's beauty than by his tour of Paradise,[14] that she has to call him to order using, paradoxically, that famous smile of hers:

> Vincendo me col lume d'un sorriso,
> ella mi disse: 'Volgiti e ascolta;
> ché non pur ne' miei occhi è paradiso'. (*Par.* XVIII, 19–21)

[Winning me over with a flash of her smile, | she said to me: 'Turn and listen; | for Paradise is not in my eyes'.]

It is interventions of this kind that truly make Beatrice in the *Commedia* 'quella donna ch'a Dio mi menava' [the lady leading me to God] (*Par.* XVIII, 4): she speaks and she tells Dante how to be a good Christian. This, on the part of Dante, is extremely innovative for two reasons. First, within the context of Dante's own literary output, the fact that Beatrice speaks at all is a radical change: in the *Vita nuova* she was only spoken of. This change of circumstances in the *Commedia* is signalled from as early as *Inferno* II, when Beatrice's speech to Virgil is reported verbatim and, as observed by Barolini (2003 and 2006: 360–78), includes the words 'Quando sarò dinanzi al segnor mio, | di te mi loderò sovente a lui' [When I will be before my Lord, | I will offer much praise of you to him] (*Inf.* II, 73–74), thus turning Beatrice from a passive object of praise ('loda', as in 'stilo de la loda') into an active giver of praise. The second radical innovation applies not only to Dante's literary output, but to his historical context. The religious authorities of Dante's time agreed that women should not minister for the Church, yet in spite of this, Beatrice is cast as the poem's religious authority. This authority is already suggested in the *Purgatorio*, where Virgil regularly refers Dante to her greater understanding (*Purg.* VI, 44–46; XV, 76–78; XVIII, 47–48, 73–75). In the *Paradiso* Beatrice speaks as an expert in theology, correcting the opinions of several male philosophers and theologians, qualifying her judgment as infallible ('Secondo mio infallibile avviso', *Par.* VII, 19). Moreover, in the episode of the earthly paradise, Beatrice acts as a priest by taking Dante's confession and absolving him (Ferrante 1992).

Beatrice's remonstrance in the earthly paradise, to which I shall return in Chapter 4, truly expresses the coming together of the Beatrice of duecento lyric and the guide of the *Commedia*. Her accusations are based on events recounted in the *Vita nuova*, thus showing continuity between the characters and re-establishing love for Beatrice as leading to virtue: Dante's sinful turning away from Beatrice after her death had already been the subject of the 'donna gentile' episode in the *Vita nuova* (Barański 1995). But the fact that Beatrice, who is compared to an admiral (*Purg.* XXX, 58) whose speech cuts like a sword (*Purg.* XXX, 57; XXXI, 2–3), recounts these events and puts Dante on trial breaks the courtly gender conventions to which the *Vita nuova* had subscribed. Beatrice criticizes Dante not as a woman, but as a religious authority. Her critique of Dante's behaviour after her death follows an Augustinian model of misdirected desire, according to which love for earthly things is inherently inferior to love for God, since all that is earthly is perishable.

Beatrice is the source both of Dante's poetry and of his piety. His beginnings as a love poet, as recounted in the *Vita nuova*, are all based on his love for Beatrice. This love, as well as making him write poetry, brings him to a new understanding of the divine, as articulated in the *Vita nuova*'s final poem 'Oltre la spera' (*VN*, LXI, 10–13). As a result, Beatrice makes him a better Christian. After this acknowledgement of the new understanding brought by his love for Beatrice, the *Vita nuova* ends with Dante's promise to write something worthy of her, in other words, to become a better poet.[15] In the *Commedia* Beatrice supersedes Virgil as the guide who will not only lead Dante closer to God, but also tell him what to write and for whom (*Purg.* XXXII, 103–05; XXXIII, 52–54). In *Paradiso* XXV, a canto whose famous opening includes the words 'ritornerò poeta',[16] Beatrice is described as: 'quella pïa che guidò le penne | de le mie ali a così alto volo' [the pious woman who guided the quills | of my wings to such lofty heights] (*Par.* XXV, 49–50). We saw in Chapter 2 that flight imagery in Dante conflates the journey to God with the journey to poetry. More specifically in this example, the reference to the 'alto volo' creates an echo with Ulysses's 'folle volo' of *Inferno* XXVI, and the word 'penne' can, as in *Purgatorio* xxiv, be read as a reference to the quill of the poet, as well as to the feathers of his metaphorical wings, the 'quill' reading being further encouraged by the pause created by the enjambment after 'penne'. In other words, these two verses are saying that Beatrice is both the saintly woman leading Dante upwards to God, and also the person guiding his pen, thereby combining the religious and the literary.

Beatrice in the *Paradiso* also takes on the pedagogical role of university lecturer (*lector*). Casting a woman as a *lector* is as unusual a move on Dante's part as casting her as a priest, seeing as this authoritative role was the privilege of men. Elena Lombardi emphasizes the originality of Dante's Beatrice by contrasting her with Jean de Meun's allegorical female figures of 'La Vieille' and 'Nature' in the *Roman de la rose*, the former being a parody of the figure of the university lecturer and the latter, though a convincing lecturer, being undermined by admissions of women's illogicality: 'No such strategies are at work with Beatrice, who is fully subsumed into her role of university lecturer, which seems to be enhanced rather than weighed down by her being a woman' (2018: 147). Lombardi indeed demonstrates how Dante and Beatrice across the *Paradiso* interact as pupil and university teacher, with Beatrice not only lecturing Dante, but also dialoguing with him in a format best described as a tutorial (for instance in *Paradiso* ii, iv, and v), and on occasion even assigning him 'homework' (*Par.* v, 37–42).

Beatrice in the *Commedia* therefore is more than an unattainable female whose looks inspire love poetry.[17] While remaining feminine through the erotic descriptions of her beauty, she is an authoritative guide and mentor, a role normally assigned to male characters. I believe it is because of a profound misunderstanding of this role that Proust scholars have only posited Albertine and Mlle de Saint-Loup as Beatrice figures.[18] The comparison is drawn on the basis that these are young women who inspire the narrator-protagonist to write. Albertine, who is his lover, does so by causing him pain, which in the Proustian world is key to artistic development — indeed, the narrator-protagonist argues in *Le Temps retrouvé* that a writer should be grateful for all that which makes his love an unhappy one (iv, 480–84). Mlle de Saint-Loup's lineage makes her the embodiment of the coming-together of the different threads of the narrator-protagonist's life (iv, 606–07), which spurs him on to writing: 'Enfin cette idée du Temps avait un dernier prix pour moi, elle était un aiguillon, elle me disait qu'il était temps de commencer' [Finally, this idea of Time had one further price for me: it was an incentive, reminding me that it was time to begin] (iv, 609).

Mlle de Saint-Loup's role is different from Beatrice's in so far as she only appears fleetingly at the end of the novel, unlike Beatrice who is Dante's beloved from the opening pages of the *Commedia*. The narrator-protagonist's relationship with Albertine is at odds with Dante's relationship with Beatrice for two reasons. First, far from being an untouchable object of admiration, her relations with the protagonist become sexual from as early as *Le Côté de Guermantes* (ii, 661–62), and there is even a scene in which the protagonist masturbates by her sleeping body (iii, 580–81). Moreover, their cohabitation leads him to speak of her with condescension: 'elle avait cessé d'être une Victoire, elle était une pesante esclave dont j'aurais voulu me débarrasser' [she had ceased to be an allegorical Victory, she was now a heavy slave that I would have loved to get rid of] (III, 873). Secondly, it is the protagonist who educates and shapes his female beloved, and not the contrary. This is made obvious, for example, in the pages of *La Prisonnière* devoted to their conversation on literature (IV, 877–83), which rather than a conversation is a lecture given by the narrator-protagonist to Albertine (addressed as 'ma petite' [my pet], 'petite fille' [little girl], and 'ma petite Albertine' [my little Albertine]), in which Albertine only participates by asking questions and admitting her ignorance: 'Je vous avoue que je n'ai pas compris' [I must admit I don't understand] (III, 880). On the occasion where she does demonstrate wit and eloquence by pastiching the narrator-protagonist's own language, this is presented as an uncomfortable moment (III, 635–37).

The character of the grandmother, who functions as a moral compass and encourages her grandson's literary activity, is far more pertinent to a study of guide figures in Proust. The fact that she dies during the course of the narrative and provides the narrator-protagonist with his first experience of mourning, moreover, creates a further parallel with Beatrice.[19] Critics concentrating on the question of art in Proust tend to agree that the figure of the grandmother plays the important role of uniting moral and artistic values. For example, George Strambolian notes:

> Throughout Proust's work, the absence of artifice is a mark of both artistic and moral perfection. In *A la Recherche*, Marcel learns this particular aesthetic from his grandmother, who values works like the Combray church and people for their natural grace and lack of pretence. (1972: 73)

Carter in *The Proustian Quest* draws the connection between the grandmother's praise of the Combray church steeple '"s'il jouait du piano, il ne jouerait pas *sec*"' [if he were a pianist, his playing would not be *dry*] (I, 63), and the writer Bergotte's self-critique on the threshold of death: '"mes derniers livres sont trop secs"' [my latest books are too dry] (III, 692), arguing that the dying Bergotte and the grandmother's shared critique of 'spiritual or artistic "dryness"' offer evidence of 'the grandmother's importance as a moral and artistic mentor' (1992: 202). She has also been studied by Hughes as 'an effective foil to the Narrator himself' (1983: 85), and by Anna Elsner (2009), who argues that the guilt with which she fills the narrator-protagonist fuels his writing. The following section will develop all of these insights by analyzing the extent to which the grandmother can be read as a guide figure.

Grand-mère as Beatrice?

Just as the implications of Virgil's failed journey were predominantly Christian and those of Swann's predominantly to do with artistic sensitivity, so are the influences of Beatrice and of the grandmother to be distinguished. The grandmother's moral stance cannot be accounted for as succinctly as Beatrice's as it is not based on an accepted religious doctrine. She values authenticity, contact with nature, and literature, and she wishes to counteract her grandson's physical weakness and lack of will power. She offers an alternative set of values to those of the socially conventional father. This is established early on in 'Combray', first when she disagrees with the father telling his son to stay in his room: '"Ce n'est pas comme cela que vous le rendrez robuste et énergique, disait-elle tristement, surtout ce petit qui a tant besoin de prendre des forces et de la volonté." Mon père haussait les épaules' ['That's no way to make him robust and energetic, she would say sadly, this child could really do with some strength and will power.' My father would shrug] (I, 11). The contrast between the father and the pair formed by grandmother and mother is then further explored through the famous episode of the 'drame du coucher'.[20]

The 'drame' is caused by the father, who does not honour 'aussi scrupuleusement que ma grand-mère et que ma mère la foi des traités' [his treaties as scrupulously as my grandmother and my mother] (I, 27) and therefore tells his son to go to bed without having received the habitual goodnight kiss from his mother. The 'drame' then ends with the father telling the mother to sleep in her son's room. This surprising turn of events is explained in terms of the difference between his father, who has no firm rules governing his relationship with his son, and the mother and grandmother who will grant or refuse his wishes according to firm and consistent principles (I, 35–36). Mother and grandmother are stronger than the father because they prioritize the protagonist's education over short-term gratification: 'elles m'aimaient assez pour ne pas consentir à m'épargner de la souffrance, elles voulaient m'apprendre à la dominer afin de diminuer ma sensibilité nerveuse et fortifier ma volonté' [they loved me enough to refuse to spare me suffering: they wanted to teach me how to dominate it, so that I may become less over-sensitive and have more will power] (I, 37). At the end of the *Recherche*, in *Le Temps retrouvé*, we are told that it is from the concession of the 'drame du coucher' that 'je pouvais faire dater le déclin de ma santé et de mon vouloir, mon renoncement chaque jour aggravé à une tâche difficile' [that I could date the decline of my health and my will, my increasingly definite abandonment of a difficult task] (IV, 465); 'C'était de cette soirée, où ma mère avait abdiqué, que datait, avec la mort lente de ma grand-mère, le déclin de ma volonté, de ma santé' [It was from that night, when my mother ceded, that dated, along with the slow death of my grandmother, the decline of my will, of my health] (IV, 621).[21] These *après-coup* passages thus tell us that had the protagonist been raised solely according to his mother and grandmother's principles, with no interference from his father, he might have learned to have will power and as a result would have set to work on his writing sooner. The flip-side to this, however, is that, as we saw in Chapters 1 and 2, the narrator-protagonist's hypersensitivity and tendency to meander are part of his artistic identity. Hughes (1983: 77–85) calls the grandmother's efforts to protect and strengthen her grandson a 'war on hypersensitivity', and in this respect such efforts could be interpreted as counterproductive.

The repeated postponements recounted in *À l'ombre des jeunes filles en fleurs* are best summarized by the phrase 'renoncement chaque jour aggravé' [increasingly definite abandoning] (I, 569–70). While procrastinating, the protagonist thinks of his grandmother as the reader of his future work: 'Certain que le surlendemain j'aurais déjà écrit quelques pages, je ne disais plus un seul mot à mes parents de ma décision; j'aimais mieux patienter quelques heures, et apporter à ma grand-mère consolée et convaincue, de l'ouvrage en train' [Convinced that by the day after tomorrow I would already have written a few pages, I no longer said a word of my decision to my parents; I preferred to wait a few hours and bring to my consoled and convinced grandmother the work in progress] (I, 569). The adjective 'consolée' suggests her disappointment at his failure to write, and indeed we saw in Chapter 2 that when he mourns her, he pictures her face as being 'déçu' (III, 153).[22] While the father dislikes the idea of his son having a career in literature, the grandmother seems to point him in that direction from the beginning.[23] This is demonstrated in 'Combray' through her choice of reading material for him:

> Ma grand-mère, ai-je su depuis, avait d'abord choisi les poésies de Musset, un volume de Rousseau et *Indiana*; car si elle jugeait les lectures futiles aussi malsaines que les bonbons et les pâtisseries, elle ne pensait pas que les grands souffles du génie eussent sur l'esprit même d'un enfant une influence plus dangereuse et moins vivifiante que sur son corps le grand air et le vent du large. Mais mon père l'ayant presque traitée de folle en apprenant les livres qu'elle voulait me donner, [...] elle s'était rabattue sur les quatre romans champêtres de George Sand. 'Ma fille, disait-elle à maman, je ne pourrais me décider à donner à cet enfant quelque chose de mal écrit.'
>
> En réalité, elle ne se résignait jamais à rien acheter dont on ne pût tirer un profit intellectuel, et surtout celui que nous procurent les belles choses en nous apprenant à chercher notre plaisir ailleurs que dans les satisfactions du bien-être et de la vanité. Même [...] quand elle avait à donner un fauteuil, des couverts, une canne, elle les cherchait 'anciens', comme si leur longue désuétude ayant effacé leur caractère d'utilité, ils paraissaient plutôt disposés pour nous raconter la vie des hommes d'autrefois que pour servir aux besoins de la nôtre. [...] Même ce qui dans ces meubles répondait à un besoin, comme c'était d'une façon à laquelle nous ne sommes plus habitués, la charmait comme les vieilles manières de dire où nous voyons une métaphore, effacée [...] par l'usure de l'habitude. Or, justement, les romans champêtres de George Sand qu'elle me donnait pour ma fête, étaient pleins [...] d'expressions tombées en désuétude et redevenues imagées [...]. Et ma grand-mère les avait achetés [...] comme [...] de ces vieilles choses qui exercent sur l'esprit une heureuse influence en lui donnant la nostalgie d'impossibles voyages dans le temps. (I, 39–41)
>
> [I have learned since that my grandmother had first chosen Musset's poetry, a volume by Rousseau and *Indiana*; for though she considered futile books as harmful as sweets and pastries, she did not think that the great blasts of genius might have a more dangerous and less refreshing influence on a child's mind than the outdoors and the sea breeze. But my father having almost called her crazy when he had learned what books she was planning to give me, [...] she had fallen back on four pastoral novels by George Sand. 'My daughter, she would say to my mother, I could never bring myself to give this child something badly written.'
>
> The truth is that she would never resign herself to buying anything that did not have some kind of intellectual value — especially those beautiful objects that teach us to find pleasure beyond the satisfactions of well-being and vanity. Even [...] when she had to give an armchair, cutlery, or a walking stick, she would try to find 'antique' ones, as though their obsolescence cancelled their

> practical purpose. They seemed better equipped to tell us how people used to live than to meet our present needs. [...] And even when these pieces of furniture did meet one of our needs, since this was done in a manner to which we are no longer accustomed, they charmed her like those old sayings in which we can trace a metaphor that has become worn out [...] through usage. Now the novels by George Sand that she was giving me for my birthday were full of such [...] expressions that have become obsolete and therefore regained their colour [...]. And my grandmother had bought them [...] like [...] those old objects which exert a felicitous influence on the mind by feeding its nostalgia for impossible journeys through time.]

We are given three criteria for the grandmother's choice of books for her grandson: the works should be intellectually stimulating, well-written, and conducive to imaginary journeys through time. The first criterion is undermined not only by the father's reaction, but also by the narrator's comparison between challenging books and bracing winds, suggesting that the grandmother lacks common sense and should have chosen something age-appropriate. The third criterion is undermined by the fact that she applies it indiscriminately. Examples I have elided include her belief that prints of artworks are more useful to her grandson than photographs of artworks, and her secondhand gifts falling apart upon first use (I, 40). However, although they are slightly ridiculed, the aesthetic qualities pursued by the grandmother bear a strong resonance with those that the narrator-protagonist sets out to pursue in *Le Temps retrouvé*.

The grandmother seeks to challenge the power of habit and bring the past back to life through contact with objects from another time and styles of writing or speaking with evocative imagery. The benefit of involuntary memory in *Le Temps retrouvé* is described precisely in terms of its capacity to break habit and put us in contact with a past epoch. What is particularly striking about this early passage, is that it explicitly makes the connection between the charm of journeys through time and the pleasure brought by living metaphor. By speaking of 'expressions tombées en désuétude et redevenues imagées', the narrator refers to the process by which a metaphor, if it gains currency as an everyday figure of speech, loses its evocative power and becomes what we refer to as a 'dead metaphor', but if this figure of speech falls out of use, then the metaphor is 'resurrected' and will become living again. In *Le Temps retrouvé*, the narrator draws a parallel between involuntary memory, which in life connects different 'terms' or 'objects', and metaphor, which plays the same role in art (IV, 467–68). The consonance between the grandmother's views and those announced in *Le Temps retrouvé* is further suggested by the Combray paragraph's ending, 'dans le temps', which literally pre-announces the ending of the novel: 'dans le Temps' (IV, 625).[24]

Although *Le Temps retrouvé* ultimately confirms the grandmother's clairvoyance, she does not possess the authority of Dante's Beatrice. Moreover, she is at times treated as a comical figure, as we already saw through the account of her preference when it comes to wedding presents for furniture that falls apart. We are first introduced to the grandmother's both tragic and comical nature in a three-page paragraph at the beginning of the novel (I, 10–13). Some sentences describing her behaviour are humorous, such as, for example, the following juxtaposition of her exaltation and the practical concerns in which it results for others:

> Les mouvements divers qu'excitaient dans son âme l'ivresse de l'orage, la puissance de l'hygiène, la stupidité de mon éducation et la symétrie des jardins, plutôt que le désir inconnu d'elle d'éviter à sa jupe prune les taches de boue sous lesquelles elle disparaissait jusqu'à une hauteur qui était toujours pour sa femme de chambre un désespoir et un problème. (I, II)
>
> [The different movements that were inspired in her soul by the excitement of the storm, the power of hygiene, the stupidity of my education, and the symmetry of the garden, rather than the as yet unknown to her desire of preserving her purple skirt from the mud splatters under which it would disappear up to a height that was for her chambermaid a source of despair and a problem.]

The comic potential of her beliefs is however counterbalanced by her pathos-ridden relationship with others. In the same passage we are told of the family's habitual taunting of the grandmother: 'elle avait apporté dans la famille de mon père un esprit si différent que tout le monde la plaisantait et la tourmentait' [she had brought such a different mindset into my father's family that everyone teased her and tormented her] (I, II), a taunting to which she responds with sadness, but enduring love and kindness (I, I2). Her self-sacrificing nature invests her with moral authority and uncomfortably undercuts those moments in which we laugh at her. For example, the passage which I cited above is subverted when we are informed of what is on her mind as she roams around the garden:

> Hélas! je ne savais pas que, bien plus tristement [...], mon manque de volonté, ma santé délicate, l'incertitude qu'ils projetaient sur mon avenir, préoccupaient ma grand-mère, au cours de ces déambulations incessantes, [...] où on voyait passer [...] son beau visage aux joues brunes et sillonnées [...] et sur lesquelles, amené là par le froid ou quelque triste pensée, était toujours en train de sécher un pleur involontaire. (I, I2–I3)
>
> [Alas! I did not know that, even more tragically [...], my lack of will power, my delicate health, the uncertainty regarding my future, concerned my grandmother during these incessant peregrinations, [...] where we could see [...] her beautiful face pass by, with its brown and furrowed cheeks [...], on which, brought there either by the cold or some sad thought, there always ran an involuntary tear.]

Proust, after having led us to laugh at her walks, thus retells them with a change in focalization and as a result gives us a different story.

The grandmother's main trait throughout the novel will be her tendency for self-sacrifice, described as a mixture of sweetness and pain: 'd'un ton doux et désenchanté' [with a gentle and disenchanted tone] (I, 570); 'son grand visage découpé comme un beau nuage ardent et calme, derrière lequel on sentait rayonner la tendresse' [her broad face cut like a beautiful cloud, calm and intense, through which one could glimpse beams of tenderness] (II, 29); 'Elle trouvait un tel plaisir dans toute peine qui m'en épargnait une' [she found such pleasure in any suffering that would spare me some] (II, 29); 'le visage si soumis, si malheureux, si doux qu'elle avait' [that sad, submissive, and kind face of hers] (III, 158). The palette of cultural imagery Proust draws on to depict the grandmother often has elements of the suffering Christ. A key example of this is the importance invested in the scene in which she takes off her grandson's shoes during their stay together at the sea resort of Balbec, which bears a resonance with Christ washing his disciples' feet on the last night of his earthly life as a supreme mark of his love for them (John 13:1–17).[25] At his first night at the Grand-Hôtel de Balbec, the narrator-protagonist describes his horror at having to sleep in a new room: 'j'étais seul, j'avais envie de mourir. Alors ma grand-mère entra; et à l'expansion de mon cœur refoulé s'ouvrirent aussitôt des espaces infinis' [I was alone, I wanted to die. And then my grandmother came in and infinite spaces suddenly opened themselves up to my oppressed heart] (II, 28). The language used to describe her love for her grandson in this passage is extremely religious: 'une robe de chambre de percale [...] qui était pour nous soigner [...] son habit de religieuse' [a percale dressing gown [...] which was her religious habit for looking after us]; 'si grand chagrin qu'il y eût en moi [...] il serait reçu dans une pitié plus vaste encore' [however great a sadness I carried in me [...] it would be received with a pity that was even vaster]; 'ce monde où nous ne percevons pas directement les âmes' [this world in which we cannot directly perceive other people's souls]; 'tout ce qui pouvait ainsi être dit encore à elle, en était aussitôt si spiritualisé, si sanctifié' [anything that could be said to her would find itself immediately spiritualized, sanctified] (II, 28–29). The paragraph then ends with her helping him to take off his shoes:

> Quand, ayant vu qu'elle voulait m'aider à me coucher et me déchausser, je fis le geste de l'en empêcher et de commencer à me déshabiller moi-même, elle arrêta d'un regard suppliant mes mains qui touchaient aux premiers boutons de ma veste et de mes bottines. (II, 29)
>
> [When, having seen that she wanted to help me get ready for bed and take my shoes off, I made a gesture to stop her and start undressing, with a supplicating gaze she stopped my hands from unbuttoning my jacket and my boots.]

This self-humiliating gesture, which summarizes so vividly the nature of the grandmother's relationship with her grandson, will be the trigger for the narrator-protagonist's belated grief in 'Les Intermittences du cœur', when he removes his shoes himself (III, 152).[26]

The different ways in which Dante and Proust use the Christ motif to characterize their female guides offers us a clear insight into the differences between Beatrice and the grandmother. As is well known, Dante's Beatrice both in the *Vita nuova* and in the *Commedia* has strong Christological traits.[27] While the grandmother is a suffering Christ, Beatrice is a glorious, resurrected Christ. Proust's female guide is a creature of self-sacrifice and debasement. The fact that she is a source of comedy and a laughing-stock for other family members can be connected to the mocking of Jesus, which was a part of the Passion, most notoriously through the placing of a crown of thorns on his head in derision of his kingship (Matthew 27:28). She will die over the course of the narrative, without any certainty of a new life after this one. Beatrice speaks after death from a position of absolute saintliness and authority:

she is Christ at the height of his glory, his resurrection proving that he truly is the son of God.

Whereas in the *Recherche* the grandmother holds little authority, Dante can only obey Beatrice, who speaks to him with an abundant use of the imperative: 'non piangere ancora' [do not cry yet] (*Purg.* XXX, 56); 'Guardaci ben!' [Look at me!] (*Purg.* XXX, 73); 'dì, dì se questo è vero' [tell me, tell me if this is true] (*Purg.* XXXI, 5); 'Rispondi a me' [Answer me] (*Purg.* XXXI, 11). And, most importantly for our consideration of her role in a narrative of literary vocation: 'ritornato di là, fa che tu scrive' [when you return there, be sure to write what you have seen] (*Purg.* XXXII, 105). This contrast between the two female figures is also suggested by the *Recherche.* The Baron de Charlus, caught in the heat of a monologue on nationalists who, hitherto advocates of war, turn pacifist, throws in a reference to Dante's female guide:

> Il est persuadé que, dans toutes les civilisations guerrières, la femme avait un rôle humilié et bas. On n'ose lui répondre que les "dames" des chevaliers, au Moyen Âge, et la Béatrice de Dante étaient peut-être placées sur un trône aussi élevé que les héroïnes de M. Becque. (IV, 377)[28]
>
> [He is persuaded that, in all warrior civilizations, women held an inferior place to men. No one dares tell him that the 'ladies' of these knights, as well as Dante's Beatrice, in the Middle Ages were perhaps placed on a throne as elevated as that of Mr Becque's heroines.]

One might speculate as to whether the source for Charlus's comment has anything to do with Proust's friendship with Lucie Félix-Faure, an early Dante scholar who wrote a book entitled *Les Femmes dans l'œuvre de Dante* (1902). What is striking in the context of this study, is that it is our modern character, the grandmother, who has 'un rôle humilié et bas', and not the self-assertive medieval character. Indeed, the grandmother in the *Recherche* is never able to give her grandson any orders.

The grandmother's influence functions through guilt. This is made clear in the dream sequence of 'Les Intermittences du cœur' (III, 148–78), a section of the *Recherche* that we considered at the end of Chapter 2. One night, during the same stay which triggers his experience of mourning for his grandmother, the protagonist has a vivid dream about her, which is described as a katabasis (III, 157). In this dream, 'je cherchai en vain ma grand-mère [...] mon père n'arrivait pas qui devait me conduire à elle' [I searched in vain for my grandmother [...] my father, who was meant to lead me to her, was not there] (III, 157). With a sudden pang, the protagonist realizes: 'j'avais oublié d'écrire à ma grand-mère' [I had forgotten to write to my grandmother] (III, 157). He fails to find his grandmother, but encounters his father who tells him: 'Elle demande quelquefois ce que tu es devenu. On lui a même dit que tu allais faire un livre. Elle a paru contente. Elle a essuyé une larme' [Sometimes she asks what has become of you. We even told her that you were going to write a book. She seemed happy. She brushed away a tear] (III, 158). As has been argued by Elsner, the dream's unwritten book lies at the heart of the narrator protagonist's 'guilty conscience' (2009: 285). This guilt is returned to in *Le Temps retrouvé*, when, having decided to set to work, the narrator-protagonist reflects on the 'récompense' [reward] that this work would have been to all of his grandmother's efforts, if only she had been alive to witness it (IV, 481):

> Et ma seule consolation qu'elle ne sût pas que je me mettais enfin à l'œuvre d'art était que (tel est le lot des morts) si elle ne pouvait pas jouir de mon progrès, elle avait cessé depuis longtemps d'avoir conscience de mon inaction, de ma vie manquée, qui avaient été une telle souffrance pour elle. (IV, 481–82)
>
> [And my only consolation for her not knowing that I was at last setting to work on my art was that (such is the fate of the dead) if she could not enjoy my progress, she had at least for a long time now ceased to suffer from knowing of my passivity and my wasted life.]

But how far does this lifelong guilt affect the narrator-protagonist's decision to set to work? According to the account that we are given in *Le Temps retrouvé*, his decision is entirely drawn from the revelations brought by involuntary memory. The narrator-protagonist's aesthetic ideas at the close of the novel may be close to his grandmother's, but he does not seem aware of this.[29] The grandmother's role, as unacknowledged mentor, is perhaps instead to highlight tragically the protagonist's inadequacy and even his ungratefulness. This is made explicit by observations such as 'La nature de ma grand-mère, nature qui était juste l'opposé de mon total égoïsme' [My grandmother's character, a character that was simply the opposite of my complete selfishness] (II, 208). When in *À l'ombre des jeunes filles en fleurs* she dares ask him, 'Hé bien, ce travail, on n'en parle même plus?' [So, this project, you won't even mention it anymore?] the grandmother immediately senses the irritation with which her question is met and therefore apologizes: 'Pardon, je ne dirai plus rien' [I'm sorry, I won't say anything again] (I, 570). This is a very different picture from that of Beatrice, who shows Dante no mercy until after he has felt the burning of true repentance (*Purg.* XXX, 144–45).

One final consideration to take into account in this comparative reading of the grandmother in the *Recherche* and Beatrice is that it may seem surprising to read a grandson-grandmother relationship on a par with an amorous relationship such as that of Dante and Beatrice. The reading of the grandmother and grandson as two lovers is in fact suggested by the *Recherche* itself, specifically in *À l'ombre des jeunes filles en fleurs*, in the context of their first holiday alone together at the Grand-Hôtel de Balbec. A sudden shift from the habitual (narrated through the imperfect) into the singular (introduced by 'Une fois') introduces a surprising conversation:

> Ainsi soumettais-je à ma grand-mère mes impressions, car je ne savais jamais le degré d'estime dû à quelqu'un que quand elle me l'avait indiqué. Chaque soir je venais lui apporter les croquis que j'avais pris dans la journée d'après tous ces êtres inexistants qui n'étaient pas elle. Une fois je lui dis: 'Sans toi je ne pourrai pas vivre. — Mais il ne faut pas, me répondit-elle d'une voix troublée. Sans cela que deviendrais-tu si je partais en voyage? J'espère au contraire que tu serais très raisonnable et très heureux. — Je saurais être raisonnable si tu partais pour quelques jours, mais je compterais les heures. — Mais si je partais pour des mois... (à cette seule idée mon cœur se serrait), pour des années... pour...'
>
> Nous nous taisions tous les deux. Nous n'osions pas nous regarder. (II, 87)

> [I would thus submit all my impressions to my grandmother, for I never knew the degree to which I should respect someone until she had told me. In the evening I would bring her the sketches I had made that day of all those non-existent beings that were not her. One day I said to her: 'Without you, I could not live. — But you mustn't, she replied with a troubled voice. What would become of you if I went away on a trip? I hope on the contrary that you would be very reasonable and very happy. — I could be reasonable if you left only for a few days, but I would count the hours. — But what if I left for months... (I could feel my heart sinking at the very thought), for years... for ...'
>
> We were both silent. We did not dare meet each other's eye.]

As seen in Chapter 1, instances of direct speech from the protagonist are rare. The choice alone to have the protagonist speak therefore already makes the passage stand out. Proust beautifully conjures the weighty sense of taboo surrounding death through the grandmother's hesitant ellipses, the implications of which are emphasized through the interjection 'à cette seule idée mon cœur se serrait' marking the first one. The unspoken last word of her references to increasing periods of time is left hanging between them, the heaviness of the silence marked by the syntactic simplicity of the following two sentences. The sense that their relationship is similar to that of two lovers is conveyed by the protagonist's absolute statements of dependence on her ('je ne pourrai pas vivre'; 'je compterais les heures'). The use of 'nous' in the last two sentences, doubled through the use of reflexive verbs, also emphasizes their relationship as a couple, both overwhelmed by the emotions they feel for one another. In a rare moment of Christian orthodoxy in a novel which is for the most part God-less, the protagonist consoles his grandmother by making a reference to eschatology:

> Mais le lendemain je me mis à parler de philosophie, sur le ton le plus indifférent, en m'arrangeant cependant pour que ma grand-mère fît attention à mes paroles, je dis que c'était curieux, qu'après les dernières découvertes de la science le matérialisme semblait ruiné, et que le plus probable était encore l'éternité des âmes et leur future réunion. (II, 87)

> [But the next day I started speaking of philosophy using the most indifferent of tones, yet making sure that my grandmother was paying attention to what I was saying. I said that it was curious that after the latest scientific discoveries materialism seemed truly over and that the most likely option remained the immortality of the soul and the future reunion of souls.]

What makes the scene moving is the protagonist's desire to cheer up his grandmother, his resourcefulness in drawing on philosophy, science, and religion to this end, and the delicacy shown by the fact he deliberately avoids being explicit. It would therefore be an exaggeration to extrapolate from this passage that the grandmother, like Dante's Beatrice, leads the protagonist to be a good Christian. Rather, Christian narrative is here drawn upon in order to embellish an individual love narrative.[30]

A gloss on the nature of the relationship between grandmother and grandson is offered within the same section of the novel through a conversation ostensibly about Mme de Sévigné's letters to her daughter, which is the work of literature with which the grandmother most closely identifies. The dialogue takes place between Mme de Villeparisis and the Baron de Charlus, in the presence of the grandmother and the narrator-protagonist. Mme de Villeparisis, already cast as representing the prosaic by having been a mouthpiece for Sainte-Beuve's theories of literature, states that 'elle voyait un peu de littérature dans ce désespoir [de Mme de Sévigné] d'être séparée de cette ennuyeuse Mme de Grignan' [she saw some literary exaggeration in the despair that [Mme de Sévigné] feels at being separated from that boring Mme de Grignan] (II, 121). Separation was precisely the subject of the conversation that so upset grandmother and grandson some thirty-four pages earlier. Charlus, to the grandmother's delight, takes the defence of Mme de Sévigné. He argues that 'rien au contraire [...] ne me semble plus vrai' [nothing on the contrary [...] could seem more real to me], and quotes from Sévigné, 'dans l'absence on est libéral des heures' [during an absence, one counts hours liberally] (II, 121), faintly echoing the protagonist's earlier 'je compterais les heures' [I would count the hours] (II, 87). Mme de Villeparisis soon grows tired of her nephew's long-winded, quotation-studded defence of Sévigné. She retorts: 'Tu oublies que ce n'était pas de l'amour, c'était de sa fille qu'il s'agissait' [You are forgetting that this was not love: we are talking about her daughter] (I, 122), thus suggesting that familial relationships cannot be compared to romantic relationships. This spurs Charlus into offering the *Recherche*'s most empassioned defence of non-normative love:

> Mais l'important dans la vie n'est pas ce qu'on aime [...] c'est d'aimer. Ce que ressentait Mme de Sévigné pour sa fille peut prétendre beaucoup plus justement ressembler à la passion que Racine a dépeinte dans *Andromaque* ou dans *Phèdre*, que les banales relations que le jeune Sévigné avait avec ses maîtresses. De même l'amour de tel mystique pour son Dieu. Les démarcations trop étroites que nous traçons autour de l'amour viennent seulement de notre grande ignorance de la vie. (II, 122)
>
> [What's important in life is not what one loves, [...] but *to love*. What Mme de Sévigné felt for her daughter can far more rightly claim a resemblance to the passion depicted by Racine in *Andromaque* or *Phèdre* than the banal relationships that the young Sévigné had with his mistresses. The same goes for a mystic's love for his God. The narrow boundaries that we draw around love come from nothing else than our great ignorance of life.]

Charlus, as a closeted homosexual, in a manner similar to Oscar Wilde on trial, is ultimately defending same-sex relationships, but it is revealing that, in circumstances where homosexual love is still unspoken of, familial love and love for God are chosen as worthy emblems of non-normative love.

Women and Art

In Dante, Beatrice brings together earthly love and divine love. This is exemplified as early as in *Inferno* II when Beatrice justifies her intervention to save Dante through the hemistich 'amor mi mosse' [it was love that moved me] (*Inf.* II, 72): the 'love' that spurred Beatrice to action is both God, the 'amor che move' ('the love that moves', *Par.* XXXIII, 145), and her personal affection for Dante. Conversely, Dante's love for Beatrice, with its earthly and erotic aspects included, is part of his greater love for God. This love is the motor that makes Dante progress throughout his journey: in Purgatory his desire to see Beatrice encourages him to march on, and as he rises higher through Purgatory and Paradise, his desire to see God becomes stronger and stronger. As has been argued by Psaki (2003), love for Beatrice in the *Paradiso* is not de-sexualized, and the erotic is not a figure for divine bliss, but a part of divine bliss. The *Commedia* indeed sets out a system in which earthly love for a woman is the first step on the journey to salvation.[31]

Women in Dante are not only necessary to men for reaching salvation, they are also necessary to male poets for producing poetry. Love for women is the central topic of the vernacular lyric poetry where Dante made his beginnings. In the *Vita nuova*, as well as writing poems about women and addressing these poems to women (e.g. 'Donne ch'avete intelletto d'amore'), Dante argues that women are the very reason poets began to write in the vernacular:

> E lo primo che cominciò a dire sì come poeta volgare, si mosse però che volle fare intendere le sue parole a donna, a la quale era malagevole d'intendere li versi latini. E questo è contra coloro che rimano sopra altra matera che amorosa, con ciò sia cosa che cotale modo di parlare fosse dal principio trovato per dire d'amore. (*VN*, XXV, 6)
>
> [The first poet to begin writing in the vernacular was moved to do so by a desire to make his words understandable to ladies who found Latin verses difficult to comprehend. And this is an argument against those who compose in the vernacular on a subject other than love, since composition in the vernacular was from the beginning intended for treating of love.]

Lombardi (2018) argues that late medieval Italian authors wrote female readers into their texts because this allowed them to create a type of reader outside the traditional models of literary authority associated with Latin. Women, due to their lower level of education, were thus an ideal audience to receive the new vernacular literature.

In the classical tradition too, on which Dante draws heavily for the *Commedia*, the poet's inspiration depends on female characters: the Muses. The Muses are invoked at the beginning of each canticle so that they may assist Dante in writing his poem (*Inf.* II, 7; *Purg.* I, 8; *Par.* II, 9). He also calls upon them at particularly challenging moments, such as to describe 'fondo a tutto l'universo' [the bottom of the entire universe] (*Inf.* XXXII, 7–12), the symbolic procession of the earthly paradise (*Purg.* XXIX, 37–42), or the souls in the Heaven of Jupiter (*Par.* XVIII, 82–87). On some occasions the Muses are described through the extremely feminized image of wet-nurses breast-feeding poets. Homer is called by Virgil 'quel Greco che le Muse lattar più ch'altri mai' [that Greek whom the Muses suckled more than any other] (*Purg.* xxii, 101–02), and Dante will later invoke the great poets that came before him as:

> quelle lingue
> che Polimnïa con le suore fero
> del latte lor dolcissimo più pingue. (*Par.* xxiii, 55–57)

[those tongues | that Polyhymnia and her sisters | lathered with their sweet milk.]

It has been argued by Jeffrey Schnapp that the image of the Muses as wet-nurses, as well as Dante's feminization of poetic genealogies, for example when Statius tells Virgil that the Aeneid 'mamma | fummi, e fummi nutrice, poetando' [was my mother | and wet-nurse when it came to writing poetry] (*Purg.* xxi, 98–99), allow Dante to sidestep the otherwise inevitable oedipal rivalry he experiences in the presence of father figures (1991: 215–17).

Tenderness, support, and care were deeply embedded as feminine qualities in the Middle Ages.[32] Beatrice, for all her 'masculine' authority, remains within the limitations of her gender as Dante's otherworldly mentor. While she judges him more severely than Virgil who had deemed him saved (*Purg.* xxvii, 139–42), we are told that this is ultimately done from a position of maternal care:

> Così la madre al figlio par superba,
> com'ella parve a me; perché d'amaro
> sente il sapor de la pietade acerba. (*Purg.* xxx, 79–81)[33]

[Thus a mother may seem just as imperious to her son, | as she seemed to me; because the taste of harsh pity | is bitter.]

Both Beatrice and the Muses' existence is predicated upon offering assistance to a male poet. Dante needs the Muses to nurture him with poetic inspiration and Beatrice to guide him to salvation, but their crucial role in aiding him does not at any stage threaten his literary authority. They cause no anxiety of influence, because they themselves will never be poets.

In Proust too, despite the centuries of distance, we encounter a male creator supported by nurturing female characters. The image of breast-feeding is used to convey the manner in which the grandmother directs all of her love and energy towards the protagonist: 'Quand j'avais ainsi ma bouche collée à ses joues, à son front, j'y puisais quelque chose de si nourricier, que je gardais l'immobilité, le sérieux, la tranquille avidité d'un enfant qui tète' [When I had my mouth glued to her cheeks or her forehead like this, I extracted something so nourishing that I would remain as still, earnest and greedy as a suckling child] (ii, 28). In this image of 'tranquille avidité' we gain a sense of the protagonist literally sucking the life out of the elderly woman, who does not possess the eternal life of a Beatrice. After the grandmother's death another female character takes over as the protagonist's care-giver: Françoise the housekeeper. On top of tending to his material needs by cooking for him and generally taking care of the apartment, Françoise also does something the grandmother never had the opportunity to do: she assists the protagonist in his literary enterprise, the material aspect of which he compares to her domestic chores:

> Regardé par Françoise, comme tous les êtres sans prétention qui vivent à côté de nous ont une certaine intuition de nos tâches [...], je travaillerais auprès d'elle, et presque comme elle [...]; car, épinglant ici un feuillet supplémentaire, je bâtirais mon livre, je n'ose pas dire ambitieusement comme une cathédrale, mais tout simplement comme une robe. Quand je n'aurais pas auprès de moi toutes mes paperoles, comme disait Françoise, et que me manquerait juste celle dont j'aurais besoin, Françoise comprendrait bien mon énervement [...]. [E]lle s'était fait du travail littéraire une sorte de compréhension instinctive, plus juste que celle de bien des gens intelligents [...]. [...] Françoise [...] devinait mon bonheur et respectait mon travail. Elle se fâchait seulement que je racontasse d'avance mon article à Bloch, craignant qu'il me devançat, et disant: 'Tous ces gens-là, vous n'avez pas assez de méfiance, c'est des copiateurs.' [...] Au besoin Françoise ne pourrait-elle pas m'aider à les [mes paperoles] consolider, de la même façon qu'elle mettait des pièces aux parties usées de ses robes [...]? Françoise me dirait, en me montrant mes cahiers rongés [...] 'C'est tout mité, regardez, c'est malheureux [...]' et l'examinant comme un tailleur: 'Je ne crois pas que je pourrai la refaire, c'est perdu.' (IV, 610–11)
>
> [Observed by Françoise, since all the unpretentious beings who live by our side have a certain intuition of our tasks [...], I would work alongside her, and almost like her [...]; for, pinning an extra page here and there, I would construct my book, I dare not say ambitiously like a cathedral, but simply like a dress. When I would not have all my 'bits of paper', as Françoise called them, and I could not find the one that I needed, Françoise would understand my irritation [...]. She had developed a sort of instinctive understanding of the work of a writer, which was more exact than that of many intelligent people. [...] Françoise could tell how happy I was and respected my work. She would only get angry if I told Bloch about the article that I was writing, fearing that he would write it before me, and saying: 'All those people, you are too trusting with them: they are copiers.' [...] If necessary, would Françoise not be able to help me glue them [my bits of paper] together, just as she would replace the worn out sections of her dresses [...]? Françoise would say, holding out my tattered notebooks [...] 'It's full of moth holes, look, what a shame [...]' and examining it, like a tailor: 'I don't think I'll be able to fix that, it's gone.'

Françoise is described as the only one who understands the narrator-protagonist's working process and her help is invaluable.[34] Moreover, he compares his literary enterprise to her dressmaking, and two paragraphs later to her cooking: 'ne ferais-je pas mon livre de la façon que Françoise faisait ce bœuf mode [...]?' [would I not prepare my book in the same way as Françoise made her jellied beef [...]?] (IV, 612). Françoise's companionship, and the analogies made between their work, suggest an egalitarian move on Proust's behalf, of the kind called for by John Ruskin in 'The Nature of Gothic' (1853), where he criticized the industrial revolution's separation of manual and intellectual labour.[35] Françoise however remains in a subordinate role. She assists a writer whose level of education she will never possess, as made obvious by her erroneous 'copiateurs' (instead of *copieurs*). The passage strengthens the distinction between Françoise's social class and the narrator and implied reader's social class through the use of a plural first person ('nous' and 'nos') which excludes her: she is one of the creatures living by 'our' side, assisting us in 'our' tasks, but she is not *one of us*. The egalitarian potential of the comparison between her work and the narrator-protagonist's work is further hampered by the adverb 'presque'. The passage also upholds a clear separation of the intellectual from the primitive: while the narrator and his social equals are reasoning people ('gens', who can be either 'intelligents' or 'bêtes'), she is a being ('être'), deprived of pretension and ambition, who relies on instinct instead of knowledge ('intuition', 'instinctive'). The narrator appreciates Françoise's instinct far more than his peers' intellects,[36] and he acknowledges how important her material assistance is to his artistic enterprise. However, she will never be able to undertake a similar project. Therefore, as observed by Hughes, it is hard to tell whether we should see this passage as an egalitarian conflation of manual labour and intellectual work or as a bourgeois writer's social paternalism (2011: 224–25).

A parallel to the interaction between Françoise and the narrator-protagonist at the writing table is the relationship between the composer Vinteuil and his daughter's girlfriend. Vinteuil dies before he is able to transcribe clearly his masterpiece, a septet, leaving only messy notations which no one can decipher. This male character's masterpiece would be lost to the world, were it not for the efforts of the anonymous 'amie de Mlle Vinteuil' who is able to make sense of the notations (III, 766). Without her efforts, the piece of music would never reach an audience, and this could be interpreted as an example of a female character being invested with artistic prowess. But the fact remains that the young woman is only transmitting the work of a man. The novel's other two key artist characters, Elstir and Bergotte, seem to value women as part of their artistic process: Elstir's muse is his wife, of whom he paints many portraits and whom he worships for embodying his aesthetic ideal (II, 205–07); and Bergotte is 'généreux' with young girls because their company is conducive to writing, 'Il s'excusait à ses propres yeux parce qu'il savait ne pouvoir jamais si bien produire que dans l'atmosphère de se sentir amoureux.' [He excused himself in his own eyes because he knew that he always wrote his best work when he was feeling in love] (III, 688). The narrator-protagonist in *Le Temps retrouvé* foresees doing the same: 'de légères amours avec des jeunes filles en fleurs seraient un aliment choisi que je pourrais à la rigueur permettre à mon imagination semblable au cheval fameux qu'on ne nourrissait que de roses' [infatuations with blossoming young girls would be an exquisite fare that I might allow my imagination, just like the famous horse that was only fed roses] (IV, 565). The same idea is expressed in relation to Elstir's attraction to his wife: 'l'on compte sur les satisfactions du corps pour stimuler la force de l'esprit' [one counts on the satisfactions of the body to energize the mind] (II, 206).

The protagonist's two female love objects are also associated with the arts without themselves being artists: the young protagonist is infatuated with Gilberte, before even seeing her, because she is friends with Bergotte (I, 98–99).[37] His adult love, Albertine, paints, but does so in imitation of the male painter Elstir who remains the authority (III, 401).[38] She is associated with music in scenes in which she 'plays' the pianola (III, 874), but as the pianola is a mechanical instrument, this only involves turning a handle. When she exhibits a creative use of imagery, in a monologue in which she expresses her desire to eat ice cream, an activity which she compares, through elaborately detailed metaphors and similes, to destroying an ancient city or a mountain (III, 635–37), this is perceived as a disruption and a threat. Although the narrator-protagonist claims in strong terms that her pastiche of the narrative voice is evidence of his Pygmalian influence on her ('elle était mon œuvre' [she was my creation], III, 636), the insistence with which he claims this (three times, even interrupting her monologue), suggests a desperate need to reassert his authority. The reason behind the narrator-protagonist's discomfort is, naturally, that Albertine through her pastiche is mocking him as the novel's narrator.[39]

Although women in the *Recherche*, with the exception of actresses, tend to be marginalized in the context of artistic creation, it is suggested that aesthetic sensitivity is connected to feminine sensitivity. For instance, the homosexual Baron de Charlus is presented as having a particular appreciation of literature thanks to his 'sensibilité féminine' [feminine sensitivity] (II, 570).[40] In contrast, heterosexual men such as the protagonist's father and the career-driven Norpois disapprove of 'sensibleries' [oversensitiveness] (I, 36). They are motivated by practical concerns such as the weather (I, 91) and stocks and bonds (I, 445), and as a result lack the necessary refinement to appreciate literature. Norpois's sole criterion to judge the merit of a work of literature is whether it is relevant to current affairs (I, 464–65), and his critique of Bergotte, who does not satisfy this criterion, is expressed in terms of gender: 'au total tout cela est bien mièvre, bien mince, et bien peu viril' [at the end of the day this is all rather mawkish and lacks substance and virility] (I, 465). Femininity, sensitivity, and the arts thus all seem to be related. Moreover, in *Le Temps retrouvé* the language of motherhood is used to describe the writer's devotion to his future work, which will be 'comme un fils dont la mère mourante doit encore s'imposer la fatigue de s'occuper sans cesse' [like a son whose dying mother must still suffer the strain of continually caring for] (IV, 619). The ideal writer is thus a man in possession of what are seen as feminine qualities, but not a woman.

Despite being works from two different historical and cultural contexts, when it comes to moral and artistic guidance, the *Commedia* and the *Recherche* fall within the same gender dynamics: male guides must be surpassed and female guides nurture the male narrator-protagonists without ever threatening to rival their writing. Out of the two female guides, however, it is decidedly Beatrice who holds the greatest authority. Unlike the grandmother, who, as with most things in Proust, can be derided, Beatrice is an authoritative and respected figure. Moreover, Beatrice plays an active role in Dante's salvation, whereas in the *Recherche* it remains unclear to what extent the grandmother is able to exert a productive influence on her grandson. These divergences seem symptomatic of the two works' different attitudes towards the narrative of redemption. Virgil and Beatrice are key actors in the drama of Dante's Christian salvation; Swann and the grandmother are part of a less clear picture, in which art is pointed towards as the path to redemption, but without there being a certain end to the story.

Notes to Chapter 3

1. Admittedly the analogy is made by Proust in the mouth of Swann, who in a fit of rage calls the salon Verdurin: 'le dernier cercle de Dante' [the last circle of Dante's hell] (I, 283), and in the mouth of the narrator-protagonist, who is intimidated by the clientele of the Grand-Hôtel de Balbec (II, 24).
2. The connection has also been made by Marie Giuriceo (1983: 75–77). A fraudulent guide-figure can be found in Charlus, who, in the hope of seducing him, offers to be the narrator-protagonist's guide to high society.
3. For more detailed readings of this process see Harrison 2007 and Gragnolati 2013: 17–34.
4. On this subject see Barolini 2006: 70–101.
5. See for instance Hollander 1983 and Jacoff & Schnapp 1999.
6. Bergotte, as literary mentor, has been compared by Fowlie to Brunetto Latini, Dante's former teacher who is encountered in *Inferno* XV (1981: 225–26).
7. 'Car Swann en trouvait [du charme] aux choses, depuis qu'il était amoureux, comme au temps où, adolescent, il se croyait artiste; mais ce n'était plus le même charme, celui-ci, c'est Odette seule qui le leur conférait. Il sentait renaître en lui les inspirations de sa jeunesse qu'une vie frivole avait dissipées, mais elles portaient toutes le reflet, la marque d'un être particulier; et, dans les longues heures qu'il prenait maintenant un plaisir délicat à passer chez lui, seul avec son âme en convalescence, il redevenait peu à peu lui-même, mais à une autre' [For Swann saw so much [charm] in things ever since he was in love, just as at the time when as an adolescent he thought himself an artist [...]. He could feel the inspirations of his youth, which had been brushed aside by a frivolous lifestyle, being rekindled, but they now all bore the reflection, the mark of a single being; and in the long hours that he now found a delicate pleasure in spending home alone, in the company of his convalescent soul, he was little by little becoming himself again, but this time he belonged to her] (I, 235). The notion of 'being himself' seems to correspond to the 'soumission à la réalité intérieure' [submitting to one's inner reality] which is considered the first criterion for artistic sensitivity (IV, 461).
8. The oedipal understanding of poetic development is most famously described in Bloom 1973.
9. For a series of brief examples of the 'donna angelo' topos in Dante's Italian lyric context (namely Guinizzelli, Maestro Rinuccino, Monte Andrea, Lapo Gianni, and Cino da Pistoia), see Santagata 1999: 16–19.
10. Dante specifies: 'e dissi questo sonetto, lo quale comincia: *Gentil pensero*; e dico "gentile" in quanto ragionava di gentile donna, ché per altro era vilissimo' [And I wrote this sonnet which begins: A thought, gracious; and I say 'gracious' in so far as it involved a gracious lady, for in all other respects it was most base] (*VN*, XXXVIII, 4).
11. The final intermediary between Dante and God is another woman, the Virgin Mary, who is called on to assist Dante by St Bernard (*Paradiso* XXX). It has been argued by Lino Pertile that St Bernard comes as a surprising replacement for Beatrice: a more logical choice would have been St Lucy for instance, seeing as she, Mary, and Beatrice are the 'tre donne benedette' [three blessed women] protecting Dante (*Inf.* II, 124). 'Perhaps,' Pertile suggests, 'Saint Bernard embodies an ideal of chastity, spirituality, and mystical ardor that, deep in his consciousness, Dante feels unable to associate with Beatrice — or any woman for that matter' (2003: 113).
12. Barolini argues that *Beatrix Loquax* is a 'hybrid creature' who reflects the tension between 'the courtly tradition and the moralizing allegorical and didactic tradition in which female abstractions like Boethius's Lady Philosophy speak with authority and vigor' (2006: 367).
13. On the subject of Beatrice's erotic appeal see Psaki 2003.
14. In this context, a problematic example is *Par.* XXIII, 61–63, a famous passage known for Dante expressing difficulty at representing the unrepresentable that is Paradise. If we read the whole canto from the top, it is in fact Beatrice's smile that Dante is struggling to describe (see in particular lines 22–24 and 55–60). Despite Beatrice's warning that she is not Paradise, Dante cannot help but conflate the two.
15. 'Io vidi cose che mi fecero proporre di non dire più di questa benedetta infino a quanto che io potesse più degnamente trattare di lei. E di venire a ciò studio quanto posso, sì com'ella sae

veracemente. Sì che, se piacere sarà di colui a cui tutte le cose vivono, spero di dicer di lei quello che mai non fue detto d'alcuna' [I saw things that made me resolve to say no more about this blessèd one until I would be capable of writing about her in a nobler way] (*VN*, XLII, 1–2).

16. See the section '"Dante" and "Marcel"' in Chapter 1 for an analysis of this passage.
17. Misunderstandings of the figure of Beatrice persist today, as we can witness for instance in the *Dante's Inferno* videogame (Electronic Arts, 2010), in which Beatrice is a damsel in distress who must be rescued by Dante. The idea that a female beloved could be the authoritative figure guiding the male lover thus seems too radical a concept for twenty-first-century popular entertainment.
18. Merging fiction and biography, Borton argues: 'Each of the writers was guided by love remembered, Dante by his beloved Beatrice and Proust by his Albertine'. Borton's argument is that love for Albertine, like love for Beatrice, leads to new knowledge (1958: 37). Albertine has also been called a 'moderne Béatrice' by Kristeva (1994: 148). Balsamo (2007) suggests that Mlle de Saint-Loup is Proust's Beatrice, positing two key similarities between Dante and Proust: both works are to be read as autobiographies and in both a longed-for love is necessary to writing. The suggestion is refuted on both counts by Landy (2007): the narrator-protagonist of the *Recherche* is *not* Proust, and Mlle de Saint-Loup is no Beatrice.
19. For a comparative reading of Dante's mourning of Beatrice at the end of the *Vita nuova* and the narrator-protagonist's mourning of his grandmother in 'Les Intermittences du cœur', see Rushworth 2016: 127–39.
20. The grandmother is frequently paired with her daughter, the narrator-protagonist's mother, who shares similar values. After the grandmother's death, the narrator-protagonist's mother's efforts to emulate her mother become all the more conscious and obvious. The narrator-protagonist first becomes aware of this with a shock during the second stay in Balbec, when having heard him cry she rushes from the adjacent room, like his grandmother used to do (III, 513).
21. On these passages see the section '*Le Temps retrouvé* and the *paradiso terrestre*' in Chapter 4.
22. This is in 'Les Intermittences du cœur', a chapter analyzed in the section 'Deviations and Returns' in Chapter 2.
23. That is, until Norpois temptingly suggests that one can gain just as much influence and esteem through a literary career as one can through a diplomatic career (II, 431–32).
24. This is likely intentional since Proust began writing the *Recherche* with drafts for the first and final volume.
25. The washing of the feet on Maundy Thursday remains a liturgical rite in many Christian denominations.
26. On this episode see 'Deviations and Returns' in Chapter 2.
27. Ferrante (1992: 9) succinctly summarizes the association between Beatrice and Christ in the *paradiso terrestre* as follows: 'she is greeted with a phrase that applies to Christ and she uses his words of herself ("Modicum et non videbitis me..." ["A little while and you will not see me..."] *Purg.* 33.10); she rides on the chariot that represents the church, and Dante sees the gryphon change its nature in her eyes (*Purg.* 31.118–26).' On Beatrice in the *paradiso terrestre* see also Pertile 1998: 74–84. On Beatrice as Christ in the *Vita nuova* see Gragnolati 2013: 17–34.
28. Henry Becque was a nineteenth-century playwright who often shocked audiences by describing with wry realism late nineteenth-century bourgeois society. One social problem his theatre engaged with was the prejudice keeping women from earning a living. What is problematic is that in order to do so, he showed women who were not empowered. His two most famous plays are *Les Corbeaux* (1882), which shows a widow and her daughter being preyed upon by notaries after the death of the paterfamilias, their life only returning to a level of security after the daughter becomes engaged to an elderly man who is her father's former colleague and ambiguously concludes the play by telling her she is surrounded by crooks; and *La Parisienne* (1885), which shows the emptiness of the life of a married Parisian *bourgeoise*, a witty and charming woman whose only occupation is entertaining adulterous relationships which are as boring and deprived of romance as her marriage. It is therefore hard to tell how one should interpret Charlus's reference to the 'elevated throne' on which Becque places his female characters. If Proust did have this aspect of Becque's theatre in mind, the evidence suggests

sarcasm on Charlus's part. All we can say for certain is that Charlus's words compare the medieval condition of women with the early twentieth-century condition of women.

29. The lack of causal relation between the values which the grandmother seeks to impart to her grandson and his actions is noted by Hughes: 'the former's code of education for her grandson occasionally coincides with what he himself sees and admits to being his own urgent needs' (1983: 92).
30. This subordination of Christian narrative to individual romantic narrative can be found in modern readings of Dante, such as Borges 2001.
31. Ferrante (1975: 130–31) observes that in general terms, all men rely on the intercession of the Virgin Mary (see *Par.* xxx, 15), and on an individual level, earthly women such as for example Forese Donati's wife (*Purg.* xxiii, 85–93) act as intermediaries between God and man. Dante therefore is not the only man in the *Commedia* to be drawn towards good by a woman. See also Kay 2015.
32. For this reason maternal imagery was used in the twelfth century to speak of abbots or of Christ (Bynum 1982: 167).
33. On the maternalization of Beatrice see Jacoff 1982.
34. It is in this respect that Françoise is most obviously close to Céleste Albaret, Proust's housekeeper, who took care of him and helped him manage his manuscripts until he died.
35. On Ruskin and Proust see Hughes 2011: 71–75, and Gamble 2002.
36. As shown by Hughes, the narrator-protagonist at times even envies Françoise's 'primitive' instinctiveness and certainty (1983: 69–77).
37. Such a dynamic of relevance by proximity is also implied by the title 'Autour de Mme Swann', a choice of preposition which can be translated either as 'on the subject of Mme Swann' or as 'around Mme Swann', the latter interpretation suggesting that the true matter of interest is to be found in Mme Swann's surroundings (which include visits from Bergotte) rather than Mme Swann herself.
38. Towards the end of *Albertine disparue* we learn that Gilberte (in the guise not of the protagonist's beloved, but as his friend Robert de Saint-Loup's wife) paints, but this is not expanded upon (iv, 266).
39. Critics who have approached the passage by centring on the figure of the author, rather than the character, read it as an example of Proust's talent for self-critique through pastiche. This is the case, for example, of Milly 1970: 45, and 1985: 149. Margaret Gray argues that Proust scholarship is so eager to read this passage as an example of narratorial or authorial mastery, that it ignores that the passage is mocking and subversive (1992: 95–114).
40. Charlus is depicted according to the nineteenth-century German sexologist Karl Heinrich Ulrichs's understanding of male homosexuality as 'anima muliebris in corpore virili inclusa' [the soul of a woman inside the body of a man]. This aspect of Proust's writing on homosexuality was strongly criticized by Gide (Ladenson 1999: 39–41).

CHAPTER 4

Art and Redemption

The Redemption Narrative

Redemption, which is associated with the fulfilment of the narrator-protagonist's literary vocation, offers an overarching *telos* to Dante's and Proust's narratives.[1] The *Commedia* begins at a point at which the poet has lost his way and we are told that the journey through the three otherworldly realms is required to turn him away from the path to perdition. The *Recherche* shows us a protagonist who spends his life failing to set out on the path that would make his existence meaningful until the final twist of the revelations of the Matinée Guermantes, a section of *Le Temps retrouvé* known as 'L'Adoration perpétuelle'.[2] This section has in recent decades become unpopular among Proust scholars as a backlash against earlier criticism, which, associating the narrator-protagonist with Proust and the narrator-protagonist's projected book with the *Recherche*, understood the pronouncements of *Le Temps retrouvé* as a hermeneutic key to the *Recherche* itself.[3] Disregard for the triumph of art in *Le Temps retrouvé* is usually justified with a reference to the chronology of the *Recherche*'s composition: *Le Temps retrouvé* was first drafted around 1909–10, at the same time as the first volume of the *Recherche* (Finch 1977), consequently it could be argued that the novel, once expanded, no longer matched its intended ending. While I agree that we should draw a distinction between the *Recherche* and the narrator-protagonist's projected novel, it would in my view be short-sighted to ignore Proust's final volume, which despite its imperfections (Proust died before having time to review the draft) participates in a motif present throughout the novel: the celebration of art as a means to reach the other, and, perhaps even, to redeem an artist's earthly existence and bring a form of afterlife. Art is ascribed redemptive powers in *La Prisonnière*, one of the last volumes to be written, a fact which invalidates the suggestion that Proust with time abandoned the intention to raise art to a central role in his novel. The passages I address in this chapter are taken from across the *Recherche* (in particular *La Prisonnière* and *Le Temps retrouvé*), and are treated as equally important, regardless of their date of composition, in so far as they all play a part in the novel's overall treatment of artistic redemption.

Literature is presented in Dante as the means to redeem past sins and in Proust as the means to redeem a wasted existence (the *temps perdu* of the novel's title). This invests the act of writing with greater significance, making the narrator-protagonists' literary vocations their key to a meaningful existence. Whereas in

Dante's case this is redemption in the literal religious sense of the word, in the agnostic world of the *Recherche*, religious concepts such as redemption are used suggestively. Both works do however move in each other's direction at a profound level in so far as Dante places a strong emphasis on his identity as a poet, making his journey more than Everyman's pilgrimage to God, and Proust uses religious language in order to express the profound role that art can play in our lives, which has led critics to speak of a 'religion of art' in Proust (Bucknall 1969), at times in explicitly Dantean terms (Bales 1975: 117–38, and Cocking 1982: 91). Proust's use of Christian motifs and Dante's emphasis on his role as poet thus create strong parallels in their treatment of redemption. This chapter will explore the various ways in which the *Commedia* and the *Recherche* invest art with an importance at least equal to that of one's life on earth, which at first sight corresponds to the 'redemptive aesthetic' critiqued by Leo Bersani (1990), that is, the belief that art is a correction of life. However, I will demonstrate that although they set out an important relationship between art and redemption, Dante and Proust also question the amount of power that art does (and should) hold over human existence. Proust does so through a characteristic combination of doubt, ambiguity, and humour, and Dante by reminding his readers that no matter how artistically talented, we are all powerless before God's judgment.

Le Temps retrouvé and the *paradiso terrestre*

The *Recherche* ends at a 'point de départ vers une vie nouvelle' [starting-point for a new life] (IV, 496), in a movement pointing both backwards, to all that we have just read, the raw material of the narrator-protagonist's life which is to be 'redeemed' through artistic creation, and forwards, to the future act of creation. In the *Commedia* the scene of repentance and absolution, in preparation for a literary redemption, takes place two thirds of the way through, in a section set in the Garden of Eden (*Purgatorio* XXVIII–XXXIII). The *Recherche* has no equivalent to Dante's *Paradiso*, which is a realm beyond time and earthly concerns, in which souls find beatitude by aligning their will with that of God. In *Le Temps retrouvé* we find expressions such as 'extra-temporel' and 'en dehors du temps' [outside time] (IV, 450), but this refers not to a divine realm beyond earthly experience (as understood by Dante),[4] but to the experience triggered by involuntary memory, which is a human phenomenon, as pithily summarized by William Empson:

> Proust, at the end of that great novel, having convinced the reader with the full sophistication of his genius that he is going to produce an apocalypse, brings out with pathetic faith, as a fact of absolute value, that sometimes when you are living in one place you are reminded of living in another place, and this, since you are now apparently living in two places, means that you are outside time, in the only state of beatitude he can imagine. (1953: 131)

A more charitable perspective is offered by Malcolm Bowie, who suggests we think of Proust as 'an artful manipulator of ordinary time rather than as the harbinger of an unusual, specialised or occult temporal vision' (1998: 64). The *Recherche* is indeed a novel about time as experienced by humans on earth. This is also the self-imposed goal of the narrator-protagonist's future work, which provides the novel's concluding words: 'décrire les hommes [...] comme occupant une place [...] prolongée sans mesure puisqu'ils touchent simultanément [...] à des époques vécues par eux si distantes, entre lesquelles tant de jours sont venus se placer — dans le Temps' [describing mankind [...] as occupying a space [...] extending beyond measure since they simultaneously touch [...] periods which they have experienced so far apart from one another — periods of their lives between which so many days have come — in Time] (IV, 625). Proust's narrator in fact shows himself suspicious of an un-earthly Paradise of the kind represented by Dante:

> Oui, [...] le souvenir [...] nous fait tout à coup respirer un air nouveau, précisément parce que c'est un air qu'on a respiré autrefois, cet air plus pur que les poètes ont vainement essayé de faire régner dans le paradis et qui ne pourrait donner cette sensation profonde de renouvellement que s'il avait été respiré déjà, car les vrais paradis sont les paradis qu'on a perdus. (IV, 449)
>
> [Yes, [...] memory [...] allows us to suddenly breathe in new air, precisely because it is an air that we have breathed before, this purer air that poets have vainly sought to place in paradise and which could only ever offer this profound feeling of renewal if it has been breathed before; the real paradises are the paradises we have lost.]

Proust's 'vrais paradis' suggest that a more productive parallel is to be found in the *paradiso terrestre*, where Dante breathes an air he has breathed before and is reunited with what he had lost: Beatrice. This encounter, which was considered in the previous chapter, is the climax of the purgatorial paradigm studied by Barolini: 'forward motion is a way of recuperating and redeeming the past, of returning to lost innocence and our collective point of origin, the garden of Eden' (1992: 101). Barolini's words 'recuperating and redeeming the past' sound more than familiar to anyone who has studied Proust's *Temps retrouvé*, and she is not the only scholar to express herself in Proustian terms when studying this section of the *Commedia*. Ricardo Quinones frames one of his observations with the English title of Proust's last volume: 'Time, to be sure, is transcended and even reversed in purgatory, where the Garden is regained' (1972: 73). Piero Boitani writes of Dante's reunion with Beatrice: 'The "theophany" with which the scene opened becomes "recherche du temps perdu" and at the same time anagnorisis. [...] It is this phenomenon that Proust describes with marvelous precision and insight towards the end of *Time Regained*' (1989: 164).[5] And Francesca Southerden, in reading the *paradiso terrestre* as a moment of poetic redemption, also cites Proust:

> Having restored Beatrice from the dead, language takes on an even more profound role in a process of textual redirectioning that allows Dante to recuperate his 'temps perdu' ('lost time'), redeeming a poetic past as much as a real one. (2010: 176–77)

It is this idea of the redemption of the past through literature which I believe most closely connects the endings of Proust's *Recherche* and Dante's *paradiso terrestre*.

In the *Recherche* the (re)turn to literature comes at a point when the narrator-protagonist has lost 'la foi dans les lettres' [faith in literature] (IV, 447) and as a result given up all ambition to be a writer:

> Mais c'est quelquefois au moment où tout nous semble perdu que l'avertissement arrive qui peut nous sauver, on a frappé à toutes les portes qui ne donnent sur rien, et la seule par où on peut entrer [...], on y heurte sans le savoir, et elle s'ouvre. (IV, 445)
>
> [But sometimes it is in the very moment when all seems lost that the warning that will save us arrives. One has knocked on all the doors that lead nowhere, and then [...] we stumble upon the door that can let us in without even realizing, and it opens.]

A series of involuntary memories brought by the sensation of tripping on a stone, the sound of a spoon, and the texture of a napkin allow him to suddenly re-experience moments of his past so vividly, that for the first time he truly appreciates how interesting his ordinary life is. This leads him to regain his faith and decide to write a work that will do justice to the temporal complexity of human existence. Barbara Bucknall argues that the plot of *Le Temps retrouvé* follows the pattern of Christian conversion described by William James:

> It was a normal day like any other; I was, if anything, rather more tired and depressed than usual. But, without paying attention to what I was doing (yet at the prompting of God, all unaware and undeserving as I was), I performed a particular action which fell a little outside my normal routine, and suddenly my heart was flooded with divine grace. (1969: 155)

Proust thus assigns to involuntary memory the role played by saving divine intervention in the Christian narrative of conversion.[6] Moreover, the narrator-protagonist's dependence on the involuntary in *Le Temps retrouvé* entails an admission of the intrinsic shortcomings of volition, since no conscious attempt can recover 'le temps perdu, devant quoi les efforts de ma mémoire et de mon intelligence échouaient toujours' [lost time, before which the efforts of my memory and intelligence would always fail] (IV, 450). The insufficiency of the voluntary efforts of memory and intelligence in Proust is mirrored by the insufficiency of reason in Dante's *Commedia*, as embodied by his two guides: the pagan Virgil's counsel cannot lead Dante all the way, for it is guided by reason alone, hence the need for Beatrice, who can be read allegorically as a figure for reason illuminated by faith and/or grace.

In the *Commedia* it is Beatrice who performs the saving divine intervention in conjunction with the Virgin Mary and St Lucy, who warn Beatrice of the danger Dante finds himself in (*Inf.* II, 94–116). Having sent Virgil to guide Dante through Hell and Purgatory, Beatrice does not appear in person until *Purgatorio* XXX, in a passage which has surprised generation upon generation of readers by depicting not a tender lovers' reunion, but a harsh confrontation. Beatrice's opening words are:

> Dante, perché Virgilio se ne vada,
> non pianger anco, non pianger ancora;
> ché pianger ti conven per altra spada. (*Purg.* XXX, 55–57)
>
> [Dante, because Virgil has left, | do not cry, do not cry yet; | for you will be crying from another sword.]

The sword to which she refers are her words, which will confront Dante with his sins. Beatrice first lists Dante's offences to her attendants, speaking of him in the third person:

> questi fu tal ne la sua vita nova
> virtüalmente, ch'ogne abito destro
> fatto averebbe in lui mirabil prova.
> [...]
> Alcun tempo il sostenni col mio volto:
> mostrando li occhi giovanetti a lui,
> meco il menava in dritta parte vòlto.
>
> Sì tosto come in su la soglia fui
> di mia seconda etade e mutai vita,
> questi si tolse a me, e diessi altrui.
>
> Quando di carne a spirto era salita,
> e bellezza e virtù cresciuta m'era,
> fu' io a lui men cara e men gradita;
>
> e volse i passi suoi per via non vera,
> imagini di ben seguendo false. (*Purg.* xxx, 115–31)

[This man was such in his new life | in potential, that any positive disposition | would have born admirable results in him. | [...] | for a time I encouraged him with my appearance: | with my youthful eyes, | I led him alongside me on the right path. | As soon as I was on the threshold | of my second age and changed life | he took himself away from me, giving himself to another. | When I had risen from flesh to spirit, | and my beauty and virtue were all the greater, | I was less dear to him and less appreciated; | he turned his steps towards an untrue path, | and followed false images of good.]

In the following canto Beatrice addresses Dante directly, demanding that he confess his guilt (*Purg.* xxxi, 5–6). She then repeats her accusations once before his confession (*Purg.* xxxi, 22–30), and a second time again after his confession (*Purg.* xxxi, 43–63), so as to leave the reader with no doubt as to Dante's culpability.

As has been remarked by Anna Maria Chiavacci Leonardi, what is striking about Beatrice's accusations is that they are based on Dante's writings: 'Non solo la *Vita Nuova* è citata espressamente, come la "pargoletta" delle *Rime*, ma tutti gli eventi narrati [...] sono eventi che appartengono alla poesia, non alla biografia storica di Dante' [Not only is the *Vita nuova* expressly cited, as well as the 'pargoletta' from Dante's *Rime*, but all of the events narrated are events that belong to the realm of poetry, not Dante's historical biography] (1991: 879–80). Barański in his reading of the episode also observes, 'the viator not only confesses to having betrayed his beloved, but also to having written bad, because dishonest, literature' (1995: 12). The *Vita nuova* had shown Dante to be inconstant after Beatrice's death (*VN*, xxxv–xxxviii), but repenting after her return in a vision (*VN*, xxxix), and ended on the newly faithful Dante's promise to study so that he could write a work worthy of her (*VN*, xlii, 2–3). Beatrice's literary critique in the Garden of Eden can therefore be understood both as a critique of the parts of the *Vita nuova* in which Dante is inconstant to her and also as a critique of the works he wrote after the *Vita nuova*, such as for example the *Convivio*, in which he was not faithful to her memory. Lombardi pushes this interpretation even further, noting that Beatrice is not only critiquing Dante's subsequent infatuations, but also his love for her when she was alive, for the very attributes that Beatrice condemns in Eden (these other women are mortal, beautiful, and new), were once hers (2018: 143).

In *Le Temps retrouvé* the narrator-protagonist's fall from grace is described as follows:

> Comme à ce *François le Champi*, contemplé pour la première fois dans ma petite chambre de Combray, pendant la nuit peut-être la plus douce et la plus triste de ma vie où j'avais, hélas! [...] obtenu de mes parents une première abdication d'où je pouvais faire dater le déclin de ma santé et de mon vouloir, mon renoncement chaque jour aggravé à une tâche difficile. (IV, 465)
>
> [Like the copy of *François le Champi*, contemplated for the first time in my little Combray bedroom, during what was perhaps the sweetest and saddest night of my life when I had, alas! [...] obtained the first concession from my parents, from which I could date the decline of my health and my will, my increasingly definite abandonment of a difficult task.]

> C'était de cette soirée, où ma mère avait abdiqué, que datait, avec la mort lente de ma grand-mère, le déclin de ma volonté, de ma santé. (IV, 621)
>
> [It was from that night, when my mother ceded, that dated, along with the slow death of my grandmother, the decline of my will, of my health.]

Justin O'Brien (1964) has argued that these passages work in the same way as the religious visual art of the Middle Ages and Renaissance, reminding the viewer of the hero's fall at the moment of his redemption. Beatrice's description of Dante's fall is far from discrete as it takes up great parts of Cantos XXX and XXXI, is given in direct speech, and repeats its key points. In Proust all we have are passing comments made by the narrator: the first *François le Champi* passage is part of the realization that time can be recaptured, whereas the second one comes at the end of the novel as part of the narrator's fear of not having enough time left to live to write his work. Yet, although this allusion to the narrator-protagonist's fall is more subtle than Beatrice's remonstrance, it is highly charged due to its references to the dead grandmother, who, as we saw in the previous chapter, provides him with his moral compass and thus acts as the *Recherche*'s Beatrice figure. The suggestion that his failure to write is somehow connected to the grandmother's death is therefore a serious self-accusation.[7]

Both Dante's and Proust's protagonists sinned against the expectations of a woman whom they loved. Instead of fulfilling their potential and writing (good) literature, both followed false images of happiness that turned them away from a higher truth that was not to be found in the worldly pleasures that they pursued. This is suggested in both works through very similar vocabulary. In *Purgatorio* XXX we read, 'imagini di ben seguendo false' [followed false images of good] (line 131), and in *Purgatorio* XXXI, 'col falso lor piacer volser miei passi' [their false pleasures turned my steps away] (line 35). And in *Le Temps retrouvé* we read:

> Sur l'extrême différence qu'il y a entre l'*impression vraie* que nous avons eue d'une chose et l'*impression factice* que nous nous en donnons quand volontairement nous essayons de nous la représenter, je ne m'arrêtais pas [...]; et je comprenais que la vie pût être jugée médiocre, bien qu'à certains moments elle parût si belle, parce que dans les premiers c'est sur tout autre chose qu'elle-même, sur des *images qui ne gardent rien d'elle*, qu'on la juge et qu'on la déprécie. (iv, 448; my emphasis)
>
> [I did not dwell on the difference between *a true impression* and the *false impression* that we offer when we voluntarily seek to represent it [...]; and I understood that life could be judged mediocre, even though in some moments it seemed beautiful, because in the former case one has judged it on the basis of something else, on the basis of *images that preserve nothing of it*, and depreciated it.]

In contrast with the disappointing 'jouissance immédiate' [immediate gratification] (iv, 450) or 'novità con sì breve uso' [novelty of equally brief use] (*Purg.* xxxi, 60) encountered by the protagonists when they were 'living in sin', there exists a true and productive pleasure. In Proust's world, this is the joy that comes with the epiphanies of *Le Temps retrouvé*, which was already foreshadowed by episodes such as that of the madeleine and of Vinteuil's septet:

> Cette contemplation, quoique d'éternité, était fugitive. Et pourtant je sentais que le plaisir qu'elle m'avait, à de rares intervalles, donné dans ma vie, était le seul qui fût fécond et véritable. Le signe de l'irréalité des autres ne se montre-t-il pas assez? (iv, 454)
>
> [Though it was eternity that I contemplated, my contemplation was fleeting. And yet I could feel that the pleasure it had given me at rare intervals during my life, was the only fruitful and true one. Was the unreality of all others not manifest?]

In Dante's world, true pleasure is found in the experience of the love of God, which had already manifested itself on earth through Beatrice and his love for her. Beatrice describes herself as Dante's 'sommo piacer' [highest pleasure] (*Purg.* xxxi, 52), in contrast with the pleasures envisaged with other mortal women, which fall under the category of 'cose fallaci' [false things] (*Purg.* xxxi, 56).

It is postulated in *Le Temps retrouvé* that 'la grandeur de l'art véritable [...] c'était de retrouver, de ressaisir, de nous faire connaître cette réalité loin de laquelle nous vivons, de laquelle nous nous écartons' [the greatness of true art [...] was to find again, to recapture, to allow us to know this reality that we live so far from, that we turn away from] (iv, 474). The verb *écarter* resonates with the words 'volser miei passi' [turned me away] in Dante's confession (*Purg.* xxxi, 35): both men turned away from what would have made their life meaningful. By the end of *Le Temps retrouvé*, the narrator-protagonist is impatient to start writing the novel that will redeem his hitherto fruitless existence. *Purgatorio* ends with Dante freshly redeemed and thus 'pure' enough to ascend to Heaven (*Purg.* xxxiii, 142–45). Both the end of *Purgatorio* and the end of the *Recherche* are a 'point de départ vers une vie nouvelle' (iv, 496): Proust's protagonist will finally start writing his long anticipated 'œuvre', whereas Dante's narrator-protagonist is prepared to travel where no other mortal has travelled and to write a new kind of poetry, superior to all that he — or anyone else for that matter — has produced before, as announced in *Par.* II, 1–18. This is why, as has been observed by Barański (1995), Dante's 'new life', or in other words, new poetry, begins not at the end of the *Vita nuova*, but at the end of *Purgatorio*.

The Religion of Art

Dante's and Proust's works invest art with salvific qualities both on the level of their narrator-protagonist's spiritual fate and on the general level of their implied readers' spiritual fate. In Proust this is most forcefully done in 'L'Adoration perpétuelle', where we find pronouncements such as, 'l'art est ce qu'il y a de plus réel, la plus austère école de vie, et le vrai Jugement dernier' [art is the most real thing, the most austere school of life, and the true Last Judgment] (IV, 458) and 'La vraie vie, la vie enfin découverte et éclaircie, la seule vie par conséquent pleinement vécue, c'est la littérature' [Real life, life at last discovered and explained, the only life fully lived, is literature] (IV, 474). As well as being an act of expiation for the guilt felt towards the death of his grandmother, writing a work of literature is described as 'un égoïsme utilisable pour autrui' [a selfishness useful to others] (IV, 613), in so far as this work will serve its future readers as a heuristic tool (IV, 610). In the *Commedia*, writing his masterpiece is what allows Dante to turn from a path of error and to reject non-divinely sanctioned poetry: he redeems himself by writing a poem that will save others 'in pro del mondo che mal vive' [for the world that lives in sin] (*Purg.* XXXII, 103). The *Commedia* can also be described as an 'égoïsme utilisable pour autrui' in the sense that it can be read as an Augustinian exemplum: Dante is only talking about himself in so far as it is helpful to others.[8]

Both works suggest that artistic creation, and in particular writing, is a moral duty. In the *Commedia* this is done by having blessed souls instruct Dante to write the poem, making writing a God-willed religious duty.[9] Besides Beatrice, a key example is Dante's ancestor Cacciaguida, who tells him 'rimossa ogne menzogna, | tutta tua visïon fa manifesta' [excluding any lies, | make every part of your vision manifest] (*Par.* XVII, 127–28). By calling himself a 'scribe' rather than a 'creator' (*Purg.* XXIV, 52–54), Dante further puts himself in the position of one serving God, comparable to David 'the humble psalmist' (*Purg.* X, 65).[10] Suggesting that he is divinely sanctioned allows Dante to eschew charges of hubris, a risk that is all the greater in the *Paradiso*. The *contrapasso* (punishment) of the terrace of pride, in which the penitent souls have to carry boulders on their backs, will be turned on its head in *Paradiso* through the metaphor that Dante uses to describe the effort involved in composing his poem:

> Ma chi pensasse il ponderoso tema
> e l'omero mortal che se ne carca,
> nol biasmerebbe se sott'esso trema. (*Par.* XXIII, 64–66)

> [Anyone who were to consider the weighty subject matter | and the mortal shoulder bearing it, | would not blame it for trembling under its load.]

This tour de force breaks the mould established in *Purgatorio* XI, according to which artists who take too much pride in their skills will be punished in the afterlife by bearing a weight that makes them look down humbly. Dante, by describing his work of art as a humbling burden rather than a source of pride, implies that the act of writing a Christian poem is a form of penitence, which ultimately allows him to look upwards, to God. However, as Barolini reminds us, Dante's self-portrayal as a humble *scriba dei* should not be taken at face value, given that 'the only way to have practiced humility in writing *Paradiso* would have been not to write it' (1992: 54).

In the *Recherche* artistic creation is often invested with a moral dimension through religious similes and metaphors. For example, Swann's failure to devote himself to art is described in the language of a failed conversion. In *À l'ombre des jeunes filles en fleurs*, it is suggested that the virtue present in Bergotte's literature compensates for his sins as a man, and this is justified through the following simile, which invests the writer with the authority to provide moral guidance for others:

> Comme les grands docteurs de l'Église commencèrent souvent tout en étant bons par connaître les péchés de tous les hommes, et en tirèrent leur sainteté personnelle, souvent les grands artistes tout en étant mauvais se servent de leurs vices pour arriver à concevoir la règle morale de tous. (I, 548)
>
> [Just as the great Doctors of the Church, while remaining good, often began by familiarizing themselves with the sins of all men, and drew from them their personal sanctity, often great artists, while being bad, use their sins to create moral guidelines for the rest of us.]

However, a sense of doubt is cast on the merit of Bergotte's work when he is confronted with that of a greater artist, the painter Ver Meer.

Bergotte dies in a museum, in front of the *View of Delft*, a work of art so skilfully and attentively executed that it leads him to question the value of his own artistic output. As he stares at a detail in the painting he has the following vision: 'Dans une céleste balance lui apparaissait, chargeant l'un des plateaux, sa propre vie, tandis que l'autre contenait le petit pan de mur si bien peint en jaune' [In a celestial set of scales he could see, in one platter, his own life, while the other one bore the little section of wall so beautifully painted in yellow] (III, 692). Proust in this passage is appropriating the iconography of the 'psychostasia', that is the weighing of the soul on a set of scales, which can be traced back to Graeco-Roman and Egyptian religious art.[11] In Christian visual culture, the scales are most frequently found in late-medieval depictions of the Last Judgment (Angheben 2007). Proust would have not only encountered the image in churches, but also have read about it in Émile Mâle's *L'Art religieux du XIIIième siècle en France*, which in its chapter on representations of the Last Judgment indicates the wide-spread and varied use of the metaphor of the scales, citing examples from the churches and cathedrals of Conques, Chartres, Bourges, Amiens, and Le Mans (1898: 475–78).[12] In the *Recherche*, Bergotte expires and the image of the scales represents his individual last judgment, with Ver Meer's painting being the measure of a life well lived. In this episode, the narrator associates the artist's commitment to produce work of the highest quality with the believer's observance of religious virtues, since both forms of devotion are motivated by something that lies beyond an individual's life on earth:

> Il n'y a aucune raison dans nos conditions de vie sur cette terre pour que nous nous croyions obligés à faire le bien, à être délicats, même à être polis, ni pour l'artiste athée à ce qu'il se croie obligé de recommencer vingt fois un morceau dont l'admiration qu'il excitera importa peu à son corps mangé par les vers, comme le pan de mur jaune que peignit avec tant de science et de raffinement un artiste à jamais inconnu, à peine identifié sous le nom de Ver Meer. Toutes ces obligations qui n'ont pas leur sanction dans la vie présente semblent appartenir à un monde différent. (III, 693)
>
> [Given our conditions of life on this earth, there is no reason for us to feel the need to do good, to be delicate or even to be polite, nor for the atheist artist to feel he must start the same piece over again twenty times, the admiration that the piece will excite mattering little to his maggot-ridden corpse, just like the section of wall painted with so much science and refinement by an artist forever unknown, barely identified under the name Ver Meer. All these obligations that are not sanctioned in this life seem to belong to an altogether different world.]

The adjective 'athée' suggests that artists such as Ver Meer are committed to their art even if they do not believe in life after death. The duty to create art is thus presented as something that transcends one's life on earth, even when one does not believe in an afterlife. The passage therefore further confirms the definition of the artist's work as a selfishness useful to others, since while the work of art will be appreciated by generation after generation, this is of no benefit to the dead artist. Finally, the reference to a 'monde différent' is not to be taken lightly in a work that does not subscribe to a belief in Heaven: it raises the question of what this otherworldly source of sanction might be, if it is not the Christian God.

These types of passages have led critics to speak of a Proustian 'religion of art', in which art has come to replace God as a source of worship. Bucknall (1969: 19) and Cocking (1982: 43) have suggested that Christian motifs are used as a vehicle to stir in the reader sentiments that will give greater authority to Proust's pronouncements on the value of art.[13] Some critics go so far as to compare the goals of the *Recherche* to those of religious works. Bales, having brought our attention to the parallels made both by Proust in his correspondence and the narrator of the *Recherche* between the structure and scope of their novel and that of churches or cathedrals, compares the *Recherche* to another cathedral-like literary construction: the *Commedia* (1975: 117–38).[14] He sees Dante's and Proust's structure and goals as differing only in terms of cultural context:

> That Proust's heaven is godless (unless that god be art), while Dante's contains the Deity, is largely a matter of terminology: if one were to be rash — though to a large extent accurate — one could say that each attains to a sort of mystical state, and the frame of reference is largely irrelevant, depending mainly on the social and religious climate of the time. (1975: 134–35)

Both works, according to Bales, share a 'didactic purpose' which differs only in terms of the material that they are teaching (1975: 137). Proust, therefore, 'was right to call *A la recherche* a cathedral, for, in modern form, its function is similar' (1975: 138). Benjamin Crémieux makes a similar argument, but through a different medieval comparison, calling the *Recherche* 'l'équivalent laïque de l'*Itinerarium Mentis ad Deum* — l'itinéraire de l'âme vers Dieu — de saint Bonaventure' [the secular equivalent of the l'*Itinerarium mentis ad deum* — the soul's itinerary to God — by Saint Bonaventure] (cited in Mouton 1968: 21).[15]

Though they make an important point, these accounts of Proust's novel skirt around certain important differences. First, Proust's *Recherche* never seeks to move beyond the earthly experiences of human subjects. As we saw in Chapter 2, the most distant journey possible in the *Recherche* is not towards God, but towards other individuals' selves which can be approached, on a one-on-one basis, through the contemplation of their artworks (III, 761–62). In Dante one sins against God, but in Proust one only sins against oneself, as did Swann by failing to fulfil his potential. Instead of the shared lost point of origin that is the Garden of Eden, the *Recherche* speaks of 'paradis perdus' [lost paradises] (IV, 449) and 'patrie perdue' [lost homeland] (III, 761) as metaphors for one's individual subjectivity (the 'moi profond' [the deep self]).[16] Moreover, Dante travels beyond the 'temps retrouvé' of Eden, which is not the climax of the poem, but a stop on the way. As Mouton is forced to conclude in his book on Proust 'devant Dieu' [before God]: 'Seul Dante a pu deviner l'incandescence de Dieu, qui est insoutenable. Dante n'y est arrivé qu'après l'obscurité de l'enfer et la lueur incertaine du purgatoire; Proust n'est pas allé plus loin que cette lueur incertaine' [Only Dante could envisage the incandescence of God, which is unbearable. Dante reached it after the obscurity of hell and the uncertain glimmer of purgatory; Proust never went beyond that uncertain glimmer] (1968: 103). Secondly, as I shall argue in this chapter's concluding section, though Proust does invest art with moral and perhaps even religious qualities, this 'religion of art' is not given absolute faith. This means that even if we do call it a 'religion', the *Recherche*'s perspective on art is very different from the *Commedia*'s perspective on Christianity, written and narrated as it is by a believer. Finally, what Proustians have referred to as the 'religion of art' is critiqued by the *Commedia*, which maintains a hierarchic distinction between human achievement and the work of God. One of the rare uses of the word *artista* in the poem indeed contrasts the unsteadiness of the human hand with the perfection of God's creations: 'l'artista | ch'a l'abito de l'arte ha man che trema [the craftsman | who practices his art with a trembling hand] (*Par.* XIII, 77–78). A similar distinction is made on the terrace of pride, which is framed by God-made *basso rilievi* which are so realistic that they seem to speak (*Purg.* X, 37–39) and therefore surpass by far the man-made works that will come under discussion in *Purgatorio* XI.[17] Dante's poem, moreover, sounds a clear warning against the overpraising of artistic legacy in two important episodes: the encounter with the writer Brunetto Latini and the encounter with the illuminator Oderisi da Gubbio.

Dante's former master, Brunetto Latini stands as an example of what happens when an author's commitment to his work is stronger than his commitment to the salvation of his soul. Encountered in the *Inferno*, Brunetto still believes that he lives on in his books as made clear by his parting words to Dante: 'Sieti raccommandato il mio Tesoro, | nel qual io vivo ancora, e più non cheggio' [Hold dear my Treasure,

| in which I live on, and I shall ask for nothing more] (*Inf.* xv, 119–20). Brunetto's farewell reveals that despite his experience of the eternal tortures of Hell, made most obvious by his scorched face (*Inf.* xv, 26), his attention is not on what has happened to his soul, but only on the fate of his major work, entitled *Li livres dou Tresor.* Dante in the encounter shows a lot of affinity with Brunetto, not only from an affective point of view, but also from an intellectual one:

ché 'n la mente m'è fitta, e or m'accora,
la cara e buona imagine paterna
di voi quando nel mondo ad ora ad ora

m'insegnavate come l'uom s'etterna. (*Inf.* xv, 82–85)

[My heart breaks at the fixed image in my mind | of you, dear, kind and fatherly | when in the world, day after day, | you would teach me how man makes himself eternal.]

The notion that one can make oneself eternal through literature is revisited in *Purgatorio* xi, where Dante encounters the illuminator Oderisi da Gubbio, who is expiating his artistic pride. In a lengthy monologue Oderisi exposes the perishability of artistic renown, presenting Dante's poetic talent as a negligible asset in the greater scheme of things:

Non è il mondan romore altro ch'un fiato
di vento, ch'or vien quinci e or vien quindi,
e muta nome perché muta lato.

Che voce avrai tu più, se vecchia scindi
da te la carne, che se fossi morto
anzi che tu lasciassi il 'pappo' e 'l 'dindi',

pria che passin mill'anni? ch'è più corto
spazio a l'etterno, ch'un muover di ciglia
al cerchio che più tardi in cielo è torto.
[...]
La vostra nominanza è color d'erba,
che viene e va, e quei la discolora
per cui ella esce de la terra acerba. (*Purg.* xi, 100–17)

[Worldly fame is nothing more than a gust | Of wind, which blows here and then blows there, | And changes name because it changes direction. | What more renown will you have, if you are old when | you leave your bodily existence, than if you die | before learning to say 'daddy' or 'dindins', | before a thousand years have passed? a period | that compared to eternity is even shorter | than the bat of an eyelid to the slowest turning sphere. | [...] | Your reputation is the colour of grass, | which comes and goes, and he who discolours it | is the one who makes it grow out of the raw earth.]

The role of these encounters is however far from straightforward, and the poem contradicts Oderisi's warning more than once. This is first done by having a group of characters whose fate after death is directly influenced by their 'nominanza' [reputation], a word which appears only once outside Oderisi's speech. In *Inferno* iv we encounter the illustrious pagans Homer, Horace, Ovid, and Lucan, who reside together with Virgil in a castle in Limbo. As Virgil explains to Dante:

> L'onrata nominanza
> che di lor suona sù ne la tua vita,
> grazïa acquista in ciel che sì li Avanza. (*Inf.* IV, 76–78)

[Their honourable reputation | which resounds above, in your life, | earns them heavenly grace and advances them.]

The fate of the 'bella scola' (the fair school, as these pagan poets are collectively classified) contradicts Oderisi: the longevity of the classical authors' works protects them from the physical tortures of Hell and earns them special treatment even in Limbo, where they have a source of light and are given an amenable abode: a castle, surrounded by protective walls, a stream, and vegetation.[18]

If *Inferno* IV already suggests that Oderisi's words of warning do not apply to the 'bella scola', the rest of the *Commedia* suggests that they apply even less to Dante. Brunetto Latini's belief in a literary afterlife will eventually be validated in Dante's case through the encounter with his ancestor Cacciaguida in the *Paradiso*. As noted by Barolini (1992: 122–42), Cacciaguida recasts the 'etternarsi' of Brunetto's teachings through another neologism, 'infuturarsi' (*Par.* XVII, 22), which he applies to Dante. Moreover, Dante himself recasts Brunetto's words when he tells Cacciaguida that while, on the one hand, he fears persecution by those he will criticize in his poem, on the other hand, if he chooses to flatter rather than tell the truth, he will not be read in the future:

> s'io al vero son timido amico,
> temo di perder viver tra coloro
> che questo tempo chiameranno antico. (*Par.* XVII, 118–20)

[If I am not the loyal friend of truth, | I fear I will forfeit living among those | who will call this time ancient.]

Dante's substantive use of the verb 'viver' echoes Brunetto's 'nel qual io vivo ancora'. This parallel with the vainglorious sinner would have been avoided if the emphasis had been placed on the poem ('I fear that my work will not be read'). 'Temo di perder viver' clearly tells us that Dante believes that his work, provided it is worthy, will allow him to live on. This introduces us to an important negotiation taking place in the *Commedia*: Dante needs to square his faith in his literary talent with his religious faith, which forbids him to take pride in his artistic identity.

Transcending the Individual

The term most frequently used to refer to creative talent in the *Commedia* is 'ingegno' from the Latin *ingenium*, which referred to the natural faculties with which a human is born.[19] In Dante's case, the two things are one and the same since his natural talent is poetic creativity. Indeed, Beatrice accuses Dante of failing to live up to his poetic potential through the metaphor of the cultivation of a seed (*Purg.* XXX, 118–20), which is the same metaphor used by Charles Martel in *Paradiso* VIII when he argues that an ideal society is one in which individuals follow their own natural inclinations (*Par.* VIII, 139–48). In *Paradiso* XXII, Dante will thank his stars (specifically, the Gemini constellation), and by extension God, for the aptitude they blessed him with upon birth:

O gloriose stelle, o lume pregno
di gran virtù, dal quale io riconosco
tutto, qual che sia, il mio ingegno,

con voi nasceva e s'ascondeva vosco
quelli ch'è padre d'ogne mortal vita
Quand'io sentì di prima l'aere Tosco. (*Par.* XXII, 112–17)

[O glorious stars, o light brimming | with great power, I owe you | all of my talent, whatever it may be, | with you was born and hidden | he who is the father to all mortal beings | When I felt for the first time the Tuscan air]

But Dante also shows self-awareness when it comes to the negative potential of his 'ingegno'. This is most dramatically the case in the encounter with his alter ego, the eloquent Ulysses, whose 'ingegno' manifested itself in the cunning with which he tricked others (see Chapter 2). The very thought of Ulysses's fate leads Dante to hold back his own 'ingegno', lest he should risk having too much in common with the sinner:

Allor mi dolsi, e ora mi ridoglio
quando drizzo la mente a ciò ch'io vidi,
e più lo 'ngegno affreno ch'i' non soglio

perché non corra che virtù nol guidi. (*Inf.* XXVI, 19–21)

[I suffered then, and I suffer now again, | when I turn my mind to what I saw, | and I rein my genius in more than usual | for I do not want it to run without being guided by virtue.]

While Ulysses embodied hubris through his desire to travel beyond the limits of human knowledge, the episode of the terrace of pride in the *Purgatorio* serves as a meditation on the hubris specifically associated with artistic pride. In this context, 'ingegno' is referred to in order to describe the limitations of human agency. Wit and talent may be enough to make one a great artist, but they are of no value when it comes to the fate of the soul after death. This is made clear in the opening lines of *Purgatorio* XI, which are a rewriting of the Lord's Prayer — though we should note that the passage also exhibits Dante's 'ingegno' in so far as the reader knows that this is his own translation and adaptation of the prayer (Barolini 1992: 122–42):

Vegna ver' noi la pace del tuo regno,
ché noi ad essa non potem da noi,
s'ella non vien, con tutto nostro ingegno. (*Purg.* XI, 7–9)

[May the peace of your kingdom come to us, | for with all our wit, we cannot reach it by ourselves, | if it does not come to us.]

The word 'ingegno' will be used in a similar sense in Virgil's parting words to Dante:

e disse: 'Il temporal foco e l'etterno
veduto hai, figlio; e se' venuto in parte
dov'io per me più oltre non discerno.

Tratto t'ho qui con ingegno e con arte
lo tuo piacere omai prendi per duce'. (*Purg.* XXVII, 127–31)

[And he said: 'You have seen the temporal fire | and the eternal, my son; and you have now reached | a place beyond which I cannot see. | I have led you here with my intelligence and skill | from now on, may your pleasure be your guide'.]

Virgil's parting words tell us that human wit alone is insufficient: for all his wisdom and poetic skill, he has reached a limit that cannot be crossed without faith. The admonishments against artistic pride administered in *Purgatorio* XI and the shortcomings of Virgil therefore both remind us of the necessity of divine intervention.

The examples that we have considered reveal an important paradox in Dante's understanding of 'ingegno': it is used in some cases to refer to a God-given ability or inclination and in other cases to refer to individual agency. This reflects a divide that has remained with our modern concept of 'genius', which is derived both from the Latin words *ingenium* and *genius* (the latter being a translation of the Greek *daemon* or tutelary spirit). As observed by Ann Jefferson, this 'split etymological inheritance' is part of the reason why genius can be located 'alternately outside and inside the individual associated with the phenomenon (in the *daemon* and the disposition, respectively)' (2009: 182).[20] Dante maintains both understandings of 'genius': his poetic 'ingegno' is drawn both from an aptitude with which he was born and from personal effort. In the context of the metapoetic use of aeronautical imagery examined in Chapter 2, Dante's 'ingegno' is famously metaphorized as a sea-vessel:

Per correr miglior acque alza le vele
omai la navicella del mio ingegno,
che lascia dietro a sé mar sì crudele

e canterò di quel secondo regno. (*Purg.* I, 1–4)

[The little vessel of my genius now raises its sails | to travel over better waters, | leaving behind it the cruellest of seas | and I shall sing of that second realm.]

This passage shows an interaction between Dante's 'ingegno' or natural abilities, expressed in the third person, and his action as poet, expressed in the first person. The same distinction occurs in *Paradiso* XXIII, mentioned above, referring to a vessel, which we assume is again Dante's 'ingegno', and to a sailor, who metaphorizes the risks taken by Dante in composing the *Commedia*: 'non è pareggio da picciola barca, [...] né da nocchier ch'a sé medesmo parca' [this is no journey for a small craft, [...] nor for a sailor who spares himself] (*Par.* XXIII, 67–69). Success is thus dependent both on the means available and on the individual's intention.

Dante presents his vocation as author of the *Commedia* as being not only an expression of his 'ingegno' (in all understandings of the word), but also of his personal experiences. The sacred poem is bound up with the implied author's biography: it is inseparable from his earlier poetry, his love life, his family history, his hometown, and his exile. As was established in Chapter 1, writing is also a part of Dante's identity: it is an expression of both his personal history and his poetic agency. Indeed, although the first two lines of the opening tercet of *Paradiso* XXV claim dual authorship for the poem — ''l poema sacro | al quale ha posto mano e cielo e terra' [the sacred poem | to which both heaven and earth have lent a hand], its third line stresses the individual human effort of writing: 'sì che m'ha fatto per molti anni macro' [so that it has for many years worn me thin] *Par.* XXV, 1–3). Such emphasis on 'individual human talents' has led Ascoli to conclude that 'Dante no doubt anticipates the humanized, historicized author traditionally associated with Petrarch and a dawning age of increasingly secular culture' (2008: 405).

The narrator-protagonist's self-assertiveness as author of the *Commedia* is ultimately incompatible with the abandonment of selfhood which should be the aim of Christian *caritas*. As has been argued by Christian Moevs (2005: 8) and further developed by Manuele Gragnolati with reference to queer theory (2013: 157–61), union with God in the *Paradiso* relies on a 'dissolution' of the self, that is, a relinquishing of agency and individuality. The blessed souls of the *Paradiso* find beatitude by aligning their will with God's, in the words of Piccarda Donati: 'E 'n la sua volontade è nostra pace' [In his will lies our peace] (*Par.* III, 85). 'Ingegno' and the model of selfhood associated with it must therefore be abandoned by the narrator-protagonist in order to merge with the divine. Indeed, Dante tells us that he cannot rely on his natural abilities when confronted with Christ: 'Qui vince la memoria mia lo 'ngegno' [At this point my talent cannot match my memory] (*Par.* XIV, 103). This line foreshadows the poem's final verses, where Dante, in order to unite with the Godhead, must abandon his personal agency and poetic prowess, the latter being referred to through the metonymy 'penne' (on this term, see Chapter 2):

> ma non eran da ciò le proprie penne:
> se non che la mia mente fu percossa
> da un fulgore in che sua voglia venne.
>
> A l'alta fantasia qui mancò possa;
> ma già volgeva il mio disio e 'l *velle*,
> sì come rota ch'igualmente è mossa,
> l'amor che move il sole e l'altre stelle. (*Par.* XXXIII, 142–45)

> [But my quills were not up to the task: | were it not for a bolt of light that thundered through | my mind, making its desire come true. | The highest imagination at this remains speechless; | but already my desire and my will were being turned, | like a wheel in equal motion, by | the love that moves the sun and the other stars.]

The poem thus closes on the moment at which Dante finds beatitude through an abandonment of his agency and aligns himself, like the blessed of the *Paradiso*, with God's will. The *Commedia*, invested as it is with Dante's individuality and poetic self-awareness, can do nothing but fall silent once these are relinquished. And indeed, no human art can recreate the selfless experience of divine bliss.

While artistic genius in Dante must ultimately be surmounted in order to move beyond the limits of self-assertion, in Proust, artistic genius is the only means to transcend individualistic models of selfhood. As we saw in Chapter 2, the *Recherche* makes the central claim that a work of art is the expression of an individual's unique world vision (III, 762). Consequently, artistic genius is the ability to externalize one's individual worldview: 'le génie consistant dans le pouvoir réfléchissant et non dans la qualité intrinsèque du spectacle reflété' [genius consists in the power to mirror and not in the intrinsic quality of the spectacle being mirrored] (I, 545). However, in *Le Temps retrouvé* the narrator-protagonist tells us:

> Ce serait même inexact que de dire en pensant à ceux qui le [mon livre] liraient, à mes lecteurs. Car ils ne seraient pas, selon moi, mes lecteurs, mais les propres lecteurs d'eux-mêmes, mon livre n'étant qu'une sorte de ces verres grossissants comme ceux que tendait à un acheteur l'opticien de Combray; mon livre, grâce auquel je leur fournirais le moyen de lire en eux-mêmes. (IV, 610)
>
> [It would be incorrect to call those who would read it [my book] my readers. For, in my opinion, they would not be my readers, but their own readers, my book being nothing more than one of those magnifying glasses, like the ones that the optician in Combray would hold out to his customers; my book, which would offer them the means to read inside themselves.]

The work of art here is no longer only an expression of the artist's individuality, but an instrument through which readers can examine their own individual nature: it is 'un égoïsme utilisable pour autrui'. Contrary to Barthes's prophecy, however, the writer has not been replaced by the reader, but has fused with him: the writer's subjectivity and the reader's subjectivity intermingle through the work of art. The value of art lies precisely therein: it is the only way out of solipsism. Humans may well be described as 'l'être qui ne peut sortir de soi, qui ne connaît les autres qu'en soi, et, en disant le contraire, ment' [creatures who cannot go outside of themselves, who only know others within themselves, and who, when they say the opposite, are lying] (III, 34), but instead of a bleak end to all possibilities of exchange, this can be the beginning of an interaction in which knowing others 'en soi' becomes a valid means to reach 'ces mondes que nous appelons les individus, et que sans l'art nous ne connaîtrions jamais' [those worlds which we call individuals, and which without art we would never know] (III, 762).

Literary creation in the *Recherche* liberates the writer from the weight of his individuality, as personal experience is given 'une forme générale [...] qui fait de tous les copartageants de notre peine' [a general form [...] that makes everybody share our pain] (IV, 484). This experience will be shared in every act of reading, which relies on the interaction between the writer's and the reader's subjectivities, which brings us back to the passage from *Contre Sainte-Beuve* cited in Chapter 1:

> un livre est le produit d'un autre moi que celui que nous manifestons dans nos habitudes, dans la société, dans nos vices. Ce moi-là, si nous voulons essayer de le comprendre, c'est au fond de nous-même, en essayant de le *recréer en nous*, que nous pouvons y parvenir. (*CSB*, 221–22; my emphasis)
>
> [a book is the product of a different self from the one that we show in our habits, in society, in our vices. *That* self, if we are to try to understand it, can only be reached deep inside ourselves, by trying *to recreate it within us*.]

The act of reading implies the creation of a new self, drawn from both the 'I' of the writer and the 'I' of the reader. What we are presented with therefore is the paradox of literature as *both* a loss of individuality as all experience becomes general *and* an assertion of individuality through the intersubjective relationship between reader and writer.

Literary vocation thus brings us to the heart of the problematic relationship between the individual and the general, which expresses itself in terms of the relationship between author and reader. While both Dante's poem and the projected book of Proust's narrator-protagonist can accurately be described as 'un égoïsme utilisable pour autrui', the phrase means something different in each case. In Proust, literature is valuable because it allows for intersubjectivity, which is a one-on-one interaction between two unique individuals (the writer and the reader). In Dante the story of an exceptional poet is valuable to the 'mondo che mal vive' [world that lives in sin] (*Purg.* XXXII, 103) because it has an exemplary value as the story of a man's journey to salvation. This is possible because the medieval understanding of individuality differed from the modern understanding of it as difference from others. At the time Dante was writing, all humans were considered to be made in the image of God, and therefore every individual (*homo interior* or *seipsum*) shared a common nature with the rest of humanity (Morris 1972: 64–65; Benton 1982; and Bynum 1982: 82–109). In contrast, the *Recherche* elevates art as the only means to escape secular man's solitary and hermetic concept of individuality. Within this context, every individual is a different universe (III, 761) or book: 'livre intérieur de signes inconnus' [inner book of unknown signs] (IV, 458). The artist is the individual capable of opening his unique book to others, in a process that allows for intersubjectivity and the consequent acknowledgment that many aspects of human experience are not unique, but general:

> L'œuvre est signe de bonheur, parce qu'elle nous apprend que dans tout amour le général gît à côté du particulier [...]. En effet, comme je devais l'expérimenter par la suite, même au moment où l'on aime et où on souffre, si la vocation s'est enfin réalisée dans les heures où on travaille on sent si bien l'être qu'on aime se dissoudre dans une réalité plus vaste qu'on arrive à l'oublier par instants. (IV, 483)

> [The work of art is a sign of happiness, because it teaches us that in every experience of love, the general lies alongside the particular [...]. Indeed, as I was to experience later on, even in the very moment in which one loves and suffers, if one's vocation has finally been realized in the hours in which one works, one feels so clearly that the being one loves is dissolving into a far greater reality, that one is able to forget him or her for a moment.]

Proust Against the Religion of Art

Proust's *Recherche* has been used by Bersani (1990) as a prime case study for what he calls 'the culture of redemption', a modern aesthetic based on the compensatory logic that art makes up for lived experience, which is understood as inherently valueless. Bersani summarizes what he refers to as Proust's aesthetic in a perceptive paraphrase of the narrator's pronouncements in 'L'Adoration perpétuelle':

> In the work of art, a certain type of representation of experience will operate [...] as a justification (retroactive, even posthumous) for having had any experiences at all. In Proust, art simultaneously erases, repeats, and redeems life. Literary repetition is an annihilating salvation. (1990: 11)

Several passages of the *Recherche* exemplify the culture of redemption as defined by Bersani. For example, the moral character of Bergotte's literature, as seen above, is said to make up for his vices (I, 548). In *Le Temps retrouvé* it is suggested that one's art is more valuable than one's life, the narrator going so far as to argue that an unhappy life is a positive thing, because it makes one artistically productive:

> Car le bonheur seul est salutaire pour le corps; mais c'est le chagrin qui développe les forces de l'esprit. [...] Il est vrai que cette vérité, qui n'est pas compatible avec le bonheur, avec la santé, ne l'est pas toujours avec la vie. [...] Et c'est ainsi que peu à peu se font ces terribles figures ravagées du vieux Rembrandt, du vieux Beethoven. (IV, 484–85)
>
> [For while only happiness is healthy for the body, it is sorrow that develops the powers of the mind. [...] Indeed this truth, which is not compatible with happiness, with health, is not always compatible with life either. [...] And that is how, little by little, the faces of the old Rembrandt or the old Beethoven become ravaged.]

Art's hierarchic positioning over life is further suggested in *Le Temps retrouvé* by the fact that the narrator-protagonist fears that he will die before having completed his book (IV, 609–16). The crucial episode of Vinteuil's septet in *La Prisonnière* also seems to suggest the value of an artist's output over his life. We are told that the piece was recovered and performed thanks to Vinteuil's daughter's lover, who made him unhappy when he lived, but atoned by deciphering his manuscripts:

> L'amie de Mlle Vinteuil était quelquefois traversée par l'importune pensée qu'elle avait peut-être précipité la mort de Vinteuil. Du moins, en passant des années à débrouiller le grimoire laissé par Vinteuil, en établissant une lecture certaine de ces hiéroglyphes inconnus, l'amie de Mlle Vinteuil eut la consolation d'assurer au musicien dont elle avait assombri les dernières années, une gloire immortelle et compensatrice. (III, 766)
>
> [Mlle Vinteuil's friend was sometimes crossed by the unpleasant thought that she had perhaps contributed to Vinteuil's death. At least, by spending years deciphering the illegible scrawls left by Vinteuil, by establishing a certain reading of these unknown hieroglyphs, Mlle Vinteuil's friend had the consolation of ensuring an immortal and compensatory glory to the musician over whose last years she had cast a cloud.]

The narrator-protagonist then goes on to apply this notion of art compensating for life to himself. The possible relationship between Mlle Vinteuil's lover and Albertine may have caused him the tortures of jealousy, but this woman has put him on the path of his artistic vocation:

> C'était grâce à elle, par compensation, qu'avait pu venir à moi l'étrange appel [...] — comme la promesse qu'il existait autre chose, réalisable par l'art sans doute, que le néant que j'avais trouvé dans tous les plaisirs et dans l'amour même, et que si ma vie me semblait vaine, du moins n'avait-elle pas tout accompli. (III, 767)
>
> [It was thanks to her, as a form of compensation, that the strange calling [...] was able to reach me — a promise that there existed something else, probably attainable through art, than the emptiness that I had encountered in all pleasures and even in love, and that if my life seemed pointless, at least it still had more to achieve.]

Bersani's account of Proust's aesthetics is however problematic in so far as it is entirely based on these types of narratorial statements. A comprehensive consideration of the *Recherche*'s overall treatment of the power of art results in a more complicated picture. Indeed, although the secular nature of the *Recherche* and the moral importance which it attributes to art might tempt us to assume that the humanist afterlife sought by Dante's Brunetto Latini reigns unthreatened in Proust's novel, this is not the case. Proust's narrator is as aware as Dante's Oderisi of the perishability of all human creations, a matter that is approached through the key cases of Bergotte and Vinteuil in *La Prisonnière,* and the narrator-protagonist himself in *Le Temps retrouvé.*

The episode of Bergotte's death, which was cited above, leads the narrator to ask 'Mort à jamais? Qui peut le dire?' [Dead forever more? Who can tell?] (III, 693). After considering the question of the subsistence of the human soul, the narrator concludes:

> L'idée que Bergotte n'était pas mort à jamais est sans invraisemblance.
>
> On l'enterra, mais toute la nuit funèbre, aux vitrines éclairées, ses livres, disposés trois par trois, veillaient comme des anges aux ailes déployées et semblaient pour celui qui n'était plus, le symbole de sa résurrection. (III, 693)
>
> [The idea that Bergotte was not dead forever is not entirely unlikely.
>
> He was buried, but during the night of the wake, in the illuminated shop windows, his books, laid out in groups of three, watched over him like open-winged angels and seemed, for the one who was no more, a symbol of his resurrection.]

However, an earlier passage has in fact already informed us of the limited nature of such a resurrection:

> Peu à peu, la chaleur se retirera de la Terre, puis la vie. Alors la résurrection aura pris fin, car si avant dans les générations futures que brillent les œuvres des hommes, encore faut-il qu'il y ait des hommes. [...] [Q]uand il n'y aura plus d'hommes, et à supposer que la gloire de Bergotte ait duré jusque-là, brusquement elle s'éteindra à tout jamais. (III, 689)

> [Little by little, heat will leave the Earth, then life. And resurrection will thus have ended, for however far down future generations the works of men may shine, one still needs there to be men. [...] When there will be no more men, supposing Bergotte's glory did even last until then, it will suddenly be extinguished forever.]

Thus, Bergotte's fame, dependent as it is on human language, is certain to end with the end of the human race, and it will not necessarily last until then either. The same applies to the narrator-protagonist himself, who tells us in *Le Temps retrouvé*: 'Sans doute mes livres eux aussi, comme mon être de chair, finiraient un jour par mourir. Mais il faut se résigner à mourir' [My books too, like my fleshly being, would probably die one day. But one must resign oneself to dying] (IV, 620). The narrator thus accepts the inevitability and finality of death, even for those who have written books.

The account of the performance of Vinteuil's posthumously discovered masterpiece further complicates the notion that art offers a form of resurrection. At first, the performance leads the narrator to suggest that Vinteuil has reached immortality: 'On aurait dit que, réincarné, l'auteur vivait à jamais dans sa musique' [It seemed that, reincarnated, the author lived forever in his music] (III, 758). But he then takes issue with the notion that art should be viewed as an extension of life:

> Vinteuil était mort depuis nombre d'années; mais au milieu de ces instruments qu'il avait aimés, il lui avait été donné de poursuivre, pour un temps illimité, une part au moins de sa vie. De sa vie d'homme seulement? Si l'art n'était vraiment qu'un prolongement de la vie, valait-il de lui rien sacrifier, était-il pas aussi irréel qu'elle-même? À mieux écouter ce septuor, je ne le pouvais pas penser. (III, 759)
>
> [Vinteuil had been dead for many years; but among these instruments that he had loved, it had been made possible for him to continue, for an unlimited time, a part of his life. Of his human life only? If art was truly nothing more than a prolongation of one's life, was it worth sacrificing anything for, was it not as illusory as life itself? The more I listened to this septet, the less I could believe it.]

The rhetorical question 'De sa vie d'homme seulement?' prepares us for a negative answer, just as the question 'Mort à jamais?' did in the case of Bergotte. Art is no longer a resurrection of its creator, but something more: the effect of Vinteuil's music is far too powerful to be considered a mere continuation of Vinteuil's individual existence. This distinction between the artist's earthly life and the life of the work of art is consistent with Proust's strong stance against the biographization of works of literature, which was explored in Chapter 1. Moreover, the episode of Vinteuil's septet also presents any preoccupation with artistic glory as detrimental to the quality of the work. The artist's relationship with his inner self is described as follows: 'il délire de joie quand il chante selon sa patrie, la trahit parfois par amour de la gloire, mais alors en cherchant la gloire il la fuit' [he is mad with joy when he sings according to his homeland, betrays it at times in pursuit of glory, but by searching for glory he flees from it] (III, 761). This resonates with the account of Ver

Meer, who by far surpassed Bergotte in dedication to his art, as 'un artiste à jamais inconnu, à peine identifié sous le nom de Ver Meer' (III, 693).

The *Recherche* therefore presents us with measured views on artistic afterlife, and goes as far as to critique those who seek to live on through artistic renown ('gloire'). Moreover, these questions are explored through a language which is tentative and uncertain. Vinteuil's immortality is only a first impression ('On aurait dit que'), which is then corrected. In the case of Bergotte, while the narrator does conclude that his afterlife is more than likely, this is done entirely through grammatical constructions of possibility ('comme si' [as if], 'semblent' [seem], 'peut-être' [perhaps]), expressions of ignorance ('lois inconnues' [unknown laws], 'sans savoir qui' [without knowing who]), and finally a double negative framed as a suggestion ('l'idée que Bergotte n'était pas mort à jamais est sans invraisemblance'), followed by a 'résurrection' which is watered down by the verb *sembler* [to seem] and only justified through a sign ('le symbole') framed by an analogy ('comme des anges').[21]

The confrontation with the death of an artist brings out the doubts of an agnostic, who shows an anxious interest in spiritual questions.[22] The narrator tells us, 'Certes, les expériences spirites pas plus que les dogmes religieux n'apportent de preuve que l'âme subsiste' [Indeed, neither seances nor religious dogma bring us any proof of the subsistence of the soul] (III, 693); yet he explores the various avenues, be they Christian or secular. As a result, these passages speak of angels and a 'céleste balance' [celestial set of scales], of 'un monde entièrement différent à celui-ci, et dont nous sortons pour naître à cette terre, avant peut-être d'y retourner' [a world entirely different from this one, which we leave to be born on this earth, before perhaps returning to it] (III, 693), and of a point in the past at which the communication of souls had been a possibility: 'Et de même que certains êtres sont les derniers témoins d'une forme de vie que la nature a abandonnée, je me demandais si la musique n'était pas l'exemple unique de ce qu'aurait pu être [...] la communication des âmes' [And just as some creatures are the last remaining witnesses of a form of life that nature has abandoned, I asked myself if music was not the only example of what the communication of the souls [...] might have been like] (III, 762–63). With this wider context in mind, if we return to the example of Mlle Vinteuil's lover's act of atonement (III, 766), which had at first seemed to exemplify perfectly the compensatory logic critiqued by Bersani, we begin to notice the fissures in the novel's belief that a life can be compensated for by a work of art: when the narrator speaks of a 'gloire immortelle et compensatrice', is he telling us what he believes, or is this an instance of focalization on Mlle Vinteuil's *amie*, who tells herself these things in order to find 'consolation'? Can she assure Vinteuil immortality in a context in which entropy is an acknowledged fact of life? What do we make of 'la promesse qu'il existait autre chose, réalisable par l'art sans doute'? How solid is a promise and how convincing is a 'sans doute'?[23]

In contrast with critics who either accept or reject Proust's narrative of artistic salvation, Jennifer Rushworth (2015) has embraced its doubtfulness. Rushworth fruitfully uses Jacques Derrida's definition of the promise as 'both tenable and untenable' to account for the nature of promises in the *Recherche*, and more specifically for the protagonist's promise to write in *Le Temps retrouvé*. This allows her to offer a way out of the critical impasse of deciding whether the book we have just read is or is not the book that the protagonist will write (2015: 216). Rushworth's reading of the narrator-protagonist's promise to write can be extended to the novel's overall treatment of artistic redemption, which is consistently made up of doubts and promises. As Bersani himself observes in his introduction: 'Art, as Plato rightly saw, cannot have the unity, the identity, the stability of truth; it does not belong to the world of perfectly intelligible ideas' (1990: 2). To read the statements of the *Recherche*'s narrator as unequivocal aesthetic principles, thereby ignoring the novel's many doubts and contradictions, is to 'misread art as philosophy'. Thus Bersani ironically commits the misreading that *The Culture of Redemption* sets out to criticize.[24] The *Recherche* does present what can be called a religion of art, but the narrator-protagonist does not have absolute faith in this religion. As suggested by Bowie, Proust falls 'in and out of love with his own grand design' (1998: 124).

Humour finally provides a further important dimension to Proust's treatment of the 'religion of art'. It is present in the two key episodes on which I have drawn: Bergotte's last judgment, which is embroiled with a potato indigestion (the writer's last words being: 'C'est une simple indigestion que m'ont donnée ces pommes de terre pas assez cuites, ce n'est rien' [This is only an indigestion that those insufficiently cooked potatoes gave me, it's nothing], III, 692) as has been studied by Watt (2011: 110), and the performance of Vinteuil's septet, in which Proust mocks those individuals who worship art unquestioningly. The Baron de Charlus who intimates to the audience that 'l'heure était maintenant au grand Art' [the time had now come for great Art] is described by the narrator-protagonist as having 'quelque chose de comique' [something comical] about him (III, 752).[25] Proust then further pokes fun at those who attend concerts 'religiously' through a detailed comparison between Mme Verdurin's attitude during the concert and the attitudes of those who attend church without the ardour of faith nor of intellectual curiosity:

> La Patronne voulait-elle par cette attitude recueillie montrer qu'elle se considérait comme à l'église, et ne trouvait pas cette musique différente de celle de la plus sublime des prières; voulait-elle comme certaines personnes à l'église dérober aux regards indiscrets, soit par pudeur leur ferveur supposée, soit par respect humain leur distraction coupable ou un sommeil invincible? (III, 756)
>
> [Did the Patron want to show through this introspective posture that she felt as though at church, and did not find this music very different from the most sublime of prayers; did she want, like some people at church do, to hide from prying eyes, out of decency or putative ardour or human respect, either the guilt of their wandering mind or their invincible sleepiness?]

Within such a context it becomes hard to tell whether Proust is serious or mocking when he describes the music as a 'mystique chant de coq' [mystical cockcrow] (III, 755): musically speaking, a 'cock-a-doodle-doo' is not the most ethereal or beautiful of sounds. Mme Verdurin's belief that Vinteuil's music is just like a prayer also offers a flip-side to the narrator's later description of the septet precisely as 'prière, espérance' [prayer, hope] (III, 759). Given the instability of Proust's treatment of the parallels between art and religion, we come to see why Christopher Prendergast (2013) has described him as a 'skeptic'. Proust's expert handling of analogies is the key to much of the *Recherche*'s blurring of distinctions between the high and the low, the sublime and the everyday, and the serious and the comical. In this particular instance, we can see how in Proust's hands the analogy between art and religion can alternatively form the basis for a serious meditation on the role of art or for social satire.[26]

However, it would be amiss not to note that the lack of certainty and glory surrounding the fate of artists and their works perhaps makes Proust's account of literary vocation all the more noble. It is a form of devotion that reaps no reward for the artist, who is guaranteed neither the joys of heaven, nor a form of afterlife, and whose earnestness may at times be laughable. By undermining the religion of art, Proust thus adds to the selflessness of the artist, a selflessness which can in itself be a source of joy (IV, 483). In contrast, Dante's narrator-protagonist's faith in the Christian religion, though on the surface a guarantee of humility, is what allows him to have full confidence that his self-proclaimed sacred poem will earn him redemption and fame.

Notes to Chapter 4

1. Although, as we saw in the section 'Deviations and Returns' in Chapter 2, both works also resist teleology.
2. 'L'Adoration perpétuelle' is an abandoned title for the narrator's concluding meditations on art. The drafts for this section from the Cahiers 57 and 58 are collected in Tadié's Pléiade edition (Proust 1987–89: IV, 798–832. The term 'Adoration perpétuelle' refers to certain churches' choice to have the blessed sacrament on constant display, rather than only bringing it out during services.
3. Florian Pennanech (2009) identifies George Poulet, Jean Rousset, Jean-Pierre Richard, and Jean Starobinski as the main initiators of this interpretation of *Le Temps retrouvé* and argues that Genette's *Figures I, II*, and *III* can be read as gaining increasing distance from such a 'unified' reading.
4. Dante, as a reader of Augustine and Boethius, would have understood the experience of time as a key distinction between the human and the divine (Quinones 1972: 14).
5. 'Anagnorisis', the Ancient Greek for 'recognition', refers to the moment of denouement in a drama (*OED*).
6. The parallel between involuntary memory and grace has also been made by Georges Poulet (1949: 373).
7. In this respect I disagree with Bucknall's suggestion that the *Recherche*'s pursuit of artistic creation holds no redemptive concerns (1969: 18). I follow instead Elsner's 2009 reading (see the section 'Grand-mère as Beatrice?' in Chapter 3).
8. This is indeed the justification used in the *Convivio*, as we saw in Chapter 1.
9. As suggested by Bruno Nardi, *not* writing the *Commedia* would be a sin (1949: 337).
10. On Dante as David see Barolini 1984: 275–77, Federici 2010, and Ledda 2015.
11. On this iconography see Brandon 1967.
12. We know from Proust's correspondence that he had borrowed Robert de Billy's copy of Mâle's book in 1899, returning it to him in a pitiful state (see *Corr.* II, 456, n. 5).
13. Chaudier (2004) in contrast takes a more holistic approach, considering the many different contexts and uses of religious language in Proust.
14. On the *Recherche* and the architectural structure of cathedrals see also Fraisse 1990.

15. Angelo Caranfa uses Giotto's frescoes in the Scrovegni Chapel as the basis for a comparative reading of Bonaventure's and Proust's understanding of images (1990: 126–36).
16. This difference is acknowledged by Bales: 'The frame of reference is entirely egocentric, whereas Dante's had been theocentric' (1975: 134).
17. On their way to the terrace of pride (*Purgatorio* x), Dante and Virgil see God-made representations of examples of humility: the Virgin Mary (lines 28–45), David (lines 46–69), and Trajan (lines 70–96); on their way out of the terrace of pride (*Purgatorio* xii) they see representations of examples of punished pride, both from Christian narrative, such as Lucifer, and from classical mythology, such as Arachne (lines 25–63).
18. On the uniqueness of Dante's depiction of Limbo, see Iannucci 2005: 63–82.
19. For an etymological overview of the uses of the words *genius* and *ingenium* and their derivates in romance languages, see Vallini 2002.
20. On the origins of 'genius', see Nitzsche 1975.
21. Jean Mouton has also noted that when approaching the question of life after death, the *Recherche* shows uncertainty, framing its postulations with expressions such as 'peut-être' and 'sans doute' (1968: 17–18.)
22. Marguerite Yourcenar contrasts Proust with his contemporaries in this respect: 'En dépit de cet agnosticisme un peu mou qui est de sa génération, et qui ne laisse de place ni au refus, ni à l'acceptation, Proust me semble bien plus profondément engagé dans la tradition chrétienne-catholique que d'autres écrivains étiquetés comme tels' [Despite the soft agnosticism that is typical of his generation and which leaves no room for rejection, nor acceptance, Proust to me seems far more deeply engaged with the Catholic-Christian tradition than other writers who are labeled as such] (quoted in Mouton 1968: 23).
23. 'Sans doute', though literally meaning 'without a doubt', is an idiomatic expression for 'probably'. It appears in other passages of this ilk, such as 'Sans doute mes livres eux aussi, comme mon être de chair, finiraient un jour par mourir' [My books too, just as my physical body, would probably die one day] (iv, 620), or 'ma part de bonheur dans la seule vie qu'il y ait sans doute' [my opportunity for happiness in what is probably the only life there is] (i, 713).
24. As has been observed by L. Scott Lerner: 'Bersani sharply distinguishes the — aesthetic — theorizing of Proust's narrator from the novelistic density of the work as a whole. [...] That he fully heeds his own admonition, however, is less certain' (2007: 43). For Bersani on Proust, see also Hughes 2011: 223–28.
25. Proust also shows Charlus sacralizing art in a passage in which the baron waxes lyrical on an 'homme de goût' who said that the saddest event in his life was the death of Balzac's fictional character Lucien de Rubempré (iii, 437–38). The comment is generally attributed to Oscar Wilde, though Michael Lucey clarifies that it is actually found in the mouth of a fictional character (Vivian) in a dialogue by Wilde entitled 'The Decay of Lying' (2006: 202). Proust was in fact highly sceptical of this statement, writing in a letter to Robert Dreyfus (16 May 1908) that Wilde 'disant que le plus grand chagrin qu'il avait eu c'était la mort de Lucien de Rubempré dans Balzac, et apprenant peu après par son procès qu'il est des chagrins plus réels' [saying that the greatest sorrow that he had had was the death of Lucien de Rubempré in Balzac, and learning soon after through his trial that there exist far more real sorrows] (*Corr.* viii, 123).
26. On the subject of Dante's and Proust's use of analogies, see my 2017 article. Chaudier (2004) has shown the varied use Proust makes of religious imagery across his writings.

CONCLUSION

In the opening chapter of Proust's *Recherche*, the village priest encourages the child's aunt Léonie to visit the bell tower of Saint-Hilaire, Combray's medieval church. The tower according to the priest is the church's most striking feature since it offers a fantastic viewpoint (I, 104). From it, 'on embrasse à la fois des choses qu'on ne peut voir habituellement que l'une sans l'autre' [one can embrace together things that one is usually only able to view one without the other] (I, 105). Unfortunately — or, from the perspective of the narratable, by necessity — the protagonist does not follow this recommendation, and therefore will not discover until late in life that what he had always thought of as two separate worlds (the bourgeois sphere of his family, focused on in the volume *Du côté de chez Swann* and embodied by the walk by Swann's house at Méséglise, and the sphere of high society, focused on in the volume *Le Côté de Guermantes* and embodied by the walk by the Guermantes's estate) were related all along. This is first hinted at by Gilberte's revelation that one can combine both 'côtés' [ways] within the same walk: 'nous pourrons alors aller à Guermantes en prenant par Méséglise' [we could then go to Guermantes via Méséglise] (IV, 268), but the narrator-protagonist at the time does not fully realize the radical change in his ideas that this discovery entails. The deferral is rendered metaphorically through his postponing of the visit to the church ('je n'avais pas été une seule fois revoir l'église de Combray' [I had not once gone back to see the church of Combray], IV, 285), whose unexplored bell tower looms on the horizon from the first page of *Le Temps retrouvé* (IV, 275).[1] The anticipated change of perspective comes at the end of *Le Temps retrouvé*, when he meets Gilberte's daughter Mlle de Saint-Loup, the physical manifestation of the 'fils mystérieux' [mysterious threads] that connect the numerous people and events which he had thought of as completely separate (IV, 606–07). The realization that every point of his life is interconnected constitutes not an accretion of knowledge, but a complete revolution in his understanding of the world. Mlle de Saint-Loup offers a new perspective on his entire life, in the same way as the bell tower of Saint-Hilaire offers a new perspective on Combray's physical surroundings by bringing together 'des choses qu'on ne peut voir habituellement que l'une sans l'autre'.

The bell tower of Combray is an appropriate metaphor for the epistemological principle of this book. The topics approached in each chapter have been vantage points from which to consider Dante and Proust together, rather than separately as is the habit. In so doing, I have not merely sought to add to our existing knowledge of each author, but to change our perspective on them, following the process of analogy, which by making us see one thing in light of another, makes us look at both items afresh. The change of perspective created by the joining of Proust and Dante has challenged expectations across this monograph. We saw Proust's introspective 'I' undermine the reader's desire to ascribe him a definite identity and Dante's Everyman claim authorship of the poem recounting his journey. We saw the teleology of the literary journeys to God and to the self be resisted in both works through deviations and returns, human identity remaining both in Dante's medieval poem and in Proust's twentieth-century novel a complex negotiation between the past and the present. We saw an enduring oedipal anxiety, which requires both male protagonists to surpass other men with the support of an unthreatening female figure, and we saw a feminist Beatrice who puts Proust's bicycle-riding New Women to shame. We saw that if art is presented as the key to intersubjectivity in Proust, this does not necessarily make it a religion, and that Dante's final mystical experience must come at the price of the poem, which cannot subsist divorced from his individuality.

These are only a few of the many insights which can be gained by going to Proust 'en prenant par Dante', or to Dante 'en prenant par Proust'. The pages of this book are intended as a contribution to Dante studies, to Proust studies, and to the field of comparative literature. But they are also there to spark reflection beyond these fields of research in terms of the various possible uses of first-person narration, the importance of spatial metaphors in conceptualizing progress and temporality, the pervasiveness of gender dynamics, the attractiveness and the limitations of the 'redemption aesthetic', and the heuristic value of metaphor. I hope that my analogies between Dante and Proust have encouraged readers to question their assumptions not only about both authors, but also perhaps about their respective periods: if, as argued by Fowlie (1981: 4), 'the relating of Dante to contemporary literature is an obligation' in so far as it re-invigorates our engagement with texts written at a time in many ways different from our own, this book also suggests that analyses of modern literary texts can gain in nuance when we relate these works to their earlier counterparts. Finally, if I have led a few Proustians to pick off from their bookshelf the customary copy of the *Divine Comedy*, or convinced the odd Dante scholar to wait no longer and set out on a Ulyssean journey across the three thousand pages of Proust's *Recherche*, then that is an achievement in itself.

Note

1. Proust's awareness of this metaphorical significance can be surmised from the narrator-protagonist's account of Stendhal in *La Prisonnière*: 'un certain sentiment de l'altitude se liant à la vie spirituelle, le lieu élevé où Julien Sorel est prisonnier, la tour au haut de laquelle est enfermé Fabrice, le clocher où l'abbé Blanès s'occupe d'astrologie et d'où Fabrice jette un si beau coup d'œil' [a certain feeling of altitude is connected to spiritual life, the elevated place where Julien Sorel is emprisoned, the tower at the top of which Fabrice is locked, the bell tower where the abbot Blanès practices astrology and from which Fabrice has such a beautiful viewpoint] (III, 879). The 'beau coup d'œil' offered by Blanès's 'clocher' echoes 'le point de vue qu'on a du clocher et qui est grandiose' [the viewpoint one has from the top of the bell tower, which is magnificent] in 'Combray' (I, 104).

BIBLIOGRAPHY

❖

Primary Works

DANTE ALIGHIERI. 1967. *Dante's Lyric Poetry*, ed. by Kenelm Foster and Patrick Boyde 2 vols (Oxford: Oxford University Press)

—— 1980. *Vita nuova*, ed. by Domenico De Robertis, (Milan: Ricciardi)

—— 1991. *Purgatorio, Commedia*, ed. by Anna Maria Chiavacci Leonardi (Milan: Mondadori)

—— 1992. *Vita Nuova*, trans. by Mark Musa (Oxford: Oxford University Press)

—— 1994. *La commedia secondo l'antica vulgata*, ed. by Giorgio Petrocchi, 2nd edn, 4 vols (Florence: Le Lettere)

—— 1995. *Convivio*, ed. by Franca Brambilla Ageno, 3 vols (Florence: Le Lettere)

—— 1998. *The Banquet*, ed. and trans. by Richard Lansing (New York: Garland)

PROUST, MARCEL. 1970–93. *Correspondance*, ed. by Philip Kolb, 21 vols (Paris: Plon)

—— 1971. *Contre Sainte-Beuve précédé de Pastiches et mélanges et suivi de Essais et articles*, ed. by Pierre Clarac (Paris: Gallimard)

—— 1971. *Jean Santeuil précédé de 'Les Plaisirs et les jours'*, ed. by Pierre Clarac and Yves Sandre (Gallimard: Paris)

—— 1987–89. *À la recherche du temps perdu*, ed. by Jean-Yves Tadié, 4 vols (Paris: Gallimard)

Secondary Works

Works on Dante and Proust

BALES, RICHARD. 1975. *Proust and the Middle Ages* (Geneva: Droz)

BALSAMO, GIAN. 2007. 'The Fiction of Marcel Proust's Autobiography', *Poetics Today*, 28.4: 573–606

BORTON, SAMUEL. 1958. 'A Tentative Essay on Dante and Proust', *Delaware Notes*, 31: 33–42

CONTINI, GIANFRANCO. 1976. 'Dante come personaggio-poeta della *Commedia*', in *Un'idea di Dante: saggi danteschi* (Turin: Einaudi), pp. 33–62

GIURICEO, MARIE. 1983. 'The Dante-Virgil Relationship in Nineteenth and Twentieth Century French Fiction', *Studies in Medievalism*, 2.2: 67–79

HARTLEY, JULIA CATERINA. 2015. 'Reading in Dante and Proust', *MLN*, 130: 1330–49

—— 2017. 'L'Analogie chez Dante et Proust', in *Marcel Proust, roman moderne: perspectives comparatistes*, special issue of *Marcel Proust Aujourd'hui*, 14: 76–86

LANDY, JOSHUA. 2007. 'A Beatrice for Proust?', *Poetics Today*, 28.4: 607–18

PAPPOT, GEMMA. 2003. 'L'Inferno de Proust à la lumière de Dante: remarques sur les renvois à la Divina Commedia de Dante dans À la recherche du temps perdu', *Marcel Proust aujourd'hui*, 1: 91–118

PERRUS, CLAUDE. 2014. 'Dante du côté de chez Proust', in *Non dimenticarsi di Proust: declinazioni di un mito nella cultura moderna*, ed. by Anna Dolfi (Florence: Firenze University Press), pp. 413–25

RUSHWORTH, JENNIFER. 2016. *Discourses of Mourning in Dante, Petrarch, and Proust* (Oxford: Oxford University Press)

STEINER, GEORGE. 1978. 'Dante Now: The Gossip of Eternity', in *On Difficulty and Other Essays* (Oxford: Oxford University Press), pp. 164–85

STIERLE, KARLHEINZ. 2008. *Zeit und Werk: Prousts 'À la recherche du temps perdu' und Dantes 'Commedia'* (Munich: Carl Hanser Verlag)

TEULADE, ANNE. 2010. 'Proust et l'épopée de Dante', in *Proust, l'étranger*, ed. by Karen Haddad-Wotling and Vincent Ferré (Amsterdam: Rodopi), pp. 15–36

WATT, ADAM. 2013. '"L'Air de la chanson": Dante and Proust', *La Parola del Testo*, 17.1–2: 101–10

Works on Dante

BOSCO, UMBERTO (ed). 1970–78. *Enciclopedia dantesca*, 6 vols (Rome: Istituto della Enciclopedia italiana)

ASCOLI, ALBERT RUSSELL. 2008. *Dante and the Making of a Modern Author* (Cambridge: Cambridge University Press)

AUERBACH, ERICH. 1959. 'Figura', in *Scenes from the Drama of European Literature: Six Essays*, trans. by Ralph Manheim (New York: Meridian Books), pp. 11–76

——2000 [1953]. 'Farinata and Cavalcante', in *Mimesis: The Representation of Reality in Western Literature*, trans. by Willard R. Trask (Princeton, NJ: Princeton University Press), pp. 174–202

——2001 [1961]. *Dante: Poet of the Secular World*, trans. by Ralph Manheim (Berlin: De Gruyter)

BARAŃSKI, ZYGMUNT. 1987. 'La lezione esegetica di *Inferno* I: allegoria, storia e letteratura nella *Commedia*', in *Dante e le forme dell'allegoresi*, ed. by Michelangelo Picone (Ravenna: Longo), pp. 79–97

——1995. 'The "New Life" of "Comedy": The "Commedia" and the "Vita Nuova"', *Dante Studies*, 113: 1–29

——1999. 'Notes on Dante and the Myth of Orpheus', in *Dante, mito e poesia: atti del secondo Seminario dantesco internazionale (Monte Verità, Ascona, 23–27 giugno 1997)* (Florence: Cesati), pp. 133–54

——2004. '"Per similitudine di abito scientifico": Dante, Cavalcanti and the Sources of Medieval "Philosophical" Poetry', in *Science and Literature in Italian Culture: From Dante to Calvino, a Festschrift for Patrick Boyde*, ed. by Pierpaolo Antonello and Simon A. Gilson (Oxford: Legenda), pp. 29–36

BAROLINI, TEODOLINDA. 1984. *Dante's Poets: Textuality and Truth in the 'Comedy'* (Princeton, NJ: Princeton University Press)

——1992. *The Undivine Comedy: Detheologizing Dante* (Princeton, NJ: Princeton University Press)

——2003. 'Beyond (Courtly) Dualism: Thinking about Gender in Dante's Lyrics', in *Dante for the New Millennium*, ed. by Teodolinda Barolini and H. Wayne Storey (New York: Fordham University Press), pp. 65–89

——2006. *Dante and the Origins of Italian Literary Culture* (New York: Fordham University Press)

BOITANI, PIERO. 1989. *The Tragic and the Sublime in Medieval Literature* (Cambridge: Cambridge University Press)

BORGES, JORGE LUIS. 2001. 'The Meeting in a Dream', in *The Total Library: Non-Fiction 1922–1986*, ed. by Eliot Weinberger, trans. by Esther Allen, Suzanne Jill Levine, and Eliot Weinberger (London: Penguin), pp. 298–301

CONTINI, GIANFRANCO. 1970. 'Preliminari sulla lingua del Petrarca', in *Varianti e altra linguistica* (Turin: Einaudi), pp. 169–92

CROCE, BENEDETTO. 1921. *La poesia di Dante*, 2nd edn (Bari: Laterza)

DURLING, ROBERT M., and RONALD, L. MARTINEZ. 1990. *Time and the Crystal: Studies in Dante's Rime Petrose* (Berkeley, Los Angeles, & Oxford: University of California Press)

FEDERICI, THERESA. 2010. 'Dante's Davidic Journey: From Sinner to God's Scribe', in *Dante's 'Commedia': Theology as Poetry*, ed. by Vittorio Montemaggi and Matthew Treherne (Notre Dame, IN: University of Notre Dame Press), pp. 180–209

FÉLIX-FAURE GOYAU, LUCIE. 1902. *Les Femmes dans l'œuvre de Dante* (Paris: Perrin)

FERRANTE, JOAN M. 1975. *Woman as Image in Medieval Literature, from the Twelfth Century to Dante* (New York: Columbia University Press)

—— 1992. 'Dante's Beatrice: Priest of an Androgynous God', CEMERS Occasional Papers, 2 (Binghamton, NY: State University of New York Press)

FERRUCCI, FRANCO. 1990. *Il poema del desiderio* (Milan: Leonardo)

FRECCERO, JOHN. 1986. *The Poetics of Conversion*, ed. by Rachel Jacoff (Cambridge, MA, & London: Harvard University Press)

FRISARDI, ANDREA. 2009. 'Dante, Orpheus and the Poem as Salutation', *Temenos Academy Review*, 12: 116–39

FORTUNA, SARA, MANUELE GRAGNOLATI, and JÜRGEN TRABANT (eds). 2010. *Dante's Plurilingualism: Authority, Knowledge, Subjectivity* (Oxford: Legenda)

FOWLIE, WALLACE. 1981. *A Reading of Dante's Inferno* (Chicago, IL: Chicago University Press)

GIUNTA, CLAUDIO. 2002. *Versi a un destinatario: saggio sulla poesia italiana del Medioevo* (Bologna: Il Mulino)

GRAGNOLATI, MANUELE. 2012. '*Inferno* V', in *Lectura Dantis Bononiensis* 2, ed. by Emilio Pasquini and Carlo Grilli (Bologna: Bononia University Press), pp. 7–22

—— 2013. *Amor che move: linguaggio del corpo e forma del desiderio in Dante, Pasolini e Morante* (Milan: Il Saggiatore)

HARRISON, ROBERT POGUE. 2007. 'Approaching the Vita nuova', in *The Cambridge Companion to Dante* (Cambridge & New York: Cambridge University Press), pp. 35–45

HAWKINS, PETER S. 1980. 'Virtuosity and Virtue: Poetic Self-Reflection in the *Commedia*', *Dante Studies*, 98: 1–18

—— 2006. *Dante: A Brief History* (Oxford: Blackwell Publishing)

HOLLANDER, ROBERT. 1975. '*Purgatorio* II: Cato's Rebuke and Dante's scoglio', *Italica*, 52.3: 348–63

—— 1980. *Studies in Dante* (Ravenna: Longo)

—— 1983. *Il Virgilio dantesco: tragedia nella 'Commedia'* (Florence: Olschki)

—— 1999. 'Dante's "Dolce Stil Novo" and the *Comedy*', in *Dante, mito e poesia: atti del secondo Seminario dantesco internazionale (Monte Verità, Ascona, 23–27 giugno 1997)*, ed. by Michelangelo Picone and T. Crivelli (Florence: Cesati), pp. 263–81

IANNUCCI, AMILCARE A. 2005. 'Dante's Limbo: At the Margins of Orthodoxy', in *Dante and the Unorthodox: The Aesthetics of Trangression* (Waterloo, ON: Wilfrid Laurier University Press)

JACOFF, RACHEL. 1982. 'The Tears of Beatrice: *Inferno* II', *Dante Studies*, 100: 1–12

JACOFF, RACHEL, and JEFFREY SCHNAPP (eds). 1999. *The Poetry of Allusion: Virgil and Ovid in Dante's Commedia* (Stanford, CA: Stanford University Press)

KAY, TRISTAN. 2015. *Dante's Lyric Redemption: Eros, Salvation, Vernacular Tradition* (Oxford: Oxford University Press)

LEDDA, GIUSEPPE. 2002. *La guerra della lingua: ineffabilità, retorica e narrativa nella 'Commedia' di Dante* (Ravenna: Longo)

——2015. 'La danza e il canto dell' "umile salmista": David nella Commedia di Dante', in *Les Figures de David à la Renaissance*, ed. by Élise Boillet, Sonia Cavicchioli, and Paul-Alexis Mellet (Geneva: Droz), pp. 225–46

LOMBARDI, ELENA. 2012. *The Wings of the Doves: Love and Desire in Dante and Medieval Culture* (Montreal: McGill-Queen's University Press)

——2018. *Imagining the Woman Reader in the Age of Dante* (Oxford: Oxford University Press)

MARTINEZ, RONALD. 1983. 'The Pilgrim's Answer to Bonagiunta and the Poetics of the Spirit', *Stanford Italian Review*, 3: 37–63

MAZZOTTA, GIUSEPPE. 1979. *Dante: Poet of the Desert* (Princeton, NJ: Princeton University Press)

MOEVS, CHRISTIAN. 2005. *The Metaphysics of Dante's 'Comedy'* (Oxford: Oxford University Press)

MONTEMAGGI, VITTORIO. 2010. 'In Unknowability as Love: The Theology of Dante's *Commedia*', in *Dante's Commedia: Theology as Poetry*, ed. by Vittorio Montemaggi and Matthew Treherne (Notre Dame, IN: University of Notre Dame Press), pp. 60–94

NARDI, BRUNO. 1949. 'Dante profeta', in *Dante e la cultura medievale* (Bari: Laterza), pp. 336–416

PERTILE, LINO. 1994. 'Il nodo di Bonagiunta, le penne di Dante e il Dolce Stil Novo', *Lettere italiane*, 1: 44–75

——1998. *La puttana e il gigante* (Ravenna: Longo)

——2003. 'Does the Stilnovo Go to Heaven?', in *Dante for the New Millennium*, ed. by Teodolinda Barolini and H. Wayne Storey (New York: Fordham University Press), pp. 104–14

——2005. *La punta del disio: semantica del desiderio nella Commedia* (Fiesole: Cadmo)

——2012. '"Trasmutabile per tutte guise": Dante in the *Comedy*', in *Desire in Dante and the Middle Ages*, ed. by Manuele Gragnolati and others (Oxford: Legenda), pp. 164–78

PICONE, MICHELANGELO. 2000–01. 'Leggere la *Commedia* di Dante', in *Lectura Dantis Turicensis* ed. by Georges Güntert and Michelangelo Picone, 3 vols (Florence: Cesati), I, 13–25

PSAKI, REGINA. 2003. 'Love for Beatrice: Transcending Contradiction in the Paradiso', in *Dante for the New Millennium*, ed. by Teodolinda Barolini and H. Wayne Storey (New York: Fordham University Press), pp. 115–30

SANTAGATA, MARCO. 1999. *Amate e amanti: figure della lirica amorosa fra Dante e Petrarca* (Bologna: Il Mulino)

——2011. 'Introduzione', in Dante Alighieri, *Opere*, 3 vols (Milan: Mondadori), I, xi-cxxxii

SCHNAPP, JEFFREY. 1991. 'Dante's Sexual Solecisms: Gender and Genre in the *Commedia*', in *The New Medievalism*, ed. by Kevin Brownlee, Marina Brownlee, and Stephen Nichols (Baltimore, MD: Johns Hopkins University Press), pp. 201–25

SCOTT, JOHN A. 1977. 'L'Ulisse dantesco', in *Dante magnanimo* (Florence: Oslchki), pp. 117–93

SHANKLAND, HUGH. 1975. 'Dante "aliger"', *The Modern Language Review*, 70.4: 764–85

SINGLETON, CHARLES. 1977. *Dante's 'Commedia': Elements of Structure* (Baltimore, MD, & London: Johns Hopkins University Press)

SOUTHERDEN, FRANCESCA. 2010. 'Performative Desires: Sereni's Re-staging of Dante and Petrarch', in *Aspects of the Performative in Medieval Culture*, ed. by Manuele Gragnolati and Almut Suerbaum (Berlin: De Gruyter), pp. 165–96

THOMPSON, DAVID. 1967. 'Dante's Ulysses and the Allegorical Journey', *Dante Studies*, 85: 33–58

Works on Proust

Azérad, Hugues. 2002. *L'Univers constellé de Proust, Joyce et Faulkner: le concept d'épiphanie dans l'esthétique du modernisme* (Oxford: Peter Lang)

Baudry, Jean-Louis. 1984. *Proust, Freud et l'autre* (Paris: Minuit)

Bayard, Pierre. 1996. *Le Hors-sujet: Proust et la digression* (Paris: Minuit)

Bersani, Leo. 1990. *The Culture of Redemption* (Cambridge, MA: Harvard University Press)

Bouillaguet, Annick, and Brian G. Rogers (eds). 2004. *Dictionnaire Marcel Proust* (Paris: Champion)

Bowie, Malcolm. 1987. *Freud, Proust and Lacan: Theory as Fiction* (Cambridge: Cambridge University Press)

—— 1998. *Proust Among the Stars* (New York: Columbia University Press)

Bucknall, Barbara. 1969. *The Religion of Art in Proust* (Urbana, Chicago, & London: University of Illinois Press)

Caranfa, Angelo. 1990. *Proust: The Creative Silence* (Lewisburg, PA: Bucknell University Press; London: Associate University Presses)

Carter, William C. 1992. *The Proustian Quest* (New York & London: New York University Press)

Chaudier, Stéphane. 2004. *Proust et le langage religieux: la cathédrale profane* (Paris: Champion)

Cocking, J. M. 1982. *Proust: Collected Papers on the Writer and his Art* (Cambridge: Cambridge University Press)

Elsner, Anna Magdalena. 2009. 'Tracing the Presence of an Absence: Mourning and Creation from "Les Intermittences du cœur" to *Le Temps retrouvé*', in *Le Temps retrouvé: Eighty Years After/80 ans après: Critical Essays*, ed. by Adam Watt (Oxford: Peter Lang), pp. 279–92

—— 2017. *Mourning and Creativity in Proust* (New York: Palgrave MacMillan)

Finch, Alison. 1977. *Proust's Additions: The Making of 'À la recherche du temps perdu'*, 2 vols (Cambridge: Cambridge University Press)

Fraisse, Luc. 1990. *L'Œuvre cathédrale: Proust et l'architecture médiévale* (Paris: Corti)

—— 2011. *La Petite Musique du style: Proust et ses sources littéraires* (Paris: Classiques Garnier)

Fraisse, Luc, and Françoise Létoublon. 1997. 'Proust et la descente aux enfers: les souvenirs symboliques de la nekuia d'Homère dans la *Recherche du temps perdu*', *Revue d'histoire littéraire de la France*, 6: 1056–85

Freed-Thall, Hannah. 2015. *Spoiled Distinctions: Aesthetics and the Ordinary in French Modernism* (New York: Oxford University Press)

Gamble, Cynthia. 2002. *Proust as Interpreter of Ruskin: The Seven Lamps of Translation* (Birmingham, AL: Summa)

Gray, Margaret. 1992. *Postmodern Proust* (Philadelphia: University of Pennsylvania Press)

Haddad-Wotling, Karen, and Vincent Ferré (eds). 2010. *Proust, l'étranger* (Amsterdam: Rodopi)

Hägglund, Martin. 2012. *Dying for Time: Proust, Woolf, Nabokov* (Cambridge, MA: Harvard University Press)

Hassine, Juliette. 1994. *Marranisme et hébraïsme dans l'œuvre de Proust* (Fleury-sur-Orne: Minard)

Hughes, Edward J. 1983. *Marcel Proust: A Study in the Quality of Awareness* (Cambridge: Cambridge University Press)

—— 1994. 'Prisons and Pleasures of the Mind: A Comparative Reading of Cervantes and Proust', in *Cervantes and the Modernists: The Question of Influence*, ed. by Edwin Williamson (London: Tamesis), pp. 55–72

—— 2011. *Proust, Class, and Nation* (Oxford: Oxford University Press)

KRISTEVA, JULIA. 1994. *Le Temps sensible: Proust et l'expérience littéraire* (Paris: Gallimard)

LADENSON, Elisabeth. 1999. *Proust's Lesbianism* (Ithaca, NY: Cornell University Press)

LANDY, JOSHUA. 2004. *Philosophy as Fiction: Self, Deception, and Knowledge in Proust* (Oxford: Oxford University Press)

LARGE, DUNCAN. 2001. *Nietzsche and Proust: A Comparative Study* (Oxford: Oxford University Press)

LERNER, L. SCOTT. 2007. 'Mourning and Subjectivity: From Bersani to Proust, Klein, and Freud', *Diacritics*, 37.1: 41–53

LUCEY, MICHAEL. 2006. *Never Say I: Sexuality and the First Person in Colette, Gide, and Proust* (Durham, NC, & London: Duke University Press)

MILLY, JEAN. 1970. *Les Pastiches de Proust* (Paris: Colin)

—— 1985. *Proust dans le texte et l'avant-texte* (Paris: Flammarion)

MOUTON, JEAN. 1968. *Proust*, Les écrivains devant Dieu (Brussels: De Brouwer)

MULLER, MARCEL. 1979. *Préfigurations et structure romanesque dans 'À la recherche du temps perdu'* (Lexington, KY: French Forum)

O'BRIEN, JUSTIN. 1964. 'Fall and Redemption in Proust', *MLN*, 79.3: 281–83

PENNANECH, FLORIAN. 2009. '*Le Temps retrouvé* et la Nouvelle Critique: le problème de l'achèvement', in *Le Temps retrouvé: Eighty Years After/80 ans après: Critical Essays*, ed. by Adam Watt (Oxford: Peter Lang), pp. 239–53

POULET, GEORGES. 1949. 'Proust', in *Études sur le temps humain* (Edinburgh: Edinburgh University Press), pp. 366–401

PRENDERGAST, CHRISTOPHER. 2013. *Mirages and Mad Beliefs: Proust the Skeptic* (Princeton, NJ: Princeton University Press)

RUSHWORTH, JENNIFER. 2013. '"Alors la résurrection aura pris fin": Visions of the End in Proust's *À la Recherche du temps perdu*', in *Visions of Apocalypse: Representations of the End in French Literature and Culture*, ed. by Leona Archer and Alex Stuart (Bern: Peter Lang), pp. 153–64

——2015. 'Derrida, Proust, and the Promise of Writing', *French Studies*, 69.2: 205–19

STRAMBOLIAN, GEORGE. 1972. *Proust and the Creative Encounter* (Chicago, IL: University of Chicago Press)

TADIÉ, JEAN-YVES. 2003 [1971]. *Proust et le roman: essai sur les formes et techniques du roman dans 'À la recherche du temps perdu'* (Paris: Gallimard)

—— 1998. *Proust, le dossier* (Paris: Belfond)

——2012. *Le Lac inconnu: entre Proust et Freud* (Paris: Gallimard)

TOPPING, MARGARET. 2006. 'Artists and Alchemists in Proust's *À la recherche du temps perdu*', *French Studies*, 60.4: 466–78

——2011. 'Errant Eyes: Digression, Metaphor and Desire in Marcel Proust's *In Search of Lost Time*', in *Digressions in European Literature: From Cervantes to Sebald*, ed. by Alexis Grohmann and Caragh Wells (Basingstoke: Palgrave Macmillan), pp. 106–17

TRIBOUT-JOSEPH, SARAH. 2008. *Proust and Joyce in Dialogue* (Oxford: Legenda)

WATT, ADAM. 2005. 'The Sign of the Swan in Proust's *À la recherche du temps perdu*', *French Studies*, 59.3: 326–37

——2011. 'Proust: Poet of the Ordinary', in *Au seuil de la modernité: Proust, Literature and the Arts, Essays in Memory of Richard Bales*, ed. by Nigel Harkness and Marion Schmid (Oxford; New York: Peter Lang), pp. 97–111

Other Works

ANGHEBEN, MARCELLO. 2007. *Le Jugement dernier: entre orient et occident*, ed. by Valentino Pace (Paris: Cerf)

BARNES, JULIAN. 2013. *Levels of Life* (London: Random House)

BARTHES, ROLAND. 1968. 'La Mort de l'auteur', in *Le Bruissement de la langue: essais critiques IV* (Paris: Du Seuil, 1984), pp. 63–69

BAUDELAIRE, CHARLES. 1975–76. *Œuvres completes*, ed. by Claude Pichois, new edn, 2 vols (Paris: Gallimard)

BENTON, JOHN F. 1982. 'Consciousness of Self and Perceptions of Individuality', in *Renaissance and Renewal in the Twelfth Century*, ed. by Robert L. Benson, Giles Constable, and Carol Dana Lanham (Oxford: Clarendon Press), pp. 263–95

BLACK, MAX. 1993 [1979]. 'More about Metaphor', in *Metaphor and Thought*, ed. by Andrew Ortony, 2nd edn (Cambridge: Cambridge University Press), pp. 19–41

BLOOM, HAROLD. 1973. *The Anxiety of Influence: A Theory of Poetry* (New York: Oxford University Press)

BOITANI, PIERO. 1994. *The Shadow of Ulysses*, trans. by Anita Weston (Oxford: Clarendon Press; New York: Oxford University Press)

BRANDON, SAMUEL GEORGE FREDERICK. 1967. *The Judgment of the Dead: An Historical and Comparative Study of the Idea of a post-mortem Judgment in the Major Religions* (London: Weidenfeld & Nicolson)

BROMBERT, VICTOR. 1999. *In Praise of Antiheroes: Figures and Themes in Modern European Literature 1830–1980* (Chicago, IL, & London: University of Chicago Press)

BROOKS, PETER. 1984. *Reading for the Plot: Design and Intention in Narrative* (Oxford: Clarendon Press)

BURKE, SÉAN. 1992. *The Death and Return of the Author: Criticism and Subjectivity in Barthes, Foucault and Derrida* (Edinburgh: Edinburgh University Press)

BYNUM, CAROLINE WALKER. 1982. *Jesus as Mother: Studies in the Spirituality of the High Middle Ages* (Berkeley, CA: University of California Press)

——2001. *Metamorphosis and Identity* (New York: Zone Books)

CHAMBERS, ROSS. 1999. *Loiterature* (Lincoln & London: University of Nebraska Press)

CONTINI, GIANFRANCO (ed.). 1960. *Poeti del Duecento*, 2 vols (Milan: Ricciardi)

CURTIUS, ERNST ROBERT. 1953. *European Literature and the Latin Middle Ages*, trans. by Willard R. Trask (New York: Pantheon Books)

DONOGHUE, DENIS. 2014. *Metaphor* (Cambridge, MA, & London: Harvard University Press)

EMPSON, WILLIAM. 1953. *Seven Types of Ambiguity* (London: New Directions)

GENETTE, GÉRARD. 1972. *Figures III* (Paris: Du Seuil)

HOLMES, OLIVIA. 2000. *Assembling the Lyric Self: Authorship from Troubadour Song to Italian Poetry Book* (Minneapolis & London: University of Minnesota Press)

JAKOBSON, ROMAN. 1987. *Language in Literature*, ed. by Krystyna Pomorska and Stephen Rudy (Cambridge, MA: Harvard University Press)

JEFFERSON, ANN. 2009. 'Genius and Its Others', *Paragraph*, 32.2: 182–96

JUNG, CARL GUSTAV. 1968. *Analytical Psychology: Its Theory and Practice (The Tavistock Lectures)* (London: Routledge & Kegan Paul)

LADNER, GERHART. 1967. '"Homo Viator": Mediaeval Ideas on Alineation and Order', *Speculum*, 42.2: 233–59

LEJEUNE, PHILIPPE. 1975. *Le Pacte autobiographique* (Paris: Du Seuil)

LI, XIAOFAN AMY. 2015. *Comparative Encounters between Artaud, Michaux and the Zhuangzi* (Oxford: Legenda)

MÂLE, ÉMILE. 1898. *L'Art religieux du treizième siècle en France: étude sur l'iconographie du Moyen Âge et sur ses sources d'inspiration* (Paris: Leroux)

MINNIS, ALISTAIR J., *Medieval Theory of Authorship: Scholastic Literary Attitudes in the Later Middle Ages*, 2nd edn (Philadelphia: University of Pennsylvania Press, 1988)

MORRIS, COLIN. 1972. *The Discovery of the Individual 1050–1200* (London: S.P.C.K. for the Church Historical Society)

NITZSCHE, JANE CHANCE. 1975. *The Genius Figure in Antiquity and the Middle Ages* (New York & London: Columbia University Press)

PRESSBURGER, GIORGIO. 2008. *Nel regno oscuro* (Milan: Bompiani)

QUINONES, RICARDO J. 1972. *The Renaissance Discovery of Time* (Cambridge, MA: Harvard University Press)

RICHARDS, IVOR ARMSTRONG. 1936. *The Philosophy of Rhetoric* (Oxford: Oxford University Press)

RICŒUR, PAUL. 1975. *La Métaphore vive* (Paris: Du Seuil)

RUSKIN, JOHN. 1851–53. 'The Nature of Gothic', in *The Stones of Venice*, 3 vols (London: Smith; Elder), II, 151–231

SCOTT, CLIVE. 2000. *Translating Baudelaire* (Exeter: University of Exeter Press)

SHRODER, MAURICE. 1961. *Icarus: The Image of the Artist in French Romanticism* (Cambridge, MA: Harvard University Press)

SPITZER, LEO. 1946. 'A Note on the Poetic and the Empirical "I" in Medieval Authors', *Traditio*, 4: 414–22

TALAMO, ROBERTO. 2013. *Intenzione e iniziativa: teorie della letteratura dagli anni Venti a oggi* (Bari: Progedit)

VALLINI, CRISTINA. 2002.'*Genius/ingenium*: derive semantiche', in *Convegno internazionale di studi su 'Ingenium propria hominis natura: atti del convegno internazionale di studi (Napoli, 22–24 maggio 1997)*, ed. by Stefano Gensini and Arturo Martone (Naples: Liguori), pp. 3–26

ZACHER, CHRISTIAN K. 1976. *Curiosity and Pilgrimage: The Literature of Discovery in Fourteenth-Century England* (Baltimore, MD: Johns Hopkins University Press)

ZUMTHOR, PAUL. 1975. 'Le *je* du poète', in *Langue Texte Énigme* (Paris: Du Seuil), pp. 163–213

INDEX

CPSIA information can be obtained
at www.ICGtesting.com
Printed in the USA
BVHW011144230421
605724BV00004B/46

9 781781 888438